MAKE ROOM
FOR TWINS

MAKE ROOM FOR TWINS

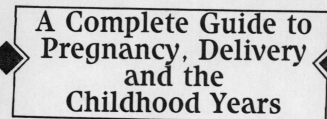

A Complete Guide to Pregnancy, Delivery and the Childhood Years

Terry Pink Alexander
Illustrated by Todd Pink

BANTAM BOOKS
NEW YORK • TORONTO • LONDON • SYDNEY • AUCKLAND

MAKE ROOM FOR TWINS
A Bantam Book / August 1987
2nd printing . . . September 1988

Library of Congress Cataloging-in-Publication Data

Alexander, Terry Pink.
Make room for twins.

Including index.
Bibliography: p. 396
1. Pregnancy, Multiple.   2. Birth, Multiple.
3. Twins.   4. Infants—Care.   5. Infants—Health
and hygiene.   I. Title.
RG567.A44   1987   618.2'5   85-48050
ISBN 0-553-34207-X

Published simultaneously in the United States and Canada

PRINTED IN THE UNITED STATES OF AMERICA

FG   11   10   9   8   7   6   5   4   3

For David, Peter, Becky, and Kevin
and for families of twins everywhere

Contents

◆ Acknowledgments ◆

When our twins were born, family, friends, and even mere acquaintances rallied to help us. Somehow, everyone seemed to sense our need for assistance. Now, many years later, when the dust has finally settled and the whirlwind of sleepless nights and our constant exhaustion are just a memory, I once again remember with gratitude and affection these wonderful volunteers. These special people gave generously of their time and energy, never expecting more than a hug or a smile in return.

So, too, when the book was in its infancy I was surrounded by a knowledgeable, willing, and supportive network of friends—old and new. Parents happily offered their wisdom and professionals generously contributed their expertise. Although I had never met many of these individuals before, they wholeheartedly supported my efforts, never expecting more than a nod or a handshake.

Many physicians worked closely with me to verify the accuracy of the medical information given in the book. I owe a special debt of gratitude to one of these doctors, Richard Oken, my pediatric consultant, and to his wonderful and supportive partners, associates, nurses, and staff. Dr. Oken spent many hours reading and re-reading the manuscript in its various stages of completion and revision. He also provided information on pertinent new research as it came to his attention. Dr. Aaron Chinn, my consultant on obstetrics, was also very helpful from the time I began work on the book. He proofed and checked the sections on obstetrics and gynecology for medical accuracy. Drs. Richard Bass, Jacob Epstein and William Hoddick, and Howard Gordon provided detailed information on their respective areas of specialization—anesthesiology, radiology, and perinatology. Dr. Melvin Cohen and Dr. Richard Umansky also read the manuscript and were kind enough to lend their names to my project.

I am indebted to a number of other specialists whose professional expertise has helped expand the depth and scope of the book's coverage. Nutritionist Sally Cohenour, R.D., M.S., not only researched and developed the book's nutrition program but was also available on repeated occasions to review new research in an effort to keep the book's information current while it was awaiting publication. I am grateful for her constant and undaunted dedication to my project. For permitting me to adapt material from her book, *The Total Nutrition Guide for Mother and Baby: From Pregnancy Through the First Three Years,* I am grateful to that book's author, Alice White. My appreciation also extends to Janet King, R.D., Ph.D., for her suggestions, recommendations, and advice, and for reviewing the nutrition program and its later revisions.

My sincere thanks also go to Mary Snyder, M.S., R.P.T., for thoroughly researching and developing the physical activity programs for multiple pregnancy and the postpartum period, and to James DeWeese, Ph.D., for his assistance in documenting this program. Madeleine Shearer, R.P.T., also gave generously of her time to review the manuscript's activity and exercise sections upon their completion, and I was delighted to receive her blessing.

For several years, I worked closely with Donald M. Keith, M.B.A., co-founder and executive director of The Center for Study of Multiple Birth (CSMB). I am grateful to him for providing me with numerous research papers, for suggesting ways to make the book more comprehensive, and for believing in the project from the first time he saw the manuscript. I also wish to thank the members of the CSMB board who, at Donald Keith's request, read the manuscript and offered their own helpful suggestions.

Patricia Malmstrom, M.A., executive director of Twinline, Services for Multiple Birth Families, was a great friend and a good ear throughout my years of work on the book. She, Denise Harter, president of the Twinline board, and the entire Twinline staff provided me with valuable resources on numerous occasions.

Other specialists to whom I would like to express my appreciation include Helen Harrison (prematurity), Joanne Ikeda, R.D. (nutrition), and Sheila Luengen (breastfeeding).

My gratitude further extends to Howard Nemerovski for his counsel and his wit, and to Alan Goodman for his persistent efforts on my behalf. And, for their tremendous help with the preparation of the manuscript, I am grateful to Steven LaPorta for his editorial wizardry, and especially to my brother Todd Pink for his artistic renderings and graphic skills, to my mother Ella Pink for her thoughtful suggestions and encouragement, to Faye and Joel Alexander for their emotional support, to Eileen Van Matre for the months of evenings she gave up to word process the manuscript, and finally to my editor, Toni Burbank, and her editorial assistant, Andrew Zega, without whom this book would never have been born.

Hundreds of families participated in the survey and/or interviews providing the backbone of the book. I particularly wish to thank the following mothers of twins clubs: Contra Costa MOTC, Coastside MOTC, and East Bay MOTC.

Additional thanks go also to parents Karen Andrade, Miriam Halpern, M.D., and Martha Holmes, for their personal help in documenting the activity and exercise program. Families who gave inordinate amounts of their time include: the Andrades, the Bakers, the Benvenutti-Pearlmans, the Donnelleys, the Ferreiras, the Fritzes, the Harters, the Holmeses, the Latimers, the Lauries, the Quans, the Rabkins, the Rubensteins, the Turners, and the Woons; and the individuals include: LaVerne Carroll, Kevan Jane Fitzgerald, and Michael J. Uhes, and Catherine Ronneberg. I am grateful to Diana Vallario and *The Herald* for generously providing several photos and to Elizabeth Crews for her photographic skill.

Most of all I want to thank my husband David who gave me his total support, especially when the long hours of research began to take their toll on me, and my three children Peter,

Becky, and Kevin, who gave me the inspiration to write the book and who loved me even on those days when I only had time for my typewriter.

Writing a book of this scope has involved many years of work, and the list of those whom I would like to thank has now grown beyond the limit of these few pages. As for those of you whose names may have escaped my pen, your kindness has not escaped my memory. I am very grateful to all of you—those whose names I mention here and those whose names I carry with me in my thoughts—for sharing my enthusiasm in bringing my idea to its realization.

Foreword

Make Room For Twins is a book for parents to treasure. Until its appearance there was no single source book for the thousands of U.S. parents making their way through the complexities of birthing and rearing twins and triplets.

As she worked on this manuscript, Ms. Alexander frequently called the Twinline staff to check facts, find references, or ask for an update on research. She asked pertinent questions about issues ranging from the wisdom of bedrest during twin pregnancy to the placement of twins in school. Her thorough research and attention to detail have created a comprehensive guide to known facts and scientific theories about the management of twin pregnancy and the birth and care of multiple birth children.

These are some of the features which make *Make Room For Twins* such a special resource. It presents recent statistics on the incidence of twinning in relation to maternal age and race and whether the twins are identical or fraternal (zygosity). Since vital statistics about multiple birth are not recorded in the same way in each state, these data are difficult to find and compile. The section on the use of drugs to prevent preterm delivery reviews their effectiveness and potential side effects, so that parents will be able to discuss this important, sometimes bewildering issue with their obstetricians. Ms. Alexander's pregnancy diet and exercises for women carrying multiples are moderate programs women can use to design individual approaches to these controversial topics.

The developmental sequence for twins' first year includes unique twin phenomena never mentioned in books about single children. Fathers of multiples are frequently neglected in books for parents. A chapter devoted to their needs reports strategies for coping with the tremendous life change, strategies which were developed by fathers in a variety of family situations.

Parents agree that single siblings are the most vulnerable family members when twins arrive. The sensitive discussion of ways that single children react and successful methods parents have used to help them is a good guide for parents in similar circumstances.

The guidelines for deciding whether or not to start twins in the same or separate classrooms challenge the conventional wisdom that separation is best. The detailed discussion of the factors to be considered in this complex decision will help parents make informed choices.

Expectant parents of multiples and parents who are already absorbed in the challenge of rearing them will find *Make Room For Twins* a wonderful resource—informative, practical, and stimulating.

> Patricia Malmstrom, M.A., Director
> Twinline, Services for Multiple Birth
>   Families
> Berkeley, California
>
> December 1986

Foreword

My first experience with multiple births was at the age of seventeen months when I had to "make room for twins" —boy-girl twins with whom I shared childhood in my own family. My experience as the brother of twins, however, did not prepare me for the tasks of counseling parents of twins as a pediatrician. In fact, there was little mention in either medical school or formal residency of the phenomenon of twinning. I can well recall the first day of internship, when faced with very sick premature triplets, feeling the weighty complications of a multiple birth upon the doctor.

Private practice has been an experience in which parents have become my teachers. As a pediatrician, I am expected to be doctor, counselor, and educator for the parents as their families grow. Certain answers cannot be found in the standard textbooks of pediatrics as parents inquire about the practical and behavioral aspects of childrearing. In essence, their experiences become my educational materials for future generations of parents.

As a parent of twins and an educator, Terry Alexander has created the definitive text on twin parenthood. She has organized the current major reference for both parents and physicians. The text is well-written, thoroughly researched, and comprehensive in the treatment of the topic. Illustrations, tables, and references augment the value of this important guide. I am honored that our practice had some small role to play in the genesis of the data for her research.

The opening chapters provide well-referenced and current factual material on the medical aspects of twin pregnancy. Diagnostic and therapeutic advances are described, as well as the preventive aspects essential to mitigate the possible complications of multiple pregnancy. A parent can understand and a professional can learn from this comprehensive treatment.

The practical aspect of how to prepare for twins is covered in the middle sections. A simple illustration of the "football hold" is worth a thousand words in the explanation to a fearful mother who wonders how one woman can ever nurse twins. In this section, the "recipes" for twin parenting are shared with the novice and the strategies are covered in checklist detail.

The final chapters are essential for understanding the impact of twins upon the family. The experience of twins has been carefully sampled in personal interviews and questionnaires. We are able to watch each parent, each twin, and other siblings as the effects are measured and described within the family unit.

How do the parents of twins survive, as we consider the difficult task of raising even a singleton? *Make Room for Twins* debunks the myth that all twins are alike and establishes the guideposts for parents and professionals on how to understand, organize, prosper, and enjoy the twin as an individual.

Richard L. Oken, M.D., F.A.A.P.
Associate Clinical Professor of Pediatrics
University of California, San Francisco
January, 1987

Preface

I am often asked whether our three children were all planned. My standard answer is, "Yes, but not so close together." Twins are, at most, only half-planned, but caring for them requires twice the time and work of any single baby. Speaking from personal experience, however, I know that twins offer their families double the enjoyment and gratification.

Nobody really expects to have twins. Even a woman who is taking fertility drugs or one whose family has a history of multiple births is surprised, shocked, or even overwhelmed when she is told that she will soon be the mother of more than one baby. At first, expectant parents of twins experience a rush of natural fears, wondering, "Can anyone give enough love to two infants?" and "Do we have enough space for both babies?" Many an expectant mother whose emotional state is already subject to the hormonally induced moods of pregnancy worries: "Will my marriage suffer?" A father's concerns are typically financial: "How much more will it cost to care for twins?" Together, parents try to anticipate how their older child or children will adapt to not just one but two new babies, and the children themselves are sometimes fearful of what is happening to mommy (preschoolers) or resentful of the impending changes in the family (school-age children).

Over four years ago, when I first searched for books relating to twins, I had very little success. My interest in the subject began when, at three-and-a-half-months pregnant, I learned that I was expecting twins myself. I was stunned, but nonetheless enthusiastic. Of the many contests I must have entered in my life, this was the first time I had ever "won the lucky number," and I envisioned how our family life would be enriched by two more. It would be a challenge, but I was confident we could handle it. My husband and I had our share of apprehensions and sleepless nights anticipating the twins' arrival, but we soon became so accustomed to the idea that we could no longer imagine having only one baby. We felt we were special, but also a bit odd, as no one we knew had twins. Since the birth of our babies, hardly a day goes by without at least one person telling me he or she has twins, is a twin, or has twin siblings or a parent who is a twin. Having twins is like joining a secret society where you do not know who the members are until you have joined.

Before delivery, my husband and I knew no one who had experienced a multiple pregnancy and delivery, so we had no one to guide us through the difficult pregnancy or to ease us into a comfortable home life with our new babies. Our initial enthusiasm for the expected double birth was clouded by friends and acquaintances who repeatedly quipped, "Congratulations, you really have my sympathies." My husband and I were told we would never survive the first year and that our older son would be permanently traumatized by the arrival of the twins. Refusing to believe this, we welcomed our new babies home and have now had eight gratifying years of twin parenthood.

The early months were fatiguing, but I never felt defeated or depressed, and I began to pass along my own suggestions to other new parents of twins. Soon pediatricians and obstetricians alike were referring expectant and new families of twins to me for advice, and I was receiving regular invitations to speak at various parents of twins clubs. Many of these families and clubs were aware of my writing experience and urged me to write a book on my own twin pregnancy and double-birth experience.

When I began work on *Make Room for Twins,* my own twins were only nine months old. I wrote when the children were napping or late into the evening, and had drafted five chapters by the time the babies celebrated their first birthday. I began by relating my personal experiences, supplemented by helpful hints gathered from other mothers of twins. Then, over the next three and a half years, as I continued to work on the book, it gradually evolved into a complete guide to twin parenthood, based on surveys and interviews with families of twins, physicians, and health professionals and on new research on multiple birth, twin development, and twin care. The book in its finished form focuses on the whole family's adjustment when twins arrive and on life with twins during infancy and the toddler and preschool years. Throughout the project, I was determined for two reasons to finish the book and to see it published. I was convinced that families of twins, as well as medical and health professionals, need the help and support of a single major resource book, and I wanted to prove to myself that a mother of twins could not only survive the early years but could even live to write a book about it.

Make Room for Twins is designed to be the only book families will need from the moment twins are diagnosed until the children are finished with preschool. For this reason, the book also offers general information on pregnancy, labor and delivery, breastfeeding, and on child development and parenting. I hope that parents of triplets and larger multiples will also find the book to be a useful tool. Information was gleaned from conversations with hundreds of parents of multiples and from questionnaires distributed with the help of numerous mothers of twins clubs and my children's pediatrician. The survey reached a cross-section of families of various races, ethnic backgrounds, and income levels. The book gives information about multiple pregnancy and traces the development and care of twins from infancy through preschool by discussing how others have successfully handled the challenges of multiple parenthood.

Much of the book is written as a direct conversation with you, the parents of twins, and I have tried to keep your concerns in mind even in the more technical and clinical sections. The fears you may have stem largely from your own uncertainty and anxiety about the unknown. Throughout the course of this book, I will try to help you identify those concerns. Your questions have probably been voiced by others before you. A wealth of materials is available on the subject of pregnancy and infant care, but very little of it focuses on the unique problems faced by parents of twins. My suggestions are intended to help you handle those times of additional stress, frustration, and fatigue unique to families of twins. The ideas, shortcuts, and home remedies are designed to bolster your self-confidence and to promote your positive feelings about your family and your relationship with your children. I hope that the book will help you meet the challenges of multiple parenthood with greater energy, enthusiasm, and success as you "make room for twins" in your own home.

CHAPTER I

Twinning: Fact and Fiction

Interest in twins is rekindled with each discovery of a pair separated since birth or with the announcement that twins were born to a movie star, politician, or sports figure, to a neighbor down the block, or most particularly to your own family. Perhaps it is the physical resemblance and the close interpersonal relationship that twins share that make the phenomenon so bewildering to others, yet so unique and special. The multifaceted nature of twinship can be particularly mystifying to new parents and families of twins, especially those with little or no previous exposure to multiple births. The composite of fact and fiction presented in this chapter will give you a better overall understanding of twins, especially your own.

Past and Present Names and Legends

Twins hold a peculiar fascination for the public. The very idea of two babies born to the same mother from a single pregnancy invites curiosity. Twins are often and unfairly treated as oddities, yet they are not a new phenomenon; they have been recorded throughout history among the various ancient societies and primitive cultures of the world. Although a double birth is still not commonplace, neither is it extraordinary. Thus, it is hard to believe that even today the public still sees twins as unusual.

Legends can be traced back to ancient times. Numerous pairs are celebrated in legend and myth. The Bible tells of dissimilar fraternals, Jacob and Esau, sons of Isaac and Rebecca. Tradition dictates that their aging father's power and inheritance should be granted to the elder son, Esau (Isaac's favorite). Through trickery, Rebecca aids her preferred son, Jacob, in stealing his brother's birthright, and Jacob becomes the founder of the nation of Israel.

Roman mythology relates the tale of Romulus and Remus, born to the vestal virgin Sylvia in her forced union with Mars, the god of war. This pair of unwanted infants is set adrift in a basket on the River Tiber until rescued and nurtured by a she-wolf and later raised by a shepherd family. In manhood, the twins set forth to build a great city, and Remus is killed by his brother in a dispute over the site. Romulus then goes on to become the founder and ruler of Rome, giving his name to the city.

Mythological twins need not be rivals, however. According to a Greco-Roman myth, Castor and Pollux are each twins, but not part of the same pair. Both pairs were born of the same mother, but one pair was fathered by a mortal and the other by Jupiter, immortal king of all gods. Thus, the first set, Castor and Clytemnestra, is mortal, and the second, Pollux and Helen, immortal. When Castor is accidentally killed in battle, Pollux is consumed with grief. Out of love for Pollux, Jupiter grants immortality to Castor, too, and directs that the brothers should eternally spend one day on earth and the next in the heavens. They travel the heavens even today as the constellation Gemini (the twins) and form the astrological sign Gemini, which corresponds to the one-month period falling from late May to late June.

This same period is represented by paired figures in other ancient zodiacs. The Peruvian symbol was a man and a woman, the Mayan sign was two generals, and twin children were found in the ancient zodiacs of Europe and Mexico. Whether the ancient Greeks and Romans had reason to choose twins to represent this part of the year can only be speculated. Margaret and Vincent Gaddis, in their book *The Curious World of Twins* (1972) claimed that the greatest number of multiple births actually occur under the sign of Gemini. According to the Gaddises, the famed Dionne quintuplets were not only born under the sign of Gemini but also showed Gemini rising on the horizon on their astrological chart.

More recent research on seasonal twinning is contradictory. According to one report, twin conceptions in Finland are greatest in July, suggesting a higher incidence of double births in the spring, but a New York State study did not find any seasonal effect on the twinning rate. Other studies done in Europe and in Asia found that twin conceptions were highest in spring and fall. Discrepancies in the findings of such studies, however, may reflect differences in the composition of the studied populations, among other possible factors.

Perhaps the most frequently told stories concerning twins involve mistaken identity. Shakespeare's *Comedy of Errors* relates the tale of two sets of male look-alike twins, one pair the masters and the other their servants. A similar plot can be found in an early Roman work by Plautus, from which the Shakespeare play may have been derived. Alexandre Dumas, in the nineteenth century, wrote *The Man in the Iron Mask*, which is based on the premise that Louis XIV had an identical twin who was mysteriously spirited away at birth. When the king's enemies discovered the monarch's long lost twin years later, they masterminded an exchange. The twin impersonated the king, and Louis himself was relegated to prison, where he would eternally wear an iron mask.

Mistaken identity is also the theme of more recent stories about twins. In the 1961 movie *The Parent Trap*, Hayley Mills is cast in simultaneous roles as a pair of mischievous teenage identical twins who, relying on their look-alike features, scheme to bring their estranged parents back together. Opposite sex twins are also found in literature, drama, and films. In Henry

James's *The Turn of the Screw*, both twins are possessed by the darker influences of the evil gardener. The famed boy-girl Bobbsey Twins of our parents' and grandparents' generations, however, are all-American kids whose happy adventures are told in a series of books much like the Hardy Boys. Even television capitalizes on the public's fascination with twins, as in television's identical girls in *Double Trouble*, the recent popular series *The Family Affair* with its boy-girl twins, Jody and Buffy, and in the classic *Doublemint Gum* commercials.

In the real world, many celebrated sets of twins are famous either as a pair or as separates. Some newsmakers include ski champions Phil and Steve Mahre, basketball greats Tom and Dick Van Arsdale, columnists Abigail ("Dear Abby") Van Buren and Ann Landers, and the late Shah of Iran, whose twin sister survives him. Famous parents of twins may be in the spotlight, such as singer Debbie Boone, and television anchorwoman Jane Pauley and her cartoonist husband Gary Trudeau of *Doonesbury* fame. When actor Richard Thomas became the father of triplets, he gained a new claim to fame. Other celebrities who have received less publicity as parents of twins include country-western star Loretta Lynn, British Prime Minister Margaret Thatcher, the late Vice-President Nelson Rockefeller, and the late Ingrid Bergman. William Shakespeare was also a father of twins.

Twin Types

The word *twins* evokes an image of look-alikes for most people, although at least two-thirds of all twins are fraternal and usually look no more alike than any two siblings in a family. The most frequent question mothers of twins are asked is, "Are they identical?" Some people even respond, "They're so cute! They must be identical!" Most people are uneducated about twins and are really asking, "Do your twins look alike?" Even little children in play often like to dress alike—to play twins. The medical community has also demonstrated an increasing interest in twins and the phenomenon of twinning. Since the first International Congress of Twin Studies in Rome in 1974, the International Society for Twin Studies has sponsored a congress every three years.

Identical girls

Despite this universal interest in twins, few people understand the characteristics of twinship in general or the distinctly different physiological processes that give rise to the two types of twins—fraternal and identical. This brings to mind a story related by a new mother of boy-girl twins who recalls, "While I was still in the hospital after the birth of my twins, the nurse on the afternoon shift said to me, 'Oh, a boy and a girl! Are they identical?' "

A single baby leaves little to your curiosity and imagination; it is either a boy or a girl. With twins, there are five possibilities— identical boys or girls, fraternal boys or girls, or opposite-sex fraternals. The term *twins* refers to double occupancy within the mother's womb. The prenatal development of identicals and fraternals, however, are separate physiological phenomena, although with both types the developing twins share a prenatal home.

Prenatal Differences

Fraternal twins derive from two eggs fertilized by two sperm and therefore can be either of the same or of opposite sex; identicals are the product of a single egg and sperm and must be of the same sex. In the normal development of a single baby, the fertilized egg implants in the uterine lining and grows a placenta that transmits food and oxygen from the mother's system to the embryo, soon to be called a fetus, through the umbilical cord. The fetus is protected by an outer bag called a *chorion* and an inner fluid-filled sac called an *amnion*. The walls of the chorion and amnion are the membranes that either break spontaneously or are ruptured by the doctor during labor.

Fraternals

In the case of fraternal (*dizygotic*) twins, two eggs are fertilized and then implant in the lining of the uterus, where each will share space with its developing twin but will grow individually. The eggs may come either from one or from both ovaries. Each egg will develop its own placenta, chorion, and amnion when implantation occurs. Their two placentas may grow together, however, if the eggs should happen to lodge near one another within the uterus. These fused placentas, if carefully examined, usually reveal their genetic dissimilarities. Whether or not their placentas are fused, each fraternal twin will develop a separate chorion and amnion. Because fraternal twins come from two eggs and two sperm, these babies can be of the same or of opposite sex and may or may not bear a strong resemblance to one another. At birth a doctor may not be able to determine whether a set of twins is identical or fraternal without performing laboratory tests, except in the case of boy-girl twins, who by definition must be fraternal.

Fraternal twins

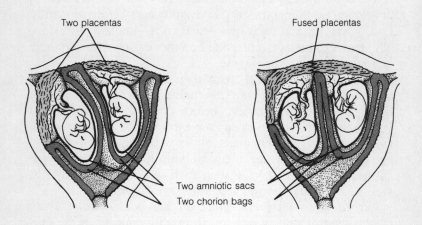

Two placentas

Fused placentas

Two amniotic sacs
Two chorion bags

Identicals

Identical (*monozygotic*) twins have a less predictable pattern of development. They begin as a single fertilized egg and split into two matched embryos either before or after implantation. The egg divides after it implants in the lining of the uterus with most identical twins, and separate umbilical cords link each fetus to the same placenta. The twins also share a chorion bag but usually have separate amniotic sacs, except in rare cases if the egg's division comes very late in this phase of development. Sometimes egg division occurs before implantation, however, and each half—each twin—implants individually, grows its own placenta, and becomes enclosed in a separate chorion bag and amniotic sac.

Each of these identical twins then continues to develop in the uterus in the same way fraternals do. Sex is determined at the moment of fertilization, before division occurs, so both babies are of the same sex and have exactly the same genes for every other physical characteristic as well, such as blood type, eye color, and hair color. Identical twins have matching physical traits, but they develop their own distinct personalities as well as individual though very similar fingerprints.

According to Elizabeth Noble in her book *Having Twins* (1980), approximately one-fourth of all identical sets are *mirror twins*, formed by a delayed splitting of the egg. Mirror twins are reflections of one another, with one side of one twin's body reflected in the opposite side of his or her twin. One is righthanded and the other a lefty, their hair whorls spiral in opposite directions, and any irregularities in their teeth patterns appear on opposite sides. Even a dimple on one's cheek can be found on the opposite cheek of the other. Occasionally some internal organs are also reversed in one of the twins. For example, the heart of one twin may be on the right side rather than the left.

In extremely rare cases division comes very late and the split into two equal halves is not complete. These *conjoined* (or "Siamese") *twins* are named for the world famous pair Chang and Eng Bunker, who were born in Siam (Thailand) in 1811

Identical twins

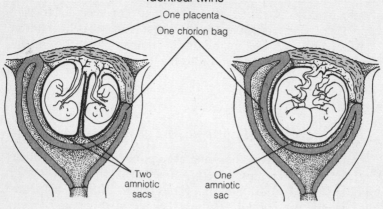

One placenta
One chorion bag
Two amniotic sacs
One amniotic sac

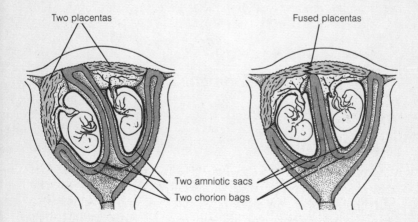

Two placentas
Fused placentas
Two amniotic sacs
Two chorion bags

and later settled in the United States. Conjoined twins occur approximately once in 50,000 births, up to 95 percent are female, and 70 percent are linked at the chest. Advances in modern medicine have enabled many sets of conjoined twins to be surgically separated and to go on to live completely normal lives.

"Half-Identical" Twins—Do They Exist?

A third type of twin has long been pondered. Could a single egg be fertilized by two sperm? If so, the resultant twin pair would have identical maternal genes but an unmatched paternal genetic prescription. If the existence of this type of twin could ever be proved, the twin type of opposite-sex as well as many same-sex pairs would have to be reconsidered. Although such a third type of twin has been identified in lower animals, including flatworms and sea urchins, doctors and scientists have not been able to confirm its existence in humans.

Growth and Development After Birth

Fraternals

Boy-Girl Pairs

Amram Scheinfeld, in his book *Twins and Supertwins* (1967), made some important observations about boy-girl twins. The girl may have a lower birth weight, but she develops at a faster rate than her twin brother. Even at birth, a girl baby's body is more mature than that of a boy by about one and a half months. Providing tangible evidence of this, her bones have already begun to harden in areas where a male baby still has soft cartilage. Boy babies are generally larger at birth than girls because males are destined to be larger than females,

Fraternal girls

according to Scheinfeld, and girls generally retain and even increase their biological lead over boys right through puberty. In addition, the likelihood of a serious defect or illness is much greater for the boy than for the girl. Scheinfeld felt that earlier physiological development may give a girl twin an advantage when it comes to walking, but the boy's more muscular body build offsets his sister's head start. This same physical strength gives boys an edge in more athletic endeavors, but girls usually talk earlier and gain small motor coordination first.

With twins as with singletons, social development may be

affected by outside influences and social pressures. For example, the expectations of family and friends condition and guide a child in socially acceptable directions for male or female behavior. At an early age, children begin to identify with their parent models. Girls become more interested in mommy's behavior and activities; boys begin to imitate daddy. This is one reason why boy-girl twins frequently discover their differences so quickly. In a more obvious way, however, boy-girl pairs rapidly learn that their bodies look different. They also find out how their organs function differently by the time they are toddlers and begin toilet training.

Perhaps because they are growing in different directions, opposite-sex twins may play well together, without as much of the rivalry that often develops in same-sex pairs, and as they grow older may find it easier to function independently. They still share a special closeness even after the first few years, though they may seem to be as separate as any two siblings in a family. Scheinfeld felt that boy-girl twins develop greater insight into the opposite sex and as a result may grow to be better-adjusted, happier adults.

Identical twin psychologists Judy W. Hagedorn and Janet W. Kizziar discuss the special concerns of boy-girl twins in their book, *Gemini: The Psychology and Phenomena of Twins* (1983). They feel that although boy-girl twins may develop a greater understanding of the opposite sex, they may also have more emotional problems related to their twinship than same-sex fraternals do. For example, if their parents preferred a girl, the boy may try to assume the role of a second girl in order to win his parents' affection. As the twins get older, their parents may make the boy twin feel responsible for his sister. This is unfair to both children and can lead to their resentment of one another and of their parents. In addition, girls generally develop earlier than boys, both physically and socially. Over the years, this can create a competitive edge for the girl, and the boy may feel inadequate. Hagedorn and Kizziar advise parents not to intervene, to avoid making comparisons between the children, and to praise the boy for his own accomplishments while ignoring his negative, attention-seeking behavior.

Boy-girl fraternals

Same-Sex Pairs

Many same-sex fraternals look very dissimilar, but some look enough alike to be mistaken for identicals. They are genetically different, however, as with other fraternal twins. One set of fraternal girls involved in the study for this book look so much alike that friends often cannot tell them apart, yet their blood types prove they are fraternal. Despite their apparent likenesses, they are developing at different rates— one began walking many months before the other. Fraternal twins' innate talents and abilities, like their physical traits, are generally no more alike than any two siblings in a family. Hagedorn and Kizziar feel that same-sex fraternals have fewer problems with emotional adjustment as they grow up than do identicals, perhaps because they find their own directions and their own interests. They are more likely than identicals to go their own ways, pursuing individual interests and making separate friendships. For this reason, same-sex fraternals may be spared the comparisons that constantly confront identicals and may not feel the pressures, especially during adolescence, to match or equal one another in every achievement. Their interests may take divergent directions, but they still have a lifetime bond which, although not as close as with identicals, is usually stronger than with two nontwin brothers or sisters. Their shared beginning provides a lasting tie.

Identicals

Identical twins are the focus of attention wherever they go and are perpetually regarded with double takes. Throughout their lives these twins are destined to be compared to one another with comments such as, "She's the talented one," or "He's the smart one." Comparative comments often stem from people's frustration at being unable to distinguish between identicals and to address them confidently as separate individuals. Even if these kinds of observations are not intended to hurt, they can be painful to twins, especially during childhood and adolescence.

Fraternal boys

Identical boys

The physiological development of identical twins seems to follow a genetic clock, and their growth charts are generally parallel. Sometimes identicals also have startling similarities in their personality traits. Comparative studies done on twins raised apart once again revive the age-old "nature versus nurture" question. That is, are correlations in their behavior, personalities, and interests due to inheritance of genetic traits or to environment before and after birth? An ongoing study being conducted by psychologist Thomas Bouchard, Jr., of the University of Minnesota, has already analyzed numerous sets of identical twins (as well as fraternals) separated at birth. Whether the correlations revealed by the study can be attributed to genes, to learned experience, or to coincidence may never be conclusively shown, but the questions posed are fascinating, particularly to parents of identical twins.

Statistics About Twins

No single source of information on the statistics of twinning is both current and comprehensive enough to provide a concise picture. Figures can help make the phenomenon more understandable, however, and some widely accepted statistics may help shed greater light on some of the areas that are of greatest concern to parents. The material is not intended as a scientific presentation but rather as an introduction to the fascinating and elusive science of twin studies. You can pursue this subject further with the help of the resources listed in Appendix I.

Incidence of Twinning

Monozygotic (one-egg or identical) twinning occurs with about the same frequency in all population groups, but the rate of dizygotic (two-egg or fraternal) twinning varies from one population group to another. M. C. Bulmer's book, *The Biology of*

Twinning in Man (1970), is still one of the most comprehensive and widely-quoted studies in this field. According to Bulmer, the incidence of one-egg twinning is 3.5 per 1000. Bulmer found the incidence of fraternal twins is generally about 8 per 1000 in Caucasians, 16 per 1000 in blacks, and 4 per 1000 in Asians, with smaller variations within these racial groups. These differences in the incidence of fraternal twinning, have a pronounced effect on the twinning rate in various parts of the world.

The search for an overall twinning rate is elusive because in each study, the results depend upon the size of the sample, the source of the information (such as national, hospital, or church birth records), the reliability of the data, and the specific years, length of time, population group, and place where the study was done. As a result, statistics may vary from one report to another and are only representative of the particular study sample.

In the United States, the late Dr. Alan F. Guttmacher analyzed eighty million births between 1928 and 1955. Although this study was concluded in the mid-1950s, it is still significant because of the size of the sample and its time span. Guttmacher found twins occurring once in 90 births, once in 93.2 white births and once in 73.2 other births (96% of which were black). A governmentally sponsored nationwide survey done in the United States in the late 1960s had similar findings, with a study population of about 45% white, 47% black, 7% Puerto Rican, and the remaining 1% of other ethnic origins. Of the 56,249 pregnancies, 615 pairs of twins were born, an incidence of 1 in 91.5 births. Twins occurred once in 100.3 white births, once in 78.8 black births, and among those of other racial or ethnic origin, once in 167.1 births.

Figures for 1950 through 1980 published by the United States Bureau of the Census show that "plural" births (all multiples) in the United States peaked in the mid-1950s when the overall birth rate was high, and reached a 30-year low in the early 1970s when total live births were beginning to decline. Since that time the plural birth ratio has been gradually increasing, with slight and occasional fluctuations.

In the figures for 1978 published by the United States Public Health Service in 1982, of the 3,333,279 births recorded nationwide, 64,163 infants were born in twin deliveries, a ratio of approximately 1 in 104 births. This agency reports a decrease in the live births in multiple deliveries from approximately 19.6 per 1000 total live births in 1978 to 19.3 per 1000 in 1980. But Public Health Service figures for the early 1980s show an increase in the multiple birth rate, with a 3% increase from 1980 to 1981, and a 2% increase from 1981 to 1982.

At least one recent American sample, however, revealed a considerably lower twinning rate. This twin study conducted by Northwestern University from 1971 to 1975 and recorded at 13 hospitals in the Chicago metropolitan area, reported 82,229 live births, of which 588 were twin deliveries—a rate of 1 in 140.

Internationally, the rate of dizygotic (two-egg or fraternal) twinning began to drop in the late 1950s in the world's developed countries. Researchers studying this phenomenon have speculated on possible reasons for this decline. Their hypotheses include environmental, nutritional, and socioeconomic effects, as well as the possible effects of oral contraceptives (birth control pills). Although some researchers identify a stabilizing trend in the international twinning rate since the mid-1970s, others are more skeptical.

According to Guttmacher's calculations, in the United States, two-thirds of all twin births are fraternal, and only one-third are identical. The frequency among white Americans is approximately 66% fraternal and 34% identical. American blacks, with a higher twinning rate than whites or Asians, also have a higher incidence of fraternals, 71% fraternals to 29% identicals. African blacks reportedly have the highest incidence of twinning, especially in many tribal groups. The Yorubas of Nigeria have as many as one set of twins in every 22 pregnancies, of which eight pairs are fraternal for every pair of identicals. In Japan, where the twinning rate is only one in 154 pregnancies, the ratio of identicals to fraternals is almost two to one. According to Bulmer's report from the 1960s, twins

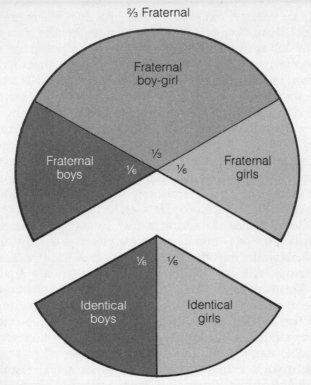

⅔ Fraternal

Fraternal
boy-girl

⅓

Fraternal
boys   ⅙   ⅙   Fraternal
girls

⅙   ⅙

Identical
boys   Identical
girls

Frequency of twin types   ⅓ Identical

occurred approximately once in 87 births, which he estimated to be about 30% identical and 70% fraternal.

If you choose to do further research on the incidence of twinning, you will discover that interpreting and comparing recent data is often difficult. Some reports show only a "plural" birth rate, which does not separate triplets and larger multiples from twins. Also, figures usually reflect actual numbers of infants born rather than sets of twins. For example, a hypothetical twinning ratio of 20 in 1000 births would really only be 10 *sets* per 1000 (or 1 set in 100). This would mean that one set of twins is born for every 100 single births. Most statistics consider only live births, so that when only one infant is born alive, the birth might be reported as a singleton, or if both are stillborn (even if delivered at term) no report might be given. Thus, the true twin-bearing chances for some women may be greater than they appear to be. Statistics show that a woman whose multiple pregnancy is closely monitored by a physician has a better chance of giving birth to live-born infants than a woman who does not receive medical care. Does this mean that a woman receiving specialized care at a major urban medical facility would have a greater chance of having twins than would otherwise be expected due to her age, racial type, and number of previous births? Similarly, would her less fortunate or less-cared for counterpart have a decreased chance of bearing twins? In short, an increase or decrease in the twinning rate in a given year may indicate more about the quality of medical care than about a change in the fertility rate. An additional variable is that most reports do not isolate multiple births induced by ovulatory-stimulating drugs ("fertility drugs") from multiple births arising from natural fertility. The use of such drugs may skew the statistical curve, artificially altering the fertility rate. The discrepancy in available statistics and the complexities involved in analyzing them make it extremely difficult to select a single, universal figure for the rate of twinning. More research is clearly needed in this area.

Influences on the Twinning Rate

Although the frequency of identical twins does not seem to be influenced by the mother's age, race, ethnic origin, or number of previous pregnancies, fraternal twinning is affected by all of these characteristics. The chances for a fraternal birth increase steadily as a woman gets older, reaching a peak at about the age of thirty-seven and then dropping off abruptly. A fraternal birth is three times more likely for women between thirty-five and forty than for those between twenty and twenty-four. In addition, the greater the number of a woman's previous pregnancies, the greater her likelihood for fraternal twins. The chances of a mother of twins giving birth to twins again are one in twenty.

Fertility drugs, first introduced in the 1960s, have artificially increased fraternal conceptions. These drugs, such as human menopausal gonadotrophin (Pergonal) and clomiphene citrate (Clomid), stimulate the ovaries and may induce production of more than one egg in a single month. The incidence of multiple fetuses following gonadotrophin therapy was reported to be as high as 20 to 40 percent in the late 1960s. Physicians are now more experienced in the use of these drugs and can better control the drugs' effects by closely monitoring the doses and their frequency. Therapy using clomiphene now has a reduced likelihood of multiples, between 7 and 8 percent, according to one laboratory's study.

Birth control pills have been linked to an increase in twin births (particularly fraternals) in several studies. A Yale University study, which was conducted between 1974 and 1976 and involved 4,428 women delivered at five large hospitals in Connecticut, reported twice the expected number of twins born to women who had become pregnant within two months after discontinuing oral contraceptives. In 1977, similar results were reported in a larger sample of 19,887 women in the Boston area among mothers who had discontinued birth control pills within one month before conception.

Twins also appear with greater frequency in certain families. Whether this increased frequency is due to heredity or environment is not clear, and may be different for identicals than for fraternals. Contrary to popular belief, however, twins do not necessarily skip generations.

Sex Ratio

In the United States, among single births, approximately 105 boys are born for every 100 girls. With twins, this frequency decreases. Almost one-third of all twins are boy-girl sets. The remaining two-thirds, the same-sex pairs, fall almost equally among boys and girls. In Guttmacher's analysis of 125,000 twin pairs born in the United States, the ratio of males to females among twins was 101.6 to 100.

Size at Birth

Twins at birth are generally smaller than singletons. Although the average weight for a singleton is seven and a half pounds (approximately 3,402 grams), the Northwestern University Multihospital Study found an average weight of approximately 2,388 grams (about five pounds, four ounces) for the first-born twin, and approximately 2,314 grams (about five pounds, two ounces) for the second twin. Among the twins in the study, 51 percent of those born first and 47.4 percent of those born second weighed 2,500 grams (about five pounds, eight ounces) or more.

The disparity in the birth weights of a set of twins may actually be greater with identical pairs than with fraternals. Because identicals generally share a placenta and chorion bag, they are not only compromised by crowding in the womb but must also compete for the same nutritional benefits. Sometimes one is well nourished and the other somewhat deprived, resulting in significant birth-weight differences, in some cases more than one and a half pounds.

The variation in size and weight becomes less and less pronounced with identicals because of their matched developmental time clock. Fraternals who have distinct developmental patterns, however, may start out about the same size but may grow increasingly different in size and weight as time goes by. In boy-girl pairs, the girl averages only three ounces lighter at birth than her twin brother. Twins generally catch up with singletons in height and weight by the age of eight.

Diagnosis of Twin Types

An examination of the afterbirth (the placenta and chorion) if it remains relatively intact is standard procedure with same-sex pairs, which may be either fraternal or identical. The twins are considered identical if the doctor finds only one placenta with no evidence of fusion and only one chorion. The presence of two placentas (or a single fused placenta) and two chorions can indicate either identicals or fraternals. The reliability of these tests, however, depends on the expertise of the examiner, as well as the presence of an intact placenta and chorion. Blood tests are generally performed to confirm or clarify the findings of the afterbirth examination.

Blood analysis is considered the most effective method currently available for diagnosing twin type. Identical twins' blood samples match for every blood group, major and minor. A doctor or trained technician can compare blood samples from a same-sex pair utilizing the ten major blood groups and can determine that twins are fraternal with approximately 97 percent accuracy. Accuracy has been increased to 98.5 percent when tests have been available to compare additional blood groups as well as enzymes taken from the placenta.

Other diagnostic techniques include fingerprinting, which is less conclusive, and questionnaires regarding visible physical traits and general resemblance when blood samples are not available. One study involving questionnaires, which was published in the early 1960s, was accurate in diagnosing identical twins in up to 93 percent of same-sex pairs. Various other methods have also been used, and some are more reliable than others. These include tests of tissue compatibility, analysis of electrocardiograms to measure differences in heart function, and the detailed examination of comparative tooth form and structure in older twins.

Even a series of tests may not always conclusively prove that a twin pair is identical or fraternal. The identification of twin type may not be essential in every case, but from a medical point of view, the knowledge could be helpful under some circumstances. For example, a doctor may be concerned about possible genetic abnormalities, which in the case of an identical pair would necessarily occur in both twins. Also, an identical twin is a perfectly matched potential donor should any tissue or organ transplant ever be required by his or her twin. Positive proof that a pair is identical could save the life of the ailing twin in such an emergency.

"Supertwins": Triplets, Quadruplets, and More

Amram Scheinfeld in his book *Twins and Supertwins* (1967) popularized the term *supertwins* as a convenient catch-all word to refer to multiples of three or more. Supertwins are formed in much the same way as twins, but with more variables. For example, triplets can all be identical, formed from a single egg; can be formed from two eggs so that two are identical twins and the third is a fraternal sibling; or can all be fraternal, formed from three separate eggs. The reported incidence of single-egg triplets (identicals) is one out of every ten cases; two-egg triplets (identical twins and a singleton) occur in six out of ten cases; and three-egg triplets (fraternals) are observed in three cases in ten. Fertility drugs alter the natural chance factors. Ovulatory-stimulating drugs can cause more than one egg to be released in a single cycle, increasing the incidence of fraternal births. As with triplets, quadruplets, quintuplets, or more can arise from one or more eggs. The Dionne quintuplets originated as a single egg, and when they were born in May 1934 they made history as the first known set of identical quintuplets to survive to maturity.

Triplets occur once in 9,300 and quadruplets once in 490,000 births, according to Guttmacher's study (see above). The frequency of triplets is considerably lower among whites, 1 in 10,200, than among blacks and other racial groups, 1 in

Supertwins

5,800. A study of multiple births in the United States in 1964 found that triplets, like twins, occur with greater frequency as maternal age increases and also as the number of a woman's previous pregnancies increases (up to six previous pregnancies in the case of black women). Among supertwins, the number of males decreases as the number of fetuses increases. A study published in 1946 found 51.59 percent males among singletons, 50.85 percent among twins, 49.54 percent among triplets, and only 46.48 percent among quadruplets.

Supertwin researcher, Helen Kirk, has been collecting data on multiple births worldwide since 1939. "Miss Helen," as she likes to be called, is a member of the International Society of Twin Studies and welcomes correspondence from supertwins and their families as well as from families who have two or more sets of multiples (see Appendix I for the address).

CHAPTER 2

Diagnosis and Pregnancy

Early diagnosis is extremely important in a twin pregnancy because of the greater physical demands on the expectant mother. Up to one-half of twin pregnancies, however, go unrecognized. According to *Williams Obstetrics* (1985), a widely respected medical text, multiple pregnancy often goes undetected "not so much because it is unusually difficult, but because the examiner fails to keep the possibility in mind."*

Doctors are becoming more attentive to the symptoms, however. One mother involved in the survey for this book said her twins were "diagnosed at the first OB [obstetrical] exam with the pregnancy." Another's doctor "heard two heartbeats at four months, and took a sonogram at five months."

It is not unusual however, for parents to suspect twins even before the doctor does. This was one woman's experience: "My twins were officially detected in an ultrasonogram done in the fourth month of pregnancy. I had suspected something unusual because I was much larger at this stage than in my first pregnancy. At fourteen weeks I could feel movements

---

*Jack A. Pritchard, M.D.; Paul C. MacDonald, M.D.; and Norman F. Grant, M.D., eds. *Williams Obstetrics*, 17th ed. (Norwalk, CT: Appleton-Century-Crofts, 1985), p. 510.

around my navel instead of near my pubic bone. When I touched my abdomen, I could feel that the top of my uterus was above my navel. The books I read said this doesn't happen until five months. In addition, I already had to wear maternity clothes. After I mentioned all of this to my doctor, he used an ultrasound stethoscope and thought he heard two separate heartbeats. Then he ordered a sonogram, which showed there were definitely twins."

This woman was able to identify many of the symptoms of a twin pregnancy and was able to bring this information to her doctor's attention, helping to bring about a timely diagnosis. This story illustrates the importance of communication between an expectant mother and her doctor. If a woman observes any of the telltale signs of twin pregnancy listed later in this chapter, she should alert her doctor.

Diagnosis

Reasons to Suspect Twins

A woman who has a family history of twins or who has taken drugs to stimulate ovulation is more likely to have a multiple birth. Her physician will monitor her pregnancy with this possibility in mind. A woman who does not have this background, however, can also have twins. The following symptoms are often associated with multiple pregnancies:

A uterus that is unusually large for the particular stage of pregnancy and that continues to grow at a rapid rate

A rapid increase in the mother's weight that cannot be attributed to a previous overweight condition or to water retention in either her own tissues or in the fetal amniotic sac

The mother's awareness of fetal movements that are markedly more pronounced than those experienced in a previous pregnancy

A small part of a fetus that presents itself in the pelvis causing cervical dilation four weeks or more before term with no evidence of the onset of labor

Any of these signs could have another explanation, but the presence of separate fetal heartbeats differing by ten or more beats per minute in two distinct areas of the abdomen, or the detection of two heads or two breeches (buttocks) in an abdominal exam are considered definite indications of multiple pregnancy.

Importance of Early Detection

The timeliness of diagnosis is constantly improving due to increased medical awareness of the importance of early detection and because of advancements in diagnostic techniques. Nevertheless, in almost half of the 588 twin pregnancies in the Northwestern University Multihospital Study mentioned in Chapter 1, the second baby was not detected until twenty-eight weeks, and not until after labor had begun or after the first twin had been delivered in 25 percent of the pregnancies. According to the Center for Study of Multiple Birth in Chicago, 20 to 50 percent of twin births are undiagnosed until after delivery of the first twin, and this causes concern because "there is often no opportunity to institute intensive care prior to the time of delivery." This national organization and another which primarily serves Northern California called Twinline, Services for Multiple Birth Families, are making great strides to educate doctors and health professionals as well as parents on the medical risks and unique problems presented by a twin pregnancy.

Tests for Confirmation

Diagnostic ultrasound is a relatively new procedure that enables the doctor to examine structures that lie beneath the surface of the skin. If the doctor suspects twins, ultrasound is currently the most effective diagnostic tool and is the usual method of confirming a multiple pregnancy. Ultrasound is also routinely used by some doctors to monitor pregnancy, whether single or multiple. As with any other clinical procedure, however, many years of study will be necessary before long-range effects can be assessed and benefits can be weighed against risks.

The process involves the reflection of ultrahigh frequency sound waves off a pelvic or intra-abdominal structure. In early pregnancy, the woman is asked to drink up to a quart of water at least an hour before the sonogram is taken. This is impor-

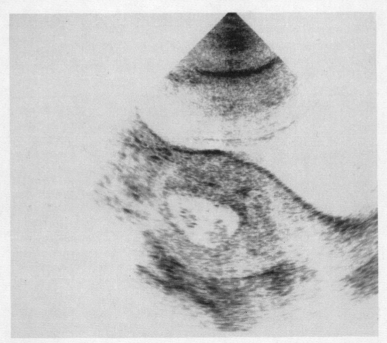

At 6½ weeks, a first look in utero at in vitro fertilization [test tube] twins.

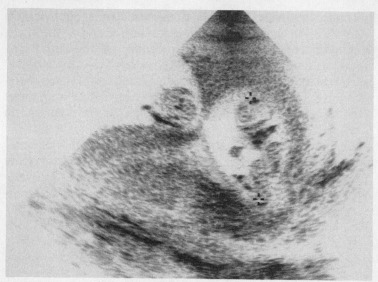

At 12½ weeks, in vitro fertilization twins with separate amniotic sacs and chorion bags. Head of twin on left, and full fetal image of twin on right are visible.

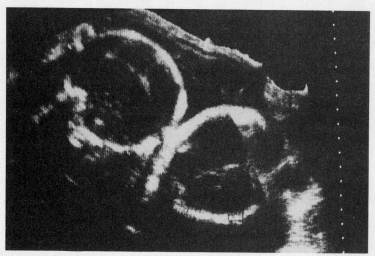

At 32½ weeks, twin heads measuring 8.5 and 8.7 centimeters. Babies weigh about 4 lbs. each.

tant for two reasons. The fluid fills the bladder, pushing the woman's uterus up above the pubic bone, and the full bladder enhances the sound, providing a clearer "view" of the contents of the uterus. The skin of the abdomen is then lubricated with mineral oil, and a technician slides the ultrasonic transducer (a wandlike object connected by a wire to a large machine) across the abdomen at regular intervals, usually in the range of one centimeter.

The intra-abdominal image of each vertical and horizontal scan is revealed on a video screen. Fetuses in different areas of the uterus can be easily detected by this technique. After this procedure, the technician may give the expectant mother a photograph of the video image. Advances in ultrasound technology have now made it possible to detect a second twin even when it is obscured by the first baby. With the introduction of "realtime" ultrasound, it is possible to see a motion picture of the contents of the uterus, and even to see the area behind a baby. This technique also confirms that both babies are alive.

Using ultrasound, diagnosis of multiple pregnancy has been made as early as the fifth to seventh week, though accuracy is not reliable before the twelfth week. According to recent studies, the findings of ultrasound examinations done in the early stages of pregnancy, however, would seem to indicate that many more twins are actually conceived than are born.

Sometimes with a multiple conception, particularly in the first trimester (the first three months), loss of one embryo or fetus takes place, accompanied only by slight vaginal bleeding. Although the mother has not lost much blood, she may fear that she has miscarried and may be relieved when a follow-up ultrasound scan reveals that she is still pregnant. She may not even have realized that she had conceived twins.

What becomes of the lost twin is somewhat of a mystery, especially when no trace of an embryo or fetus can be subsequently identified by ultrasound, and when following the resultant birth of a single infant, no evidence of a second twin can be found in the afterbirth. This is known in the medical literature as the "vanishing twin" phenomenon, occurring late in the first trimester of pregnancy or early in the second. Doctors studying the phenomenon believe that in many cases the embryo or fetus of the vanishing twin may be reabsorbed into the uterus. For this reason, if an early ultrasound exam detects a multiple pregnancy, a subsequent scan may be recommended later in the pregnancy to verify the presence of two developing fetuses.

Before the development of ultrasound, doctors generally relied on their own suspicions for diagnosis of a multiple pregnancy (as listed above under "Reasons to Suspect Twins"). Occasionally multiple fetuses were identified by X-ray, but this was usually not why the X-ray was being taken. Even today X-rays are rarely utilized during pregnancy to diagnose twins or for any other purpose. This is because even small amounts of radiation can be hazardous to a developing fetus, especially during the early months. In addition, during the first eighteen weeks X-rays are not always reliable as a diagnostic tool for obstetrics because at this stage they reveal only bony matter and the immature fetal skeleton may not as yet be visible.

An elevated level of certain hormones in a pregnant woman's blood or urine is sometimes an indication that a woman is carrying twins. Measuring the level of these hormones, however, is more often used to rule out the possibility of a multiple birth as an alternative to ultrasound, which could present a potential risk and which is also expensive. If hormonal tests are positive, ultrasound can be used, at the discretion of the woman and her doctor, to confirm diagnosis.

Pregnancy

Emotional Concerns

Mother

Once twins have been diagnosed, you may be stunned or bewildered, not knowing what to do next or how to prepare yourself. The babies do not have names or personalities yet, so although sometimes you may feel attached to them, at other times you may feel resentful. On these latter occasions you may think of twins as an imposition disfiguring your body and intruding on your marriage, your family, or both. You may even think of yourself as abnormal or freakish because you are carrying two babies. One woman remembers, "During my pregnancy I spent a good percentage of my waking hours feeling sorry for myself. 'Twins! Why me?' What was I going to do?"

Talking to experienced mothers of twins is excellent therapy. By contacting the local mothers of twins club you can get the names of women who are eager to give moral support to others. As an expectant mother, you are invited to visit the club. In some clubs, expectant mothers are welcome to join; in others you will become eligible once the twins are born. The National Organization of Mothers of Twins Clubs (NOMOTC), listed in Appendix I, can refer you to your local chapter.

Father

Fathers typically have different concerns. Those surveyed for this book had mixed feelings when first informed that their wives were carrying twins. Most were amazed and excited, but they also expressed feeling greater pressures, especially financial. Not only did fathers worry about how to provide for the costs of two infants, but they even prepared a will, bought life insurance, and tried to tighten the budget in order to save extra dollars. These types of concerns, which arc natural to all expectant fathers, were magnified twofold for men awaiting the arrival of twins.

One man reacted by buying the biggest station wagon he could find and a large freezer to store the anticipated "tons of food" he expected his expanding family to consume. An expectant father of triplets thought "the idea [of three babies] was great, but how was I going to afford this?" The men, like their wives, had to adjust psychologically to the notion of twins.

As with expectant fathers of singletons, most of the men surveyed seemed to adjust more easily than their wives because the fathers were not physiologically affected by the pregnancy and could stand back and observe the entire process. Said one man, "I was curious to see how the experience would affect our lives." For others, however, the very idea of twins was overwhelming, particularly in the case of an unplanned pregnancy. Some became angered in the presence of a situation that was completely beyond their control. Others felt left out during the months that preceded the birth of the twins.

These are normal reactions, and you may have them, too. Relatives and friends may be especially attentive, concerned, or anxious about your wife while paying little attention to you. You, in turn, may feel increasingly displaced and unneeded and may vent your frustrations in the form of jealousy or resentment. Your wife may be less interested in sexual intercourse toward the end of her multiple pregnancy. Because she is carrying twins, the larger size of her abdomen and the greater crowding of her internal organs may make her uncomfortable sooner than if she were expecting only one baby. You may even be temporarily disinterested in sexual intercourse, too, though for different reasons. One father was exhausted by "a combination of work and taking care of meals and the house while my wife was bedridden for about eight weeks." (See also "Sexual Activity" in Chapter 5.) You and your wife should openly discuss these feelings. A comfortable rapport between expectant parents is essential.

Both Parents

A subject that frequently concerns both parents of twins is the quality of medical care their babies will receive, particularly if they are born prematurely or with complications. Since twins often arrive early, you should begin the process of selecting a pediatrician well in advance of your due date.

Schedule an appointment for a consultation to discuss the history of the pregnancy. Interview more than one doctor if you feel this will help you make the best decision. Be sure that you feel comfortable with the kind of care the doctor recommends for the babies and with the other doctors who may be "on call" from time to time. Discuss any subjects that are especially important to you.

If the doctor you select is associated with the same hospital where the babies will be delivered, ask if he or she can be present at the birth. If you belong to a clinic or special health care facility, be sure to meet and talk with the doctor who will regularly see your babies. The better he or she is acquainted with you, the better your rapport will be later. Many physicians develop a special closeness with their families of twins. As one relieved mother recalls, "Our pediatrician was terrific! He came to the hospital at five o'clock in the morning when our babies were born, and he wasn't even on call."

Preparing for Childbirth

Classes

For expectant parents of twins, childbirth classes where both parents attend or classes on how to be a parent can be very helpful in maintaining the lines of communication between the expectant mother and father. Be sure to tell your childbirth instructor that you are expecting twins. Your instructor can give you information on the conduct of a twin birth as well as about the birth process in general. Be sure to enroll in a class that begins no later than the sixth or seventh month of pregnancy because twins are frequently born early.

Three childbirth programs that are popular today are described below. These methods are also generally appropriate for twin pregnancy. Consult your physician before enrolling in childbirth classes.

The Read Method

The term natural childbirth was first coined in the 1930s by the English doctor Grantly Dick-Read, author of *Childbirth Without Fear*. Dick-Read theorized and set out to prove that fear and apprehension magnify the natural pain or discomfort of childbirth. He argued that by educating the pregnant woman in the normal bodily functions during labor and delivery, she could have pain-free, even exhilarating childbirth. He believed that fear and tension are the primary sources of pain and adopted the term *contraction* in place of *labor pain*. Dick-Read felt a woman could avoid much of the usual tension through relaxation exercises. He also recommended that a woman not be left alone during labor because solitude breeds fear. Dick-Read was the first to develop a method of psychological pain relief, now known as the Read method.

The Lamaze Method

Perhaps the most popular childbirth program using psychological pain relief techniques is the *Lamaze method*. The technique is named after Dr. Fernand Lamaze, who, in the early 1950s, introduced this Russian-derived system of *psychoprophylaxis* (mind-over-body pain relief) to France. In the following few years the method was introduced in the United States, where it has gradually come to be widely practiced and accepted. The method is not really "natural" at all, as it requires careful preparation, which is accomplished through special classes in Lamaze training and through supplemental recommended readings.

The method involves education on what to expect during labor and delivery, a series of simple exercises to help the mother relax, and learned breathing patterns that work to displace pain or discomfort. The Lamaze method does not require that a woman endure discomfort without the assistance of drugs, but it does make it easier for her to feel comfortable without any painkilling medications. The husband or a coach helps the woman monitor her contractions. A woman having a Caesarean section can also use Lamaze preparation to feel more relaxed and have a greater understanding of the childbirth process.

The Bradley Method

Based on the philosophy of Dr. Robert A. Bradley, as described in his book, *Husband-Coached Childbirth*, the Bradley method helps the husband and wife work together for a joyful birth experience. The pregnant woman learns to "tune in" to her body without using distraction techniques or prescription drugs to relieve the discomforts of labor. The expectant couple plans a positive approach to labor and delivery, the hospital stay, and the complex feelings and emotions surrounding the birth experience.

Planning an "Alternative Birth"?

For parents-to-be, a warm, personal birth environment is very important. For those who are expecting only one baby this may be best realized with a home delivery. A home birth with twins, however, may be just a dream for most who want it because of the high risk of complications associated with the delivery of twins. Home deliveries are becoming increasingly popular for single births, but few doctors or midwives are willing to risk delivering twins at home since they cannot be assured of the immediate availability of emergency medical care and life support equipment. In some states, midwives cannot be certified to preside at any kind of home deliveries. Alternative birth centers at many hospitals or clinics are generally designated for low-risk births, specifically excluding twin deliveries.

One option that those expecting twins can sometimes arrange at a hospital is a labor support advocate. This individual is usually a nurse, midwife, or childbirth instructor who has previously met with the expectant couple to discuss their childbirth preferences. Parents become physically and emotionally involved during a twin delivery. The labor advocate who is present during labor and delivery can speak to the medical team on the parents' behalf. For example, the mother may want to touch or hold the first twin if time permits before delivery of the second, or the parents may want to see the babies together before they are sent to the nursery to be examined (if they do not require emergency care). Hospitals that permit a labor support advocate to be present generally require that special arrangements be made in advance.

Managing the Pregnancy

Medical Care

Selecting an obstetrician whose medical judgment you respect and with whom you can have a good rapport is especially important with a twin pregnancy. Once twins have been diagnosed certain dietary changes, modifications in your daily activities, and more rest will be necessary. Talk to your doctor about how to adapt your current routine to meet the additional demands of a multiple pregnancy. Ask what procedures he or she anticipates when you arrive at the hospital. Find out your doctor's attitude about a vaginal delivery with twins, and whether your husband or coach can be present. Does the hospital have an intensive care nursery if the babies are born prematurely or need special medical attention? These questions are especially important because twins have a greater percentage of complications at birth than singletons do. Do not be afraid to ask if you do not understand or do not agree with your physician's recommendations.

Frequent visits are essential not only to monitor your condition at each stage but also to be sure your doctor is familiar with the history of this pregnancy before delivery. The doctor will want to monitor your progress closely because multiple pregnancies are prone to certain complications. *Hydramnios,* excessive fluid in one or both of the fetal sacs, for example, can cause the abdomen to become more distended and uncomfortable.

Toxemia is another complication that may develop in late pregnancy. The first stage of toxemia is called *pre-eclampsia,* a combination of edema (fluid retention in the body tissue), protein in the urine, and high blood pressure. This serious condition, if not treated, can lead to *eclampsia,* the more severe second stage of toxemia that is marked by convulsions, coma, and sometimes even death. Toxemia is three to five times more common in women carrying twins than in those carrying a singleton, and the condition occurs in as many as 20 to 30 percent of all twin pregnancies.

Spotting or bleeding, particularly during the first trimester, is also more likely to occur with a multiple pregnancy. Prematurity is another risk that in the presence of certain warning signals can sometimes be averted with medical treatment (see Chapter 4). These are all reasons why women expecting twins have a responsibility to themselves and to their babies to be regularly checked by a doctor throughout the pregnancy.

In those families for whom genetic counseling is recommended, a genetic analysis of the fetal cells can be done by examining a sample of the amniotic fluid removed through a procedure called *amniocentesis.* This procedure is more involved with twins, who in most cases develop in separate amniotic sacs. Tissue cultures of the fetal cells found in the amniotic fluid can be used to identify genetic disorders and chemical or enzyme deficiencies that may be present in a fetus. It is not completely risk-free and is an expensive procedure because the tissue studies (of the cultured fetal cells) can cost several hundred dollars.

Genetic amniocentesis may be appropriate in the presence of one or more of the following circumstances:

An expectant mother who is thirty-five years of age or older (statistically the risk of chromosomal abnormalities increases after the age of thirty-five)

Parents who are known carriers of structural rearrangements of chromosomes

Parents who have previously had a child with a chromosomal abnormality, a chemical or enzyme deficiency, or a neural tube disorder

Parents who are known carriers of disorders of the X-chromosome

Parents who are known carriers of hemoglobin abnormalities

This list of criteria is constantly increasing with the growth of knowledge about genetic defects and with the advances in medical technology that make diagnosis possible. Genetic amniocentesis can currently identify such conditions as Down's syndrome (a chromosomal abnormality), Tay Sachs disease (an enzyme deficiency), thalassemia and sickle cell anemia (hemoglobin abnormalities), spina bifida (a neural tube disorder), and other less familiar genetic disorders. (The National Genetics Foundation in New York provides information and referrals to individuals and families with known or suspected genetic problems. See "Pregnancy and Childbirth" in Appendix I.)

Because twin conceptions are highest among women over thirty-five, the high-risk age group for chromosomal abnormalities, a discussion of amniocentesis seems appropriate. In addition, as has already been explained, testing both fetuses can be complicated. Understanding how the procedure is performed may help you consider your own options if an amniocentesis is recommended.

Between fifteen and seventeen weeks into the pregnancy, calculated from the last menstrual period, is the optimal time to perform an amniocentesis. By this time the volume of amniotic fluid is sufficient to permit the safe removal of an adequate sample. About 10 percent of the fluid in the sac is withdrawn. This quantity is replaced naturally by the body within a few hours. Earlier sampling, even when possible, carries a higher risk of abortion and infection. When amniocentesis was first developed it was not recommended for use in conjunction with multiple pregnancy. Repeated attempts were often necessary in order to remove fluid from each baby's amniotic sac (in the presence of two sacs), and the same baby's amniotic fluid was sometimes tapped twice. This frequently led to fetal or placental injury, or to miscarriage. Today, in most cases, ultrasound is used to locate the placenta(s) and fetal sac(s). A dye can be used to temporarily stain the fluid in the first sac after a sample is removed. This identifies the first sac in case it is inadvertently tapped a second time.

Amniocentesis can be performed on an outpatient basis. First, ultrasound is used to locate the placenta(s) and fetal sac(s). Then the mother's abdomen is cleansed with an antiseptic solution. A local anesthetic may or may not be administered to desensitize the abdominal wall. A long, thin, hollow needle is inserted into one amniotic sac, and several milliliters of fluid are withdrawn. If two sacs are present, a small amount of dye is injected into the sac just tested, without removing the needle. A second needle is then inserted in the area of the second sac (as identified by ultrasound), and a few milliliters of fluid are removed. The first sac has been reentered if the fluid is colored by the dye. Ultrasound is used again to check the babies' condition after amniocentesis. Some of the fluid in the sample can be tested for enzymatic abnormalities. Some can be centrifuged in order to make a culture of the fetal cells to determine the fetal genetic makeup. Multiplication of the fetal cells requires from three to forty days.

If a genetic abnormality is identified in either or both of the fetuses, parents are given information as to the nature of the disorder and the prognosis. The family is told whether the defect is likely to recur in subsequent pregnancies. At this point, the family may prefer to continue with the pregnancy or may elect to terminate it (if the law permits). Either decision can cause great emotional stress. Those who continue can prepare themselves for how to handle their child's or children's disability and their own disappointment by contacting an appropriate support organization (see "Disabled Children"

in Appendix I). Those who choose abortion, even for therapeutic reasons, face difficult moral and ethical questions and
their own feelings of guilt. Selective abortion, terminating
only one fetus of a twin pregnancy, is sometimes possible
when only one is diagnosed as abnormal. Tests are done first
to identify positively which of the twins is abnormal.

Studies indicate that the risks to the mother and to the fetus
following amniocentesis are low but may be greater with
twins if repeated taps are necessary to extract fluid successfully from both sacs. Risks to the mother include possible
puncture of a blood vessel, puncture or injury to an internal
organ, and infection. Fetal risks include possible infection,
injuries to the infant that can lead to bruising or bleeding,
injuries to the placenta or to the membranes, and premature
labor that can lead to miscarriage.

Amniocentesis is not reserved for genetic diagnosis alone. It
is also sometimes used to reduce overdistension of the abdomen due to *hydramnios* (also called *polyhydramnios*), an excessive buildup of amniotic fluid, which occurs more frequently
with twins, or to determine the maturity of the fetal lungs in
late pregnancy. With hydramnios, if only one sac is affected,
fluid is removed from that sac only, and analysis of the fluid
may or may not be performed.

With twins as with singletons, ultrasound can sometimes be
used to make a diagnosis when structural abnormalities in a
fetus are suspected. Defects acquired due to the mother's exposure to environmental influences, such as drug usage, or
due to congenital infections or diseases in the mother (such as
rubella) that cannot be diagnosed by amniocentesis can often
be identified using ultrasound. (The use of ultrasound during
pregnancy to confirm the presence of twins is discussed earlier
in this chapter.)

Body Changes, Discomforts, and Remedies

The minor discomforts of pregnancy may be magnified with
twins; however, each woman's body responds differently. Listed

below are some of the familiar complaints, although you may or may not have any or all of them. These discomforts can be annoying, but they usually are not serious and do not have permanent effects.

Nausea or vomiting, often called "morning sickness," is frequently the earliest symptom of pregnancy and may begin shortly after your first missed period and last for six to eight weeks. Although some women never have this discomfort at all or are not affected equally with each pregnancy, nausea is often greater with a twin pregnancy. The queasiness associated with morning sickness, caused primarily by the hormonal changes in the body, can be aggravated by the elevated hormonal level that accompanies a multiple pregnancy, by a poor diet, or by the nervousness that you may feel at the onset of such a major life change as pregnancy.

Despite its name, morning sickness is not limited to the early hours of the day and may be just as likely to occur at four in the afternoon. The pattern often becomes predictable, striking at around the same times each day. The condition is particularly uncomfortable whenever the stomach is empty. Eating a few dry crackers or toast before getting out of bed in the morning and as needed throughout the day can sometimes remedy the situation. Take several small meals rather than three large ones, and between meals limit fluids to small quantities. Fasting or eating rich or greasy foods can aggravate nausea. Drugs that are used to relieve discomfort may also have side effects or risks. Before taking any medication, consult your doctor. This includes over-the-counter medications such as aspirins and antacids.

Breast Changes. In early pregnancy the breasts often become very sensitive as they begin to enlarge in preparation for milk production. This temporary growth in the breast tissue may be greater for you than for a woman pregnant with a single baby. The tenderness in the breasts during early pregnancy usually goes away by itself after about three months, but the fullness continues to increase, and the nipple and dark area surrounding it (the *areola*) may darken. After the birth of twins, if you choose to nurse, your breasts may become larger during the months you are breastfeeding than if you were nursing only one baby. Two nursing babies will quickly empty the breasts, so this additional breast enlargement may be most noticeable before a feeding or after a missed feeding.

Varicose veins, a common pregnancy symptom, can be aggravated by a twin pregnancy. Try to stay off your feet, and keep them elevated whenever possible. Your doctor may recommend special support hose.

Constipation, Hemorrhoids, and Gas. Greater discomfort from constipation and hemorrhoids (varicose veins in the rectal area) is also common in women expecting twins. Eating stewed prunes or drinking prune juice can help you stay regular. If this does not help, ask your doctor about a stool softener. Your doctor can give you advice on how to relieve discomfort from hemorrhoids. Your diet can also help minimize discomfort from gas. The worst offenders are fried foods, apples, corn, lettuce, cabbage, beans, dried fruits, raw fruits and vegetables, and carbonated drinks. You may have to cut down on some of your favorite foods for a few months.

"Heartburn," generally associated with the later weeks of pregnancy, frequently begins earlier in an expectant mother of twins. The crowding of the digestive organs by the growing uterus causes the stomach to regurgitate into the esophagus, creating a burning sensation. Avoid rich or greasy foods and take only moderate amounts of citrus fruits and juices and other highly acidic foods. Check with your physician before taking any antacids, particularly baking soda or other antacids containing bicarbonate of soda. The sodium in these products can cause water retention, leading to swelling of the body tissues (*edema*), a condition that is more problematic in multiple pregnancies.

Bladder pressure, common to the later months, may be exaggerated in a twin pregnancy because of the additional weight of the abdomen. You may constantly have the urge to urinate, and you may even wake up three or four times at night to dash to the bathroom. This is an inconvenience without a remedy. Do not restrict your fluids unless this is recommended by your physician.

Stretch marks (striae gravidarium) may be far more pronounced in the woman bearing twins. The connective tissues below the skin of the abdomen are subjected to tremendous stress as they are forced to expand with the growth of two babies. Baby oil can be massaged into the skin to ease the itching sensation. Many advertised products claim they can prevent stretch marks from forming, but most women seem to find these remedies ineffective.

Appetite Changes. You may feel ravenously hungry in the middle trimester of your double pregnancy, but this craving for food will quickly be replaced by a loss of appetite as the twins begin to crowd your digestive system. The food you eat, however, is still crucial to the nourishment and development of the babies, and even if you find the thought of food distasteful, it is important to maintain a regular diet of well-balanced meals. (See Chapter 5, "Maternal Nutrition and Health," for a diet and menu plan designed specifically for twin pregnancy.)

Fatigue and Sleep Problems. Fatigue, common in early pregnancy, sets in again during the last three months and is often more pronounced for expectant mothers of twins during this last trimester. Two babies can be very active *in utero,* and you may be awakened two or even three times during the night as the twins get their nightly exercise. You may begin to feel so tired that you need a rest during the middle of the day. Nap whenever possible, taking the phone off the hook to guarantee that you will not be disturbed. You need as much extra sleep as you can get during the day to bolster you for the restless nights of late pregnancy. Finding a comfortable position, however, can be difficult. (See "Activity and Rest" in Chapter 5.)

Backache is frequently greater with a twin pregnancy. (See "Physical Activity" in Chapter 5 for suggestions on how to prevent or remedy backache.)

Swelling of the body tissues, most noticeable around the joints and in the feet and legs, is generally caused by water retention (*edema*). This condition is often exaggerated by a multiple pregnancy. (See "Physical Activity" in Chapter 5.)

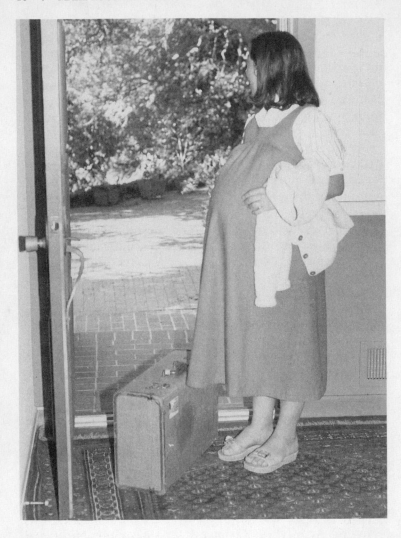

Adapting Your Wardrobe

Maternity clothes are not designed for the larger abdomen of a twin pregnancy, and finding clothes to fit can be a big problem. If you enjoy sewing, you will probably find maternity patterns that can be adapted to the fuller figure of your double pregnancy. Loose jumpers will fit longer than other styles. Pants or skirts, even with a maternity panel, seldom provide adequate room for growth. One mother remembering her own pregnancy advises, "Wear a nightgown around the house. It's much more comfortable than clothes, which can be very restrictive."

When you have to go out, especially in fall and winter, you will need something to cover your legs. Most supermarkets sell inexpensive "queen-size" pantyhose, although you will probably outgrow these before the end of your pregnancy. Your doctor may prefer that you wear specially designed pregnancy support hose, especially if you have varicose veins. These stockings can be purchased or ordered at maternity stores or in the maternity section of your local department store. Maternity and nursing brassieres are also available in these stores. Be sure that the bras are comfortable, provide good support for the breast tissue, and leave room for further breast enlargement in the advancing months of your multiple pregnancy.

If you plan to nurse your babies, you may want to buy nursing bras that you can also wear after delivery because they have flaps that can be lowered to expose each breast for the nursing babies. Some mothers of twins prefer front-fastening bras. This type of bra can be detached completely to accommodate two babies more comfortably when they are nursing simultaneously. Front-fastening bras may also be easier for you to unfasten while holding both babies.

The nursing bras you buy during pregnancy, however, may not fit properly once the babies are born and the milk comes in. Most bras are not returnable, so try them on for comfort before you buy. Your doctor may also recommend that you wear a maternity corset for support if you have a history of back problems or injury. This is a type of girdle that can usually be purchased or ordered where you buy maternity clothes.

CHAPTER 3

Labor, Delivery, and Postpartum

Labor

The last weeks of worrying how labor would begin, whether you would arrive at the hospital in time, and maybe even who would stay with your older child or children are now behind you. You may even find that labor with twins is easier to deal with than you imagined. Twins are often born early and tend to be smaller at birth, so they may be easier to push out. Thus, labor is frequently shorter than with singletons. Some twin labors can be lengthy, however, because the greater size of the uterus in a multiple pregnancy may prevent the muscles from exerting the necessary force to expel the babies.

Although this chapter more directly affects mothers, fathers are also encouraged to familiarize themselves with what to expect during labor and delivery with twins, as discussed throughout the subsequent pages.

Signs of Labor

Regular Contractions

With twins as with singletons, a certain sign of true labor is regular contractions that continue uninterrupted and increase in intensity. The last several weeks of a multiple pregnancy are usually marked by numerous series of false labor (Braxton-Hicks) contractions, which are generally more frequent and exaggerated in women expecting twins. Like true labor, Braxton-Hicks contractions may feel like an involuntary tightening of the abdominal muscles, or they may feel like painful crampish twinges in the cervical region, similar to menstrual cramps. Sometimes contractions begin as a lower backache and may come in waves that seem to start at your back and wrap around you.

True labor contractions continue at regular intervals, becoming increasingly intense and lasting for longer and longer periods. False labor, however, is usually intermittent and of varying intensity and duration, and it usually stops within an hour or so. Perhaps because the fear of complications is greater with a multiple birth, some expectant parents are inclined to alert the doctor earlier than is necessary. How far to let labor progress before calling the doctor is a question you should ask your own physician, as he or she is familiar with your specific condition. Discuss this well in advance of your due date. With twins, you may be asked to alert the doctor, clinic, or hospital earlier than you would with a single baby, particularly if you must travel a long way.

Losing the Mucus Plug

As with a single pregnancy, a plug of mucus seals off the cervix in the later months. In some women, labor begins when this plug is expelled vaginally as a thick, sometimes bloody discharge, often referred to as the "bloody show." Labor may commence immediately or may not begin for as long as a week or two afterward.

Rupture of the Membranes

In 29 percent of all twin pregnancies (12 percent of single pregnancies), the fluid-filled membrane that surrounds the first baby (the baby that is positioned to be born first) or that surrounds both babies ruptures spontaneously. This is also known as the "water breaking," and it may begin as a slow leaking of fluid or quite suddenly like a balloon bursting within you. In either case, the passage of this fluid, unlike urine, cannot be voluntarily controlled. This can happen while you are sleeping, so prepare ahead by lining your bed with an inexpensive plastic mattress cover. Keep a small towel or a few toddler-sized disposable diapers handy for protection. A feminine napkin or pad may not be sufficient to contain the flow, but do not use a tampon as it can introduce bacteria.

Call the doctor and proceed to the hospital if the membranes rupture because once a break occurs in the membranes, bacteria can enter the protective fluid-filled sac surrounding one or both babies. As with singletons, contractions usually begin within twenty-four hours. If not, and if your due date is near, your doctor may decide to induce labor. (See the section called "Induction and Acceleration of Labor" later in this chapter.) If your due date is still a long way off, however, you may need to remain in the hospital, where you may be given antibiotics to prevent infection. In the hospital, your condition will be carefully monitored, and since premature birth can be accompanied by numerous more serious problems, your doctor may try to forestall the babies' birth to give them more time to develop in the uterus. Prematurity is discussed in Chapter 4.

Hospital Procedure

Up to this point your labor has closely paralleled that of a woman carrying a single baby. Once you arrive at the hospital, however, if the doctor is aware that you are having twins, he or she will have made special arrangements for your delivery and care. Nevertheless, to avoid any possible confusion or oversight, once at the hospital, inform the staff that you are expecting twins. As with a single baby, you will be weighed, may be shaved in the perineal region (around the vaginal opening), and may be given a suppository or enema, but because you are about to give birth to twins, the labor and delivery staff will monitor your progress with special care. The procedures described below are frequently followed preceding the delivery of twins.

Sonogram or X-ray

If you arrive at the hospital in the early stages of labor with multiples, a sonogram or X-ray may be taken. Ultrasound can be used at this stage to check for suspected fetal problems, such as to detect *placenta previa* (a condition reported to occur twice as frequently in twin as in single pregnancies, where part of the placenta is covering the cervical opening and will interfere with a vaginal delivery) or to confirm the babies' positions if the doctor feels a Caesarean section may be necessary. X-rays, which present known dangers to a fetus during the early months of pregnancy, are sometimes used at term preceding a twin delivery under certain circumstances when the risk of an unsafe vaginal delivery may outweigh the risk of the X-ray. This procedure may be used instead of a sonogram to confirm the babies' presentations if the doctor feels a Caesarean delivery may be necessary and if ultrasound is not available or fails to give a clear picture of both babies' positions. X-rays are sometimes also used during labor and delivery with twins as with singletons for *pelvimetry*, measuring whether a baby's head is too large to fit through the pelvic opening. This procedure is not universally accepted, however, because physicians disagree as to whether the measurements taken can predict the ability of a woman's pelvis to deliver a specific fetal head size. Some doctors even feel that the potential risks of X-ray may not warrant its widespread use for pelvimetry.

Fetal Monitors

The conduct of labor and delivery in twin births is less predictable than in single births, with many more possible variables. An external fetal monitor is often used as a precautionary measure. Two separate monitoring machines can be used simultaneously with twins. The fetal monitor tracks a baby's heartbeats while measuring the intensity and timing of the mother's contractions. Such devices may be somewhat distracting or uncomfortable to the mother, but they can provide the doctor with valuable information about a baby's condition. Two sensors connected to a monitoring machine are strapped to the mother's abdomen and record any fetal distress that might occur during labor. Fetal distress indicates a lack of oxygen in a baby's body. This can happen if the mother's blood pressure drops (sometimes when certain kinds of anesthetics are used), or it can be caused by the pressure of the uterus itself on the mother's major blood vessels that nourish the placenta.

A normal fetal heart rate is 120 to 140 beats per minute. A baby is considered to be in distress if the amount of oxygen in the fetal bloodstream drops below a safe level. This may be due to natural causes (such as a reduction in the blood flow to the placenta or a problem with the umbilical cord causing a drop in the blood flow from the placenta to the baby), or it may be due to drugs given to the mother during labor. One twin can be in distress even when the other is not. The recording from an external monitor gives the doctor vital information about a baby's condition. Some devices have an alarm to alert the doctor if a baby's heart rate drops too low. A baby can sometimes be in distress, however, even if the alarm does not sound.

Sometimes an external monitor does not adequately record the events (such as with a woman who is obese or a baby whose position makes the heart rate difficult to monitor). In this case, an additional electrode can be placed on the head of the baby as it begins to emerge from the cervical opening into the birth canal if the baby is in a head-first (*vertex*) presentation. The sensor is inserted by a plastic tube that slips beneath the skin of the baby's scalp. If fetal distress occurs, the mother is generally asked to turn on her side to lessen the weight on the major blood vessels, and she is given oxygen. If the problem is caused by a drop in the mother's blood pressure, she may be given fluids intravenously (through a vein) and may or may not also be given drugs to raise her blood pressure to normal. A Caesarean section (C-section) can be performed if the mother's or baby's condition does not improve sufficiently. If a C-section becomes necessary for delivery of the first twin, the second twin will also be delivered by Caesarean.

Intravenous Injections

Another procedure currently used during labor and delivery is the insertion of a painless intravenous (*IV*) tube threaded into a vein in the wrist, forearm, or hand. If an emergency arises, as happens more frequently with a multiple birth, necessary fluids can be administered through this tube on split-second notice, such as blood for transfusion, hormones (such as *oxytocin*, a hormone that stimulates uterine contractions), or an anesthetic. Necessary fluids, blood, hormones, or medication may be ordered by the obstetrician during delivery and may be administered intravenously. An anesthesiologist, a doctor specializing in anesthesia, will administer pain relief medications if needed during labor and delivery. The anesthesiologist or a trained specialist called an anesthetist will attend to the IV.

Induction or Acceleration of Labor

Induced labor involves intervention by the physician to stimulate labor contractions artificially before they have begun on their own. This can be done by rupturing the membranes or by administering a labor-stimulating hormone (such as *oxytocin*), usually given as a slow intravenous drip. Some doctors prefer to deliver twins by Caesarean section rather than to use labor-stimulating drugs.

Monitoring the fetal response to these drugs is more difficult with twins. Although complications relating to the mother or to the fetus are the usual reasons to induce labor, some doctors will induce at term under certain circumstances for reasons of convenience to the mother or to the doctor.

The complexities inherent in a twin pregnancy present a greater potential for problems. Some of these problems may warrant induction of labor, such as toxemia that is not responding to treatment, diabetes, or *placenta abruptio* (a placenta that prematurely detaches from the uterine wall). Even when twin labor begins spontaneously at term, after delivery of the first twin, artificial rupture of the membranes may be necessary to initiate contractions with the second.

Accelerated labor involves the use of hormones to increase the frequency and intensity of contractions. Hormones may be used this way if labor begins to slow down or to stop altogether (a frequent occurrence with twins) or may be given to stimulate contractions during and after the third stage of labor. This helps expel the placentas and helps a uterus that is soft and toneless become firm and hard in order to avoid the possibility of hemorrhage.

Pain Relief Medications

Many expectant mothers of twins prefer not to have any pain relief medication during childbirth. Because of the complexities of a multiple birth, sometimes these medications may be necessary, even with a vaginal delivery. Three basic groups of drugs are frequently employed either alone or in combination during labor and delivery with twins as with singletons. These groups are analgesics, amnesics, and anesthetics. They are used for different purposes and may be administered in various ways.

Twins are often premature or smaller at birth than singletons. The use of pain relief medications during labor and delivery can present an additional level of risk to these infants. Otherwise, however, these drugs present no greater risks to twins than to singletons. Some level of risk accompanies the use of any drug. Discuss the subject with your physician and your childbirth educator well in advance of your due date. Your awareness of the effects of the various drugs that are often used makes you more educated during labor and delivery and lets you specify your own preferences for your care.

Analgesics

Analgesics give limited relief from discomfort or pain and help to relax the patient. (Aspirin, for example, is a mild analgesic.) They are used primarily during labor and can be administered orally, by injection into muscle tissue, or intravenously. One of the most commonly used drugs is an intravenous painkiller called Demerol that is generally given by injection. (Nisentil, a similar drug, is also widely used.) This drug usually becomes effective within five to fifteen minutes, lasting up to two hours, and is often also used postpartum as a painkiller, especially for women recovering from the discomforts of a Caesarean section.

Demerol, like other analgesics, can have side effects, however. It can cause vomiting as well as changes in blood pressure and can also depress respiration in one or both of the babies, depending upon how it is administered to the mother and how long before delivery it is given. If a significant amount of this drug is present in a baby's body at birth, the newborn liver is slow to metabolize it, and the drug's effects may last for many hours. Sometimes another drug, Narcan, is given to reverse the effects of Demerol. Narcan is generally considered safe for mother and babies.

Amnesics

Amnesic drugs cause drowsiness and do not relieve pain; instead, they act as a memory block to cause a woman to forget any discomfort or pain experienced during labor or delivery. Amnesic drugs are seldom used today with single or multiple births as more and more women want to be awake and aware during childbirth.

Anesthetics

The same anesthetics that can be used for a single birth can also be used for the birth of twins to eliminate completely any sensation of pain. Some anesthetics also prevent muscular control in the parts of the body they affect. The three types of anesthetics are: generals, regionals, and locals.

General anesthetics cause complete unconsciousness. They are rarely used for childbirth today except for some Caesarean deliveries. General anesthetics are administered intravenously, either alone or in combination with anesthetic gases that are inhaled directly into the lungs.

Regional anesthetics are used to desensitize or reduce sensation in areas of the body where the mother is experiencing pain or discomfort during labor and delivery. Regionals may block muscular control in the affected areas, depending upon the concentration of the drug. Sometimes a regional "block" may prolong the second stage of labor because it can impair the mother's ability to push out the babies. The doctor may then have to intervene and assist in extracting the babies (see "Forceps Delivery" later in this chapter).

Because of their temporary numbing effect, regional anesthetics are often given instead of general anesthetics for Caesarean deliveries. Two types of regional anesthetics frequently used for childbirth are *intrathecal*, involving the injection of an anesthetic into the spinal fluid, and *epidural*, involving anesthetics injected through a fine plastic tube placed by a needle into the space outside the dural sac that holds the spinal cord and fluid.

Two types of intrathecal anesthetics are *spinals* and *saddle blocks*. With both types a small dose of the anesthetic is injected into the spinal fluid, but a spinal is given with the mother lying on her back whereas a saddle block is administered with the mother sitting up. A saddle block is given in this position so that the anesthetic, which is heavier than the spinal fluid, will sink to the bottom of the spinal canal, numbing only the part of the body that sits on a saddle. Spinals and saddle blocks can stop contractions altogether, so they usually are not administered until labor is well established.

Intrathecal anesthetics can cause the mother's blood pressure to drop. In some cases they can also cause a temporary but painful headache if spinal fluid leaks out through the hole in the spinal canal created when the injection was given. If this should happen, a "patch" can be done to cover the hole by taking a small sample of blood from the woman's arm and injecting it into the area of the hole. The blood acts as a patch, and relief is usually rapid and permanent. Occasionally symptoms recur and a second patch is performed. The dose given with intrathecal anesthesia is so low that it generally does not cross the placenta or present risks to a fetus.

Two commonly used types of epidural anesthetics are *lumbar epidurals*, given in the small of the back, and *caudal epidurals*, injected under the tail bone (*coccyx*). Epidurals are harder to administer than spinals or saddle blocks but are often preferred by doctors and laboring women for several reasons. The temporary placement of the plastic tube provides for repeat doses of anesthetic to be easily administered with no need for continuous use of needles into the back. This can be an advantage with the birth of twins if the effects of the anesthetic begin to wear off before the second baby is delivered. Epidurals are less likely to cause a drop in the mother's blood pressure than are spinals and saddle blocks. In addition, epidural anesthetics can also give analgesic relief from the discomforts of labor and the birth process. Epidurals are effective in relaxing the perineum, the tissue at the outer opening of the birth canal, so they are especially useful for forceps deliveries, which are more common with multiples. If an epidural is not placed correctly, however, the woman may develop a headache or in rare cases may develop other more serious problems. Small amounts of the anesthetic may cross the placenta with an epidural, but normally the fetus is not adversely affected.

Local anesthetics, administered by the obstetrician, give relief to a smaller, more limited area. When used for the discomfort of labor, a local can be injected around the edge of the cervix. This is called a *paracervical block*. With a paracervical block, however, the emerging baby may get a high dose of the anesthetic. A *pudendal block* can be given to the mother for

Presentation of twins at birth

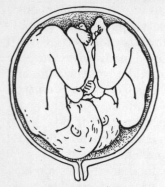

Both vertex, 39%

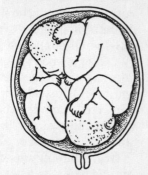

One vertex, one breech, 36%

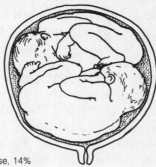

One or both transverse, 14%

Both breech, 11%

relief from discomfort as a baby's head emerges by administering a local anesthetic around the area of the pudendal nerve reached through the vagina. A local perineal anesthetic can be injected into the perineum to numb this area if an episiotomy is done.

Delivery

Your doctor will try to determine the positions of the babies in the weeks preceding labor and delivery. According to Guttmacher, usual presentations for twins are:

Both heads (called *vertex* or *cephalic*) in 39 percent of the cases

One head and one *breech* (buttocks or feet first) in 36 percent

Both breech in 11 percent

One or both crosswise (*transverse*) in 14 percent

Your doctor will probably proceed with a normal vaginal delivery if both heads are down. Some doctors will also permit a vaginal delivery if one or both babies are in a breech position. Sometimes after the birth of the first twin, the second baby is in a breech presentation. With a vaginal delivery, the doctor can sometimes manually rotate the fetus so that it presents in a vertex position. This procedure is called a *version* and is done externally by massaging the abdomen. If an external version cannot be successfully performed, the doctor may be able to extract the infant as a "footling breech." This surgical procedure, called a *podalic version*, is done internally under general anesthesia and is discussed later in this chapter.

There is no such thing as a typical twin labor and delivery.

For some women, contractions are brief and are not uncomfortable. "I didn't have labor. I was in the doctor's office when he told me to get to the hospital because I was dilated to five centimeters. I never felt a thing." For others, the opposite is true. "The labor and delivery was long—over thirty hours. There was an hour between the birth of the boys and more than five hours of pushing." For some, labor does not progress as expected. "I was in labor for twenty-two hours, but I didn't dilate beyond five centimeters, so they performed a Caesarean."

During a twin delivery, the potential risk is greater to the second twin than to the first. For example, following delivery of the first baby, the placenta of the second baby may begin to detach as the walls of the uterus readjust to their reduced volume. When the placenta begins to separate prematurely from the uterine wall, the baby's lifeline is threatened. This condition is known as *placenta abruptio* and is usually accompanied by vaginal bleeding. If the remaining twin's placenta is in jeopardy, as evidenced by fetal distress, the baby must be delivered immediately. Delivery by forceps or by vacuum extraction (see later in this chapter) may be necessary if contractions do not begin either spontaneously or with the assistance of intravenous hormones. The umbilical cord may slip through the already dilated cervix before the second twin is engaged in the pelvis. This potentially dangerous condition is called a *prolapsed cord* (see later in this chapter). Another problem may arise if the second twin is considerably larger than the first. In this case the uterus dilates to accommodate the passage of the first baby, but cervical dilation may not be adequate for a trauma-free passage of the second baby.

With these or other unforeseen complications a Caesarean section may be necessary for delivery of the second twin. If the doctor anticipates a problem before delivery of the first twin, however, a C-section may be performed. Because the conduct of twin labor and delivery is far less predictable than that of a single birth, you should be familiar with the procedures involved in both vaginal and Caesarean deliveries.

Vaginal

Three stages of labor are involved during a single or multiple vaginal delivery. During the first stage, powerful contractions of the uterine muscles increase in frequency and build in intensity exerting pressure on the cervix and causing it to dilate. The cervix dilates to approximately ten centimeters, enabling the fetal head to pass through and into the vagina. The second stage of labor begins from the time the mother bears down to push the baby through the vagina until the fetal head emerges through the perineum, the vaginal opening. Finally contractions begin again for a third stage of labor to expel the placenta from the uterus. This phase concludes when the placenta is delivered.

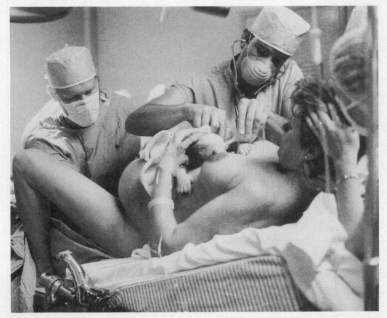

Between birth of first and second twin, pediatrician attends to first-born twin, while obstetrician awaits delivery of second

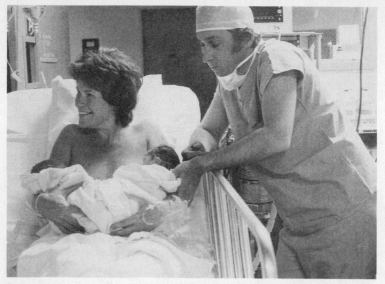

Father looks on while mother cradles their newborn twins, born fifteen minutes apart

Although with twins the first stage of labor proceeds as with a singleton, you must undergo the second stage of labor twice in order to push each baby out. The doctor may perform an *episiotomy*, a small incision in the perineum, to prevent this tissue from tearing as the head of the first baby emerges. An episiotomy is also done during a forceps delivery, a vacuum extraction, or an internal version.

You may have little time to rest after the first twin is born before labor begins with the second. "Labor was short with the second baby," says one new mother, "but I was surprised that I had to push as hard with the second as with the first." Once the head or breech of the second twin is fixed in the birth canal, the doctor will rupture the membranes. Then, if there are no complications, once normal labor has resumed, it can continue at its own pace. You will probably be able to push out the second baby without assistance because your cervix is already dilated from the exit of the first twin.

Time elapsing between the birth of both infants is ideally

five to twenty minutes, but in some cases the actual interval may be up to an hour or more. If delivery of the second twin is too hasty, this may result in trauma to the baby. Too great a delay may lead to oxygen deprivation if the placenta begins to separate or if the umbilical cord prolapses (precedes the baby). A prolapsed cord, more common with twins because of the greater frequency of abnormal presentations, can become compressed between the fetus and the bony pelvic area restricting circulation through the cord and thus cutting off or reducing the baby's supply of oxygen.

As soon as the vertex or breech of the second baby is fixed in the birth canal, the doctor applies gentle pressure to the fundus of the uterus, ruptures the membranes, and checks for a prolapsed cord. Sometimes, however, even after the membranes have been ruptured, contractions do not begin spontaneously. If labor does not begin again within a short period of time, oxytocin (the hormone that causes the uterus to contract) may be administered intravenously (see "Induction and Acceleration of Labor" above). The fetal heart rate will be closely monitored, and at the first sign of fetal distress, the baby can be delivered quickly either by forceps, vacuum extraction, or if necessary by Caesarean section.

The third stage of labor with twins is much the same as with a singleton. The first twin's placenta (if there are two placentas) is usually delivered along with that of the second, after the birth of both babies. If the placentas are not expelled spontaneously, an intravenous oxytocin drip may be administered. If this is not effective, the doctor may have to remove the afterbirth manually. Following a normal vaginal twin birth you may feel fatigued, but you will probably feel strong enough to move around comfortably within a few days if you get back on your feet soon after delivery.

Caesarean Section

Should a Caesarean section be necessary, you will want to feel confident that the surgery is indeed necessary. Some doctors feel that all twins should be delivered by Caesarean section; others deliver twins vaginally whenever possible. It is essential that you have confidence in your physician and feel comfortable with his or her philosophy before you arrive at the hospital in labor. You have the right to know the reasons for surgery and to give permission or to refuse the procedure. For this reason, it is important long before your due date to speak frankly with your doctor about your own concerns regarding surgery and anesthesia. Should complications develop in delivery, decisions must be made quickly, and you might not have time at that point to discuss your feelings with your doctor.

Many expectant mothers of twins as well as those who are expecting singletons are afraid of a Caesarean section because the procedure is unfamiliar and because surgery of any kind, especially if unexpected, is frightening. The usual fears are, "Is it safe? Will I feel anything? How will the babies respond? Will my recovery be painful?" In addition, most women are initially disappointed that they cannot have a vaginal delivery. One woman was unhappy when the hospital would not let her husband be with her in the delivery room because she and her husband "were really looking forward to the twin birth together." If you prepare yourself ahead for the possibility of a C-section, you will feel more comfortable later should the situation arise. A support group for Caesarean parents can help you cope with your concerns (see Appendix I).

As with a single birth, the need for a Caesarean delivery with twins can sometimes be anticipated, and surgery can be scheduled in advance, such as in the case of *placenta previa* (see earlier in this chapter). "Because our older child had been delivered by section, the twins were a planned C-section," recalled one woman. "My husband was there, and it was a wonderful birth experience." For some women, however, a Caesarean may be deemed necessary at the last minute due to an unnaturally long or difficult labor, fetal distress, unfavorable presentations of the babies, or other reasons.

Although emergencies are not common, they can and do arise, and in an emergency a surgical delivery can save the life of the mother as well as the infants. Sometimes complications arise after a vaginal birth of the first twin, and a C-section becomes necessary for delivery of the second baby. For example, a Caesarean for the second twin may be considered safer if the baby's position cannot be manipulated for a vaginal birth or if your uterus cannot be relaxed for such a manipulation due to the absence of readily available anesthesia.

A C-section may also be necessary if the second twin is considerably larger than the first, if the cervix contracts and thickens after the birth of the first twin and does not dilate again, or in the presence of significant uterine bleeding. If the doctor can anticipate any of these problems before delivery of the first baby, a Caesarean delivery for both twins is usually preferable.

A Caesarean section today is very safe when performed in the sterile conditions of a hospital with all the necessary medication and surgical equipment readily available. The entire operation can be done within an hour. Delivery of the first baby takes only minutes, with the birth of the second following almost immediately. The greater part of the doctor's time is spent repairing the mother's internal tissues and organs after extraction of the babies. In the past, a Caesarean delivery would leave the patient with a large vertical scar running downward from the navel. Today, most obstetricians (except in the case of certain emergencies) make a transverse cut, just above the pubic bone. Evidence of the incision is normally well disguised by pubic hair after it heals.

If your twins are delivered by C-section, you will be given either a general or a regional anesthetic. With a regional, you may experience a great deal of pressure during surgery and may even feel successively lighter after each of the twins is lifted from your abdomen. With a regional, your husband or Lamaze coach may be allowed to remain in the delivery room to offer moral support. You do not even have to watch the operation itself, as a draped sterile sheet obscures the view. Ask whether hospital regulations permit your husband or coach to be present during the birth. After delivery, you will be encouraged to get out of bed and walk a few paces as soon as possible, usually by the next day.

If you are given a general anesthetic, your progress may be somewhat slower at the beginning. In the recovery room, you may awaken feeling weak, sleepy, and achy, and you may feel like you have a hangover. Discomfort from gas pains is greatest around the third day. Otherwise progress is much the same as after regional anesthesia. The incision will be sore at first but will become less uncomfortable after the first few days, and thereafter recovery will be rapid. By two weeks after the birth, often sooner, you will probably feel quite strong and able to move about normally. Strenuous exercise is not recommended at first, but a balanced program of exercises, such as those found in Chapter 5, "Maternal Nutrition and Health," is advisable.

Caesarean newborns seldom manifest the side effects of anesthesia, as regionals do not cross the placenta, and generals usually do not reach the babies before they are removed from the uterus. Infants may be even more alert than those delivered vaginally, as they have not spent long minutes or even hours laboring to get through the pelvic opening and birth canal.

Other Surgical Procedures

You may not realize that there are other surgical delivery procedures besides Caesarean section. Two relatively common types of obstetrical surgery are forceps delivery and podalic version. A third type, vacuum extraction, is used less frequently.

Forceps Delivery

Forceps deliveries are more common with multiple births. A special instrument called a forceps, which resembles large tongs, is designed to fit the curve of an infant's head and can be employed to extract a baby if there are signs of fetal distress or if you are having difficulty pushing the baby out. One mother felt that her "uterus was so stretched that contractions were not strong enough to help me. I pushed for two hours, and at the end, the doctor helped the twins out with forceps." Forceps deliveries in general, however, are less frequent today than they were a generation ago, when women were routinely heavily sedated for vaginal delivery and thus were unable to exert the muscular control required to expel a baby. An anesthetic is used in forceps deliveries.

Podalic Version

Another surgical procedure, podalic version, is often used in the delivery of the second twin, if the second baby is in a transverse position. This procedure involves the manual rotation of a fetus in the uterus. You are anesthetized and the doctor inserts one hand vaginally to grasp the infant's feet while placing the other hand externally on your abdomen to manipulate the baby's head. The baby is then removed as a "footling" breech (feet first). If the first twin presents in a transverse or oblique position, a Caesarean section is generally considered safer because the uterus is usually too crowded to risk a version of the first baby.

Vacuum Extraction

This technique may be used particularly to deliver the second twin if spontaneous delivery does not occur within a reasonable period of time or if the fetus is in distress. The procedure involves the extraction of a baby by suction. A metal cup is applied to the baby's head, forming a vacuum seal with the infant's scalp. A rubber tube attached to the cup is used to turn the baby's head and/or to pull the baby gently out. The procedure can put excessive stress on the head.

The Babies: The Neonatal Period

The first thirty days in an infant's life are known as the neonatal (newborn) period. This is a time for parents of twins to get to know their babies' individual personalities and to begin the bonding process.

Physical Appearance

A newborn infant (*neonate*), whether a singleton or a twin, is not usually pretty to look at. Often still covered with a waxlike coating called *vernix caseosa*, a new baby may have loose, wrinkled skin and a head that is disproportionately large when compared to the body. The head may be melon-shaped and pointed in the back due to the natural molding process that takes place so that the head can pass safely through the narrow pelvic opening for a vaginal delivery. Because an infant's skull is designed to move through the bony region of the pelvis during the birth process, the bones of the skull overlap, enabling the safe passage. This happens without danger of brain damage, and the head assumes its normal shape within a few days of the birth. Pressure on the head during the molding process may, however, cause a temporary fluid-filled swelling, called a *caput succadaneum*, to form at the top of the head. This usually disappears after a week or so.

Because twins are usually smaller at birth, their heads may not need to mold significantly and may not even appear visibly misshapen after delivery. Twins at birth may however show signs of their cramped intrauterine existence. "Kenny was born with a noticeably receding jaw," recalls one mother. "The pediatrician said that this was caused when his jaw was wedged against the shoulder of his twin. The doctor said Kenny would outgrow it within a few months, and he did." Your twins' legs may be bowed and feet turned inward, outward, or to one side. Even your babies' ears may be flattened against the head or pressed forward against the cheeks. These temporary conditions will normalize within a few weeks or months.

Newborn twins may or may not look alike at birth, whether they are identical or fraternal. Much depends on the circum-

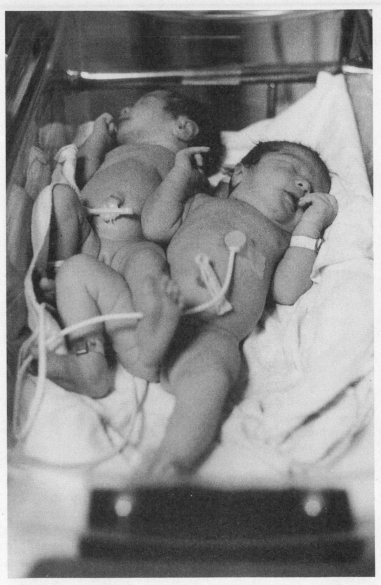

In the hospital nursery, only multiples can share a bassinette or infant seat

stances of each baby's delivery and intrauterine development. One twin may be noticeably and measurably larger than the other (see "Growth Retardation" in Chapter 4). Temporary puffiness of the face and blotches of the skin if they happen to occur in only one of the twins may also initially create a dissimilar appearance, even in single-egg twins. Caucasian babies may appear bluish, especially around the hands and feet, for the first few days. Newborns of black, Asian, or Mediterranean parents may be light in color at first, often darkening in the few days following the birth.

Assessing the Babies' Physical Condition

Because numerous factors affect an infant's physical well-being at birth, a newborn's condition is always assessed at the time of delivery. Each twin is evaluated separately. The best-known evaluation for newborn health is the *Apgar score*, given immediately after birth while an infant is still in the delivery room and then given again five minutes later to monitor the infant's progress. The Apgar score is considered to be a reliable indicator of the baby's immediate response to the environment outside the uterus. Twins may not have the same score. The rating, based on the observation and assessment of a newborn's vital signs as determined by a trained technician, evaluates a newborn's heart rate, breathing, muscle tone, color, and responsiveness. A score of seven to ten is the sign of a healthy, normal baby; three to six indicates the need for further medical attention, and less than three reveals an immediate, perhaps even life-threatening problem.

Immediately after birth, each twin is weighed and measured and is checked for vital signs (pulse, respiratory rate, and temperature). Head circumference is also measured. A suction bulb is used to remove fluid or mucus that may be present in the baby's mouth and throat. An infant may suffer heat loss at birth. This forces the newborn's body to expend more energy, compromising the baby's ability to adapt to the extrauterine environment (life outside the womb). The delivery room is

APGAR SCALE

The highest possible score is 10. Assessment of the baby's overall condition is based on the score of 1 to 10.

Indicator	Score		
	0	*1*	*2*
Appearance (skin color)	blue, pale	body pink, extremities blue	completely pink
Pulse (heart rate)	absent	below 100 beats per minute	over 100 beats per minute
Grimace (reflex irritability—catheter in nose or sole of foot stimulated)	no response	grimace, some facial movement	cough, sneeze, or vigorous cry
Activity (muscle tone)	limp, flaccid	some bending of extremities	well-flexed, active, vigorous motion
Respiration (breathing effort)	absent	irregular or slow	good, crying vigorously

usually kept at a temperature that is comfortable for adults but is too cold for a newborn. To reduce the loss of body heat, the baby, whose head and body are wet at birth, is thoroughly dried and then swaddled (wrapped tightly in a receiving blanket) or kept under a warming lamp or in an incubator until the body temperature can be stabilized.

Bonding

Parents of twins are generally encouraged to handle their newborns even while they are still in the delivery room if the infants' physical condition at birth appears to be good. As one

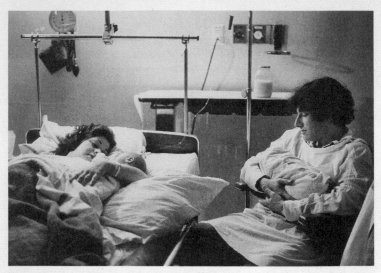

Twins three hours old

father remembers, "I held Ann while Danny was being born."
The babies may even be able to stay with you in the recovery
room if competent nursing staff is on hand to monitor your
own recovery and if the required facilities are available in this
area to observe the babies' progress. If you are planning to
breastfeed, you may want to nurse the babies while you are
still in the recovery room. This helps initiate the bonding
process and also stimulates uterine contractions, which speed
the process of reducing the uterus to its prepregnant size and
firmness. The babies' father can bottle feed or hold one baby
while you breastfeed or hold the other. This enables him also
to begin bonding with the babies during these first minutes
and hours after their birth.

Standard Nursery Procedures

During their stay at the hospital, your twins will be routinely
bathed and weighed daily, and they will be given periodic

blood tests and urinalysis. The nurses will monitor the babies' output of urine and bowel movements. Their intake of fluids will also be measured (in the case of babies on formula, water, glucose, or electrolyte fluids that contain essential nutrients) or estimated (in the case of babies who are breastfeeding). Body temperature is recorded during each nursing shift (every eight hours). A newborn's normal body temperature is generally between 97.7° and 99.5° Fahrenheit (36.5° to 37.5° Centigrade) and is usually taken rectally or in the armpit. A rectal temperature is usually considered normal between 99° and 100° Fahrenheit. An electronic device can also be used to read a baby's temperature by taping a small sensor to the infant's chest.

Preventive eye care for newborns is required in most areas. Silver nitrate drops, often causing chemically induced conjunctivitis (irritation of the eyes and swelling of the lids) has now been replaced at many centers by erythromycin ointment. Many areas now also have laws requiring hospitals to screen newborns for rare disorders that may be damaging as the child grows, such as *phenylketonuria* (PKU), an enzyme deficiency; *hypothyroidism*, the absence or inadequacy of thyroid hormone due to failure of the thyroid gland to grow properly; or *galactosemia*, another enzyme deficiency. When these disorders are diagnosed in the first weeks of life, serious consequences may be avoided through the use of special diets or medications.

"Rooming in"

With twins as with singletons, you may be able to have the babies stay with you in your own room or ward if the hospital has a rooming-in program and if the babies do not require any special care or treatment that can only be given in the nursery. Infants may room in continuously or intermittently, with nurses checking on you periodically. Although the hospital provides an excellent opportunity for you to get to know your babies and to learn to care for them, caring for twins requires twice as much energy as with a singleton.

Intermittent rooming in gives you the chance to be with the babies upon request or at designated hours. You will be able to have them either separately or together, during the day only or also at night at feeding times if you wish. Because you have twins, you may need extra help, especially at feedings. It may be easier to feed them separately, at least for now. Do not be afraid to ask the nurses to assist you. Call the nurse immediately if a baby is choking or is having difficulty breathing or if you are concerned that something may be wrong.

You, the babies' father, and/or another person you choose are the only people besides the doctors and nursing staff who will be allowed to handle your babies. Other visitors may or may not be permitted in the room when the babies are with you. The hospital will have specific instructions for proper handwashing before handling the babies. Gowns may also be required. If your twins are rooming in, you will be given enough clean diapers, newborn clothing, and receiving blankets and other supplies to care for two babies while they are in the room with you. Ask the staff for extras of these items if you need them.

Discharge from the Hospital

Before the twins are released from the hospital they will be given a complete evaluation. Sometimes an infant requires special attention or continued treatment. Often this can be done on an outpatient basis. Sometimes only one twin may require ongoing hospital care even after the mother and the other twin have been discharged. (See Chapter 4, "Prematurity, Low Birth Weight, and Twin-Related Complications.")

The Mother: The Postpartum Period

The period of several weeks following childbirth is known as the postpartum period or the *puerperium*. As you plan for labor and delivery, take a few extra minutes to familiarize yourself with the postpartum period, too. Looking ahead will help you feel more comfortable about what to expect after the much awaited delivery.

Vaginal Flow

The vaginal flow, called *locchia*, which follows childbirth, is different from menstruation; it is the expulsion of the fluid and tissue that line the uterus during pregnancy. Even if you had a Caesarean delivery, you will have this vaginal discharge. Feminine napkins, not tampons, should be used to absorb the flow, which may last several weeks, tapering off and becoming paler in color as the days progress. Initially the discharge may be greater for a woman recovering from a twin birth, particularly following a Caesarean twin delivery. After a twin delivery, the uterus may tend to relax and bleed excessively. For this reason, you will be monitored more carefully for the possibility of hemorrhage. The increase in the mother's blood volume during a multiple pregnancy is up to 50 percent greater than that of a single pregnancy. This, however, accounts for only a small amount of the excess blood lost after a twin birth—the total amount estimated to be almost twice the amount generally lost after the birth of a singleton. This additional blood loss may lead to iron-deficiency anemia. Discharge that remains heavy and red in color or the passage of large clots of blood warrants a call to the doctor.

Abdominal Stretching

Your uterus will return to its prepregnant state within about six weeks, but your abdominal muscles and skin will need additional time to recover from the enlarged and stretched condition of a twin pregnancy. Stretch marks will fade in time, as will the hormonally induced dark line running longitudinally downward from the navel that some women develop during pregnancy. Loose skin and poor muscle tone resulting from a twin pregnancy may never completely return to their previous condition. (In Chapter 5, "Maternal Nutrition and Health," you will find exercises designed specifically for new mothers of multiples that can help you regain muscle tone, firm up your abdomen, and generally help you feel better.)

Change in Body Fluids

After childbirth, the body rids itself of the two or three quarts of fluid that are normally retained during pregnancy. The volume may be even greater during a multiple pregnancy. Fluids are eliminated through increased urination and perspiration. Perspiration is most noticeable at night, when you may awaken to find your nightgown completely wet. Put a towel underneath you when you go to sleep, and keep a clean nightgown by the bed for a middle-of-the-night change. In addition, keep yourself covered with a blanket or you may become chilled. Mothers report that perspiration at night seems to last longer after the birth of twins than after a single birth, sometimes up to six weeks.

Urinary Tract

If you had a vaginal delivery, you will probably be asked to urinate before the end of the first day to be sure that your urinary tract is functioning freely. You may have difficulty emptying your bladder after a twin birth. Should this happen, a thin catheter tube may be inserted into your bladder to drain the build-up of urine. This may be required periodically until you are able to urinate at will, and your doctor may prescribe an antibiotic to prevent infection. A catheter is inserted as standard procedure following a Caesarean section.

Episiotomy

If you had a vaginal delivery, the doctor may have performed an *episiotomy*, usually as the first twin's head emerges. The stitches used to repair an episiotomy can cause discomfort for the first week or two following delivery. A heat lamp, "sitz" baths (sitting in a shallow tub of warm water), and ice packs are a few of the remedies used to relieve soreness and promote the healing process.

Caesarean Incision

If you had a Caesarean section, you will undoubtedly be more uncomfortable for the first week to ten days, but by two weeks after surgery, you may feel as strong as a woman who had a vaginal delivery. A new and widely used procedure for closing the incision involves the application of thin strips of tape that are affixed perpendicular to the wound. The tape falls off once the skin surface has healed. Unlike stitches, these "steri-strips" do not leave any marks in the skin, nor do they involve the discomfort of removal.

Constipation, Hemorrhoids, and Gas

You may be constipated at first because your internal organs were overcrowded during your multiple pregnancy. Your system will probably begin to regulate itself naturally within a day or two. After a Caesarean section, the problem may last somewhat longer. Your doctor may prescribe suppositories or oral medication to relieve constipation. If you are breastfeeding, however, medication you take orally may also cause looseness in your babies' stools. Hemorrhoids and gas can also be annoying. Cold packs sometimes relieve hemorrhoidal discomfort and may also simultaneously provide relief to the perineal region where the episiotomy is healing. Gas pain is greatest after general anesthesia. It subsides after a few days.

Breasts

Breast enlargement is normal as the milk comes in a few days after the birth of your twins. Your breasts do not yet "know" whether and how much milk to produce. If you are breast-feeding, the babies may not yet be nursing efficiently, and the breasts may become engorged with a surplus of milk at first. This may be an uncomfortable sensation. Breast tissue has no muscles, so if you are nursing, wear a comfortable supportive bra both day and night to avoid permanent sagging of the breasts. Select a specially designed nursing bra with flaps that can be lowered to expose each breast. The bra should have wide straps and a cup size large enough to support the breast tissue completely without binding it. Buy cotton bras because synthetics can irritate the skin.

Cracked nipples or general nipple discomfort are common in nursing mothers. Nipple problems can often be prevented by letting the nipples air-dry after feedings, by applying pure lanolin several times a day, and by gradually increasing the duration of each feeding. A heat lamp can be helpful, or your doctor can recommend a soothing cream or ointment to be applied to the nipples. If you were given a hormone injection because you do not wish to nurse you may have some engorgement a week to ten days later. Aspirin and a bra that fits securely will help the problem. Discomfort should not last for more than a few days.

Fatigue

After your twin delivery you will need extra rest, especially if your labor was long or difficult. Even if you had a brief labor and delivery, your body will be tired. Loss of blood and body fluids and a change in the hormonal balance within your system are greater than with a single birth, and these conditions contribute to this feeling of fatigue. Despite your need for rest, however, your hospital stay may not provide much opportunity to sleep. Nurses will monitor your blood pressure, pulse, stitches, and vaginal flow every four to six hours. The daily schedule at the hospital will also include the arrival of your meals, the babies' feedings, and visits from the obstetrician and pediatrician.

Getting as much rest as you need following a multiple birth is not easy in the midst of all the excitement. If the babies are rooming in, send them back to the nursery when you want a nap. Politely ask your roommates to try to speak quietly to their visitors and on the phone. Let the nursing staff know that you do not want to be disturbed unnecessarily.

"The Blues"

Feeling depressed or "blue" during this period after childbirth is very common, particularly with twins. Your body, which was designed for a single pregnancy, has been through additional stress, and your hormones suddenly have begun a major readjustment. In addition, the delivery that you have so anxiously awaited is over, and you now have a vast and unpredictable future to face with not one but two new babies. If you are feeling a bit depressed or even sorry for yourself at this point, be assured that you *are* a hero. After all, how many women undergo two labors and two deliveries in a single day?

As a new mother of twins, you may feel awkward and even unreceptive toward your newborns at first, and once the double arrival becomes a reality, you may also question your ability to cope with the situation. Your doctor or the nurses in the hospital can be very supportive if you discuss your anxieties with them. Your recuperation will be more rapid if you take each day one at a time, an approach that will also get you through even the most trying moments at home with your babies.

CHAPTER 4

Prematurity, Low Birth Weight, and Twin-Related Complications

Note: the photos interspersed throughout this chapter document the first three months of life for fraternal twins Steven and Timothy Laurie, born on November 17, 1980—a full three months before their February 15, 1981 due date. At birth, Steven weighed barely two pounds, and second-born Timothy weighed only one pound, thirteen ounces. Despite their small size and the large number of complications that plagued them in their early months, both boys recovered completely. In the last photo, taken on their first birthday, Steven weighed eighteen pounds, ten ounces, and Timothy weighed eighteen pounds, five ounces.

As this book goes to print, the Laurie twins are healthy, normal six-year-olds with an excellent long-range prognosis for development.

A discussion of the complications that can arise out of a multiple pregnancy, such as prematurity, low birth weight, and other twin-related or otherwise uncommon conditions is important in a book about twins because complications occur with greater frequency with multiples than with singletons. The term *prematurity* is used to describe babies who are gestationally premature, that is, born three or more weeks before term. These infants are often developmentally immature as well as small in size. Full-term infants weighing less than 5.5 pounds (2,500 grams), the international standard for low birth weight, are sometimes incorrectly labeled premature. These newborns, if well formed and developmentally mature, are actually "small for gestational age" or "small for dates."

Babies born early often seem long and thin due to the lack of fatty tissue beneath the skin. Veins are usually visible through the skin, which is generally thin and papery, wrinkled and reddish. The head of a premature baby appears elongated relative to the body size, and the abdomen may look distended. Lanugo hair, the downy "coat" covering the body of a fetus, may still be present. Ears appear tightly pinned to the sides of the head, eyes seem large, and fingernails and toenails are short and very soft. In time, as the baby grows, his or her undeveloped body will mature.

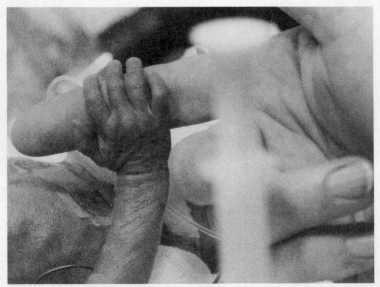

Steven's hand at four days

Prematurity and Low Birth Weight in Twins

Although forty weeks is the natural length of a human pregnancy, in the Northwestern University study of twin pregnancy and birth mentioned in Chapter 1, about one-third of the deliveries were premature, occurring before thirty-seven weeks (calculated from the mother's last menstrual period) —more than 20 percent at thirty-three to thirty-six weeks, and approximately 11 percent before thirty-three weeks.

Twins comprise about 15 percent of low birth-weight newborns. According to the Northwestern report, in a recent examination of 340 twin births and over 30,000 single births, 60 percent of the twins but less than 12 percent of the singletons weighed under 5 pounds, 8 ounces. Although the average birth weight for an infant is between 7 and 8 pounds (between 3,175 and 3,630 grams), only about 18 percent of the Northwestern twins exceeded 3,000 grams (6 pounds, 10 ounces), and almost half weighed less than 2,500 grams (5 pounds, 8 ounces).

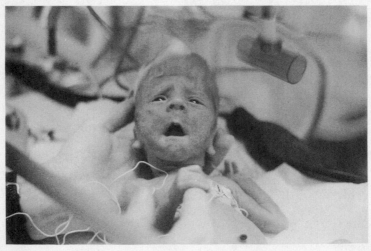

At 4 weeks, Timothy opened his eyes for the first time

Newborn twins are generally smaller than singletons for several reasons. They are often born before term, may be crowded in the womb, or may be nutritionally deprived if the mother's diet did not furnish enough calories or nutrients for two developing babies. Most twins are small at birth, even if born at term, yet some babies born before thirty-seven weeks may weigh more than five and a half pounds and still be developmentally premature. Diabetic mothers, for example, often give birth to large babies. Thus, even infants with ample weight may sometimes be gestationally premature (underdeveloped).

A premature birth can in some cases lead to loss of life in one or both twins. According to a recent report, the chances that an infant may not survive the pregnancy, birth, or newborn period are at least three times greater for a twin than for a singleton, and the majority of recorded deaths result from prematurity. Stillbirth is twice as common with twins as with singletons. Second-born twins are at greater risk than first-born.

Monitoring the High-Risk Twin Pregnancy

Identifying the High-Risk Mother

Most doctors now recognize the importance of carefully monitoring multiple pregnancies because of the greater risk of complications. A doctor may recommend an increase in the mother's daily calories and may also restrict the mother's activities or even prescribe complete bed rest in hopes of forestalling labor and delivery. Thus, the risk of premature birth may be increased with undiagnosed twin pregnancies, which may not be given the necessary additional attention. Specific conditions relating to the mother or to the pregnancy can also increase the risk of a premature birth. These include

An extreme overweight or underweight condition

Chronic infection or illness during pregnancy

Toxemia (associated with malfunction of the mother's kidneys, diabetes, or high blood pressure)

Abnormal uterine shape or an incompetent cervix (an incompetent cervix can sometimes be surgically stitched closed during early pregnancy, a procedure called *cerclage*; the stitches are removed for delivery)

Tumors of the uterus

Rh blood incompatibility between mother and baby

Heavy smoking or alcohol or drug usage during pregnancy

Poor nutrition during pregnancy

Placenta previa (a placenta that covers all or part of the cervix) or *placenta abruptio* (a placenta that separates prematurely from the uterine wall)

Your doctor will probably be able to detect any of these problems, but be sure to let him or her know if you have a history of any of the above conditions.

Common Sense Steps to Minimize the Risk

You can take several steps during your twin pregnancy that may help avert prematurity and low birthweight:

• Avoid alcoholic beverages and drugs that have not been prescribed by a doctor

• Maintain a well-balanced diet (see Chapter 5)

• Do not push yourself too hard at work or other activities

• Rest whenever tired

Premature Labor

With twins as with singletons, some babies are born prematurely even if their mother has taken every reasonable precaution. If you do go into labor prematurely, your doctor may prescribe an alcoholic beverage as a home remedy. Sometimes alcohol will arrest uterine contractions until you can be examined at the hospital. Do not take alcohol, however, without your doctor's recommendation. Once you have been examined at the hopsital, the doctor may give you a *tocolytic* drug, a drug that stops labor by relaxing the muscles of the uterus. Tocolytic drugs can be given intravenously or orally. Frequently an intravenous drip of the drug is given first. When the drip is removed, treatment may be continued with a dose given orally. You may be hospitalized overnight, for a few days, or even for a few weeks during treatment. Tocolytic drugs can produce side effects. Your doctor can discuss these with you.

If contractions cannot be stopped, you may be given a steroid to accelerate the babies' lung development, minimizing the risk of *hyaline membrane disease* (*respiratory distress syndrome*). This treatment must be administered at least forty-eight hours before delivery and may or may not be effective. The use of steroids for this purpose is generally considered safe, but the treatment is still relatively new and long-range studies are in progress.

Nurseries that Care for Premature Infants

Babies who are born prematurely or who have medical problems that require extra attention and care are sent to the nearest newborn intensive care unit (NBICU or NICU), a nursery designed with the medical equipment necessary to monitor sick newborns and to handle life-threatening conditions. Sometimes only one twin needs this special care. An infant can remain in the unit until well enough to go home. The NBICU is staffed by doctors (*neonatologists*), nurses, and other personnel trained in the care of newborns. When a newborn is in an NBICU, parents are invited and encouraged to visit and handle their babies as much as possible, given each infant's physical condition and necessary medical treatment. Frequently the newborn intensive care unit is not located in the babies' birth hospital, and may even be hundreds of miles away. Moving a premature baby from one hospital or medical center to another is done by a transport team usually consisting of a doctor, a nurse, and paramedics trained in the emergency care of newborns. Infants are transported in an ambulance or aircraft that has been equipped for interim newborn intensive care.

Twins can be transported together if both need to be moved to the NBICU. With twins, however, one baby may need to be transferred while the other is well enough to be cared for at the birth hospital. This can be particularly difficult for parents because they cannot visit both babies at the same time. Sometimes parents live many miles or hours away from the NBICU and cannot regularly visit their baby. Once the doctors feel that an infant's medical condition has stabilized, parents may request that the baby be transferred to a regular premature nursery at a hospital that is closer to home, particularly if the baby's twin is still being cared for there.

Assessing a High-Risk Newborn's Physical Condition

With premature twins who may score very low on the Apgar scale, it is also necessary to determine the gestational age (level of development) of each baby so that each can be given the kind of special care and treatment required for his or her stage of growth. One widely used method of assessment for distinguishing premature newborns from low birth-weight infants is the *Dubowitz system*. This method considers such neurological characteristics as a baby's reflexes, muscle tone, and body positioning and physical characteristics such as ear form and cartilage, skin color, texture, and thickness, configuration of the genitals, nipple formation and breast size, and the amount of lanugo hair present. The score is then plotted on a graph to determine the gestational age.

This system is not designed exclusively for twins, and it does not account for the special circumstances that may contribute to twins' size and maturity at birth. For example, because twins are usually smaller than singletons and are often small-for-dates, the Dubowitz assessment (and others like it) may give too low a score for twins when considering how birth weight relates to each baby's actual stage of development or maturity. In general, assessment methods that involve the subjective evaluation of one examiner (a doctor, nurse, or other trained individual) may not be universally applied by all examiners.

Other systems can be used in conjunction with the Dubowitz to evaluate behavior, to measure respiratory distress, or to measure neurodevelopmental age.

Complications Related to Prematurity

Throughout most of the last three months of pregnancy, most of a baby's vital organs are still undergoing structural and functional development. Thus, babies born prematurely can have a variety of complications in adjusting to life outside the womb. The presence or severity of any of these conditions varies according to each infant's particular size and degree of prematurity, and problems affecting one twin do not necessarily affect the other. Some of the complications frequently found in a gestationally premature newborn are

Respiratory disorders caused by immature lungs that cannot yet breathe on their own, depriving the blood of adequate oxygen

Low body temperature (the baby is unable to maintain its own body temperature)

Jaundice due to an immature liver that cannot yet function effectively

Blood, circulatory, and heart problems

Special nutritional needs and feeding requirements caused by an inability to suck or swallow, coupled with an under-developed digestive system

Bleeding in the brain (*intracranial hemorrhage*)

Lowered resistance to infection

Dehydration

Babies with these problems must be given special care and medical treatment in the newborn intensive care unit or the intensive care nursery to compensate for their developmental deficiencies until their bodies are mature enough to function independently. Should a newborn require surgery, pediatricians and pediatric surgeons will perform and monitor all necessary surgical procedures and will continue to supervise a baby's progress after the operation.

Respiratory Conditions

Lungs that are structurally underdeveloped or cannot function efficiently do not supply adequate oxygen to the bloodstream. Various types of equipment that mechanically monitor or assist breathing are used in the intensive care nursery. The doctor supervising a baby's care will determine the type of apparatus needed. One special device, a respiratory monitor, is used to record an infant's breathing rate and to be sure the rate remains adequate. Like a heart monitor, this device connects to a conducting plate (sensor) taped to the skin of the infant's chest. If breathing becomes too fast or slow, an alarm sounds.

In some premature babies, the air sacs in the lungs are so small that the baby cannot take in enough air with each breath. Breathing may become very irregular or may stop entirely for short periods (*apnea*). This condition may be treated with oxygen, to make breathing easier, with medication, or with the use of a mechanical respirator. If additional oxygen is needed it may be supplied through a plastic tube that goes to a clear plastic boxlike hood over the infant's head. The hood is connected by a tube to a machine that can administer a humidifying mist as well as oxygen. Humidity helps loosen mucus that may be present in the baby's lungs.

Oxygen, although essential to the survival of many premature babies, can also pose a threat to their long-range health outlook. If given in too high a concentration, it can cause *retrolental fibroplasia*, a disease of the retina of the eye that can lead to blindness. Today, hospitals with intensive care nurseries have sensitive equipment that can carefully gauge the amount of oxygen administered to premature babies. Thus, the risk of damage to the retina has now been greatly reduced.

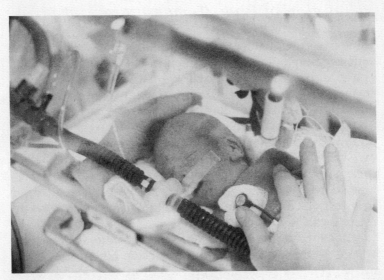

Steven is still on a respirator at 8 weeks

Hyaline membrane disease, also called *respiratory distress syndrome*, poses the greatest danger to twin infants. The underdeveloped lungs of babies who suffer from this condition collapse between breaths. A normal newborn lung is coated inside with an oily substance known as *surfactant* that allows the sacs to expand in order to exchange air between breaths. It is not until the last weeks of pregnancy that surfactant is produced by the fetus, so babies born early may lack sufficient quantities of this vital substance. A special type of respirator is required, one that regulates the pressure and volume of air reaching the baby's lungs. By means of a tube that passes through the mouth or nose to the back of the throat or into the windpipe (*trachea*), pressurized air can reach the lungs.

Sometimes air pockets form inside the chest wall but outside of the lungs. This condition, *pneumothorax*, can be treated by placing a "chest tube" through a small perforation made in the wall of the chest and by suctioning the air through this tube using a special machine.

Regulation of Body Temperature

Tiny premature infants generally cannot tolerate even a short period of heat loss. They have minimal fatty tissue beneath the skin to insulate them from cold and have much more surface area than body mass as compared with a term infant. A premature baby may not have the muscle strength to shiver or to retract arms and legs and hold them close to the body. The result is considerable loss of body heat. In addition, breathing may be inadequate to provide sufficient oxygen to the bloodstream, and continued heat loss may produce further compromise of body function. The baby may turn bluish in color (*cyanosis*) due to insufficient oxygen or may even stop breathing (*apnea*).

A small or premature baby's body temperature is monitored at least every eight hours, sometimes even more frequently. If the temperature is too low, an infant can be placed under a warmer or in an incubator that heats the body to a safe and

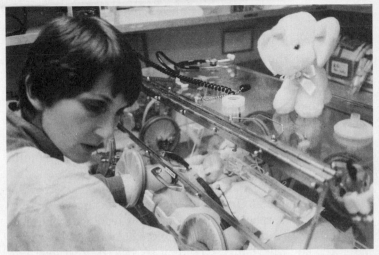

At 7 weeks, Timothy cannot yet leave his incubator

comfortable temperature. The constant heat given off by such equipment may have a drying effect on a baby's body. For this reason, infants under warmers or in incubators are frequently offered additional fluids to prevent dehydration.

Jaundice

Newborns, whether singletons or twins, frequently have some degree of jaundice, often visible as a yellowing of the skin and the whites of the eyes. Most apparent between the third and seventh day of life, the condition is caused by the normal destruction of older red cells in a baby's bloodstream. When this happens, hemoglobin in the blood turns into a yellow pigment called *bilirubin*. The liver is designed to cleanse the body of this pigment through excretion into the intestines and urine; however, it usually does not begin performing efficiently until two or three days after birth. A small amount of bilirubin may build up in a baby's body until liver function begins. This is called *physiologic jaundice*.

If an unusually high bilirubin level develops during the first few days of life (as detected through blood tests), the baby may be suffering from a more serious condition called *hemolytic jaundice*. This more severe form may be due to infection, or may occur if the infant's blood is incompatible with that of the mother (as with *ABO incompatibility*, in which the mother has "O" blood and the baby has "A" or "B," or *Rh disease*, involving an Rh-negative mother and an Rh-positive baby). During pregnancy, a small amount of fetal blood finds its way across the placenta and into the mother's system. The mother's body responds by producing antibodies to attack the foreign substance just as if it were an intruding bacterium or virus. These antibodies enter the baby's bloodstream and begin to destroy the healthy red cells. As a result, the bilirubin level in this infant may be far in excess of normal physiologic jaundice, and the baby may require special treatment. (A RhoGam injection may be given to an Rh-negative mother to prevent the formation of these antibodies in the future.)

Jaundice in newborns must be closely observed, and should it exceed a safe level, usual treatment is phototherapy. The infant is placed under bright "bili-lights," which are mounted above a special incubator so that all clothing and coverings can be removed. The baby's eyes are covered by a protective shield. The light itself breaks down the bilirubin, thus decreasing the jaundice. In severe cases, however, transfusions may be necessary to exchange the body's supply of red blood cells. A thin plastic tube (catheter) entering the umbilicus (navel) is used for this procedure.

Blood, Circulatory, and Heart Problems

Some conditions relating to the blood and circulatory system that often threaten premature babies are anemia, low blood pressure, irregular heart rate, and a deficiency of vitamin K.

Anemia involving iron deficiency in the blood is common among premature babies, especially those with other complications, such as heart and lung problems that may require transfusions. Jaundiced babies are often anemic, too. Iron, carried by the red blood cells, is periodically checked in a test called a *hematocrit*, which determines the percentage of red cells in the baby's blood serum. Routine blood tests also measure other components and characteristics, such as sugar levels, acidity, and blood gases. Only a small amount is needed for any of these tests, and it is usually taken from the infant's heel, arm, or umbilicus.

Low blood pressure, *hypotension*, which can have many causes, is carefully monitored, often with a special instrument using ultrahigh-frequency sound waves (Doppler technique) or with a thin catheter tube entering the baby's bloodstream through the artery in the umbilicus. A tube of this kind inserted into the umbilical artery or vein can also be used to give transfusions of additional blood or to administer medication if blood pressure is dangerously low.

A baby's heart rate can be recorded by a small metal probe taped to the skin of the chest and connected by a wire to a special instrument, a type of electrocardiograph. An alarm sounds an alert if the rate is dangerously high or low. Because many premature babies have a number of life-threatening problems, the heart rate of these infants must be carefully monitored, particularly if there are signs of other heart or circulatory ailments.

Vitamin K, essential to blood coagulation (blood clotting), prevents the possibility of hemorrhage. It can be found in the digestive tract once a baby begins oral feedings. Newborns are routinely given a single dose of vitamin K to be used by the body until the liver and intestines begin producing clotting factors. The healthy bacteria which then begin to grow in the stomach and intestines are responsible for converting vitamin K to a form that can be used by the body. Once this process is established, it becomes continuous. Additional vitamin K is sometimes given to premature or sick newborns whose intravenous feedings interfere with the development of normal bacteria within the digestive system. Antibiotics can also alter the natural balance by destroying healthy as well as dangerous bacteria, and small doses of vitamin K are frequently prescribed.

Feeding and Digestive Problems

Many premature babies who are too small or too weak to suck at a nipple may be deficient in calcium, phosphorous, and vitamin D and may not be able to absorb the fat-soluble vitamins given in the feedings. Babies who are not yet able to tolerate milk-based feedings must be fed intravenously through a small needle inserted in the scalp, arm, or leg.

Infants with more mature digestive systems but who still do not have an adequate sucking reflex are usually fed breast milk or formula by *gavage*. A thin tube is inserted through the nose or mouth and passed directly to the stomach or intestine. This form of feeding may be continuous or may be intermittent, every two to three hours. Breast milk expressed into sterile containers (by the baby's mother or by a donor) or formula is fed to the baby in measured quantities. Once the sucking reflex is strong enough, most babies can be nursed or bottle-fed by their mothers while still in the intensive care nursery.

Neonatologists, doctors who care for premature or sick newborns, differ on whether to feed premature infants breast milk or a special formula developed for premature babies. The breast milk produced by a woman who delivers prematurely has been reported to be different in composition from the milk of a woman who delivers at term. This "preemie milk" has nutritional qualities that are better suited to the specific nutritional needs of the premature infant. The small protein molecules in human milk also make it easier to digest than cow's milk (which is often the base ingredient in formulas) with its larger protein molecules, and breast milk also contains valuable immune factors to protect against disease. Some physicians, however, feel that human milk is too low in some essential nutrients needed by the premature infant, so breast milk is sometimes supplemented by a fortifier or by mixing it with special preemie formula. Your doctor can advise you about your own babies' special needs.

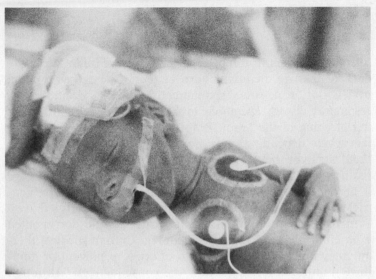

At 4½ weeks, Steven still requires gavage [tube] feedings

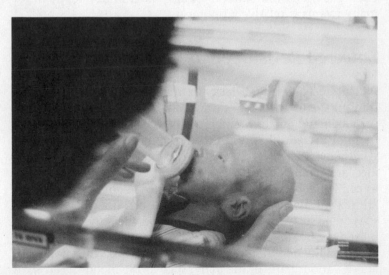

By 9 weeks, Steven is able to take a 'preemie bottle'

Bleeding in the Brain
(Intracranial Hemorrhage)

The blood vessels in the brain of a premature infant are more delicate than in an infant born at term. These fragile blood vessels can break either spontaneously or in association with respiratory distress, metabolic instability, and/or infection, causing bleeding in the brain. Brain hemorrhage can be more or less severe depending upon how much blood passes into the brain tissue or the *ventricles,* the chambers at the center of the brain where the fluid that cushions the brain and spinal cord is produced. When enough accumulates to spill into the ventricles, it is called an *intraventricular hemorrhage.*

In many instances brain hemorrhages can be documented with either ultrasound or CT scanning. Current medical therapy may involve the prescription of drugs to prevent or minimize brain hemorrhage and its consequences. Although intracranial hemorrhage can cause permanent brain damage, the long-range prognosis for all but the most severe cases is often good, and the outlook for neurological development for many infants is relatively optimistic.

Lowered Resistance to Infection

Premature babies often lack the maternal antibodies that are transmitted to the fetus during late pregnancy. In addition, their skin and mucus membranes do not have the resistance to harmful bacteria that is normally found in term infants. Previously mentioned conditions such as breathing difficulty, jaundice, and temperature instability can be indications of infection, as can lethargy, vomiting, or a distended abdomen. Symptoms are not always obvious, however, and because infants on life support systems are particularly vulnerable, these preemies must be carefully monitored. Tests are used to identify the exact origin and nature of toxic substances. Infections can attack various parts of the body, such as the blood (*septicemia*), lungs (*pneumonia*), brain tissue and spinal cord (*meningitis*), membranes of the eye (*conjunctivitis*), and intestinal tract (*necrotizing entercolitis*).

When bacterial infection is suspected, antibiotics are often prescribed until the results of a culture are available. If positive, this treatment is maintained; if negative, it may be discontinued. A baby who is contagious may be placed in isolation, generally in a special incubator called an isolette, to prevent exposing others and to be protected from other potentially contaminating airborne viruses or bacteria.

Newborns can contract an infection in a number of ways. For example, even before birth, harmful bacteria can enter the amniotic fluid if the mother's membranes have broken. For this reason, if labor does not begin within twenty-four hours, the mother may be given antibiotics or may be hospitalized unless it is close enough to term to induce labor.

Babies born to women suffering from certain diseases (such as venereal disease) are frequently born with the mother's illness. Germs can also be transmitted by improper handwashing. This is the reason why hospitals require all visitors who may come in contact with the babies, parents as well as others, to wash hands thoroughly with an antibacterial soap. The infants themselves may also be given periodic baths using a soap containing a germ-killing or antiseptic agent.

Dehydration

Newborns emerge from a fluid-filled environment inside the uterus and are expected to have some water loss as they dry out in the first several days of life. Tiny premature infants and those receiving phototherapy or in warmers or incubators, however, can lose excessive amounts, particularly if they are too small or weak to take sufficient fluid at feedings. Through analysis of the baby's blood and urine, dehydration can be identified and treatment prescribed. Excessive weight loss and a high sodium concentration in the baby's body are signs of dehydration. Usual treatment involves intravenous feedings of fluids containing electrolytes, essential nutrients, and minerals (primarily sodium, potassium, glucose, and chloride), which restore the balance of fluids in the body tissues and help the body's cells function properly.

Developmental Outcome for Premature Babies

Many very small, premature, or sick newborns recover completely with no developmental handicaps. With some babies, however, medical complications that arise during the first few weeks and months of life may affect the long-range developmental outcome. An infant may develop a life-threatening complication that must be treated immediately in order to save the baby's life. Sometimes the complication itself or its treatment could lead to future developmental problems. Doctors who care for premature or sick newborns (neonatologists) must maintain a delicate balance, carefully weighing risks of treatment against the more immediate risks presented by the infant's medical condition.

Some disabilities are not evident immediately and may not show up during the first year or more. Brain damage caused by oxygen deprivation, meningitis (infection or inflammation of the membranes surrounding the brain and spinal cord), or an excessive buildup of bilirubin (a yellow pigment formed when older red blood cells break down) can result in *cerebral palsy* or mental retardation. A lack or an excess of oxygen can lead to visual impairment or blindness, or partial or complete hearing loss. Infections can also cause brain damage, hearing loss, or other problems.

Handicaps resulting from birth trauma or from circumstances following birth may not appear equally in both twins. Sometimes only one of the twins is affected and the other is completely normal. Whether or not the twins have disabilities, they may need special care once at home. *The Premature Baby Book* (1983), by Helen Harrison, is an excellent resource for parents. This and other books and organizations are listed in Appendixes I and II.

Complications Unique to Twins

Other circumstances besides prematurity can endanger the healthy outcome of a twin pregnancy. Complications may arise out of the twins' intrauterine development or during labor and delivery.

Growth Retardation

Twins are often small for their gestational age. Frequently one will be considerably smaller than the other at birth. This is true for both fraternals and identicals, usually for different reasons.

Intrauterine Growth Retardation

Fraternal twins, or identicals who have separate chorion bags during their fetal development, sometimes have growth retardation due to crowding in the uterus. According to one report, placental growth is measurably slower than with singletons as early as twenty-two weeks into the pregnancy, and slower growth of a twin fetus is apparent between twenty-seven and thirty-three weeks. The smaller twin may also suffer from low blood sugar and at birth may have a disproportionately large head and short arms and legs. Most twins who are born with this type of initial growth retardation but who have no other serious complications, however, can develop and grow normally.

Twin-to-Twin Transfusion Syndrome

Most identical twins share a placenta. These babies may develop at different rates if one receives more nutrients than the other. Fewer than 15 percent of all identical twins while still in the womb develop twin-to-twin transfusion syndrome. Tiny fissures in the blood vessels within the twins' common placenta enable blood designated for one baby, the donor, to pass into the system of the other, the recipient. The donor is usually smaller and anemic because of the decrease in the blood supply. The larger recipient, however, generally suffers more from this syndrome, with possible jaundice, respiratory disorders, or even heart failure. Exchange transfusions for one or both twins may be necessary.

Entangled Umbilical Cords

Approximately 4 percent of identical twins occupy a single, shared amniotic sac. With no membrane to separate them in the womb, they may become entangled in one another's umbilical cords, or the cords may entwine, cutting off each baby's lifeline to the placenta. According to one report, this has been estimated to take place in approximately 50 percent of all twins who share an amniotic sac. Entangled umbilical cords often lead to death of the fetuses. As with intrauterine growth retardation and twin-to-twin transfusion syndrome, however, this condition is found in such a small proportion of all twin births that it is not a cause for concern.

Interlocking

This rare phenomenon occurs in approximately 1 out of every 1,000 twin births. If the first twin presents by breech and the second is head down in a vertex presentation or is transverse, the heads can become interlocked. An attempt to deliver the breech baby vaginally could be fatal to either or both infants. This situation is usually detected prior to delivery, however, and a Caesarean section is performed.

Supertwins

The greater the number of multiples, the greater the risk to their survival. An English study published in the early 1950s is reported to have found that the usual length of pregnancy was 280.5 days for a singleton, 261.5 days for twins, 247 days for triplets, and 237 days for quadruplets. The more fetuses, the greater the demand on the mother's uterus due to increased weight and volume. Pressure on the cervix is also stronger, and labor generally occurs prematurely. Helen Harrison, in *The Premature Baby Book* (1983), reports that crowding in the womb causes slower growth of the fetuses beginning by the thirty-fourth week with twins, the thirtieth week with triplets, and the twenty-sixth week with quadruplets. Some reports indicate that growth retardation begins even earlier.

The degree of prematurity and the birth order can significantly affect the amount of risk to each infant. One study that was published in 1979 examined fifty-nine triplet pregnancies at four major hospitals and discovered that most of the triplets were delivered vaginally. A physician, however, may feel that Caesarean delivery is safer in some cases in order to spare tiny premature babies additional stress and to maximize the chances for a healthy outcome for all three infants, particularly when the babies' positions make a vaginal delivery more risky. Because of the many and various complications that can arise during labor and delivery of supertwins, they are often delivered by physicians who specialize in high-risk obstetrics.

Emotional Strain on Parents

Parents of premature or sick newborns often wonder, "Why did this happen to me?" If twins were diagnosed early or in midpregnancy, this question may be even more difficult to answer, as the mother was probably given ample warning of the risks of prematurity and was probably restricting her activities.

"I had a premature delivery five weeks early," said one woman, "but I had gone into labor four times before, and each time the doctor stopped it." A second woman's situation was somewhat different. "I have an incompetent cervix, so my cervix was surgically closed. I was also confined to bed eleven weeks prior to delivery. Even so, the boys were born prematurely and weighed only two pounds, eight ounces; and three pounds, eight ounces." Other parents were completely unprepared, as with another woman who "delivered prematurely the night after our last Lamaze class. We were prepared for childbirth, but not for prematurity."

For parents of twins, with not just one baby but two to worry about, a premature delivery can be frightening as well as disappointing. "I was worried whether the babies would be okay, and I was also upset that I couldn't take them home immediately," was the response of one woman. Fear and dejection are magnified twofold; anger, bitterness, depression, and guilt are all natural reactions. One mother confided, "I felt so guilty and kept wondering if I could have done something to prevent this." Premature babies are often born early for reasons of nature beyond our control, and doctors cannot always explain why twins frequently arrive early, even after bed rest.

If your twins are born prematurely you may have as much trouble coping with your own emotions as dealing with the realities of your babies' medical needs. Doctors and nurses take over primary responsibility for the babies' welfare after a premature birth. This can leave you feeling helpless, depressed, or displaced, sensing you are not needed to care for your children. You may fear for your babies' safety, or worry that they will not be given individualized attention in the impersonal environment of a hospital. Newborns who require intensive care are often very small and fragile-looking and may be connected to a variety of frightening life-support devices. You may be afraid to touch your tiny infants, may think of them as imperfect, or may worry you will not be able to love them. "I had mixed emotions," recalls a woman two years later. "I was so relieved that they were healthy, but they were so small and fragile that I was afraid to hold them."

Premature newborns, like babies born at term, need love and affection, and a chance to bond with both parents. Today, because most hospitals recognize this, they urge parents to visit, touch, and participate in the care of their infants. The degree of parental involvement, however, is necessarily determined by the condition of the babies. Looking back, one mother remembers, "I worried a lot about bonding or the lack of it, whether I was holding one more than the other. At that point, and for many months thereafter, I spent many hours worrying about equalizing time with the girls." Do not be ashamed if you feel guilty, worried, or frightened. Discuss your concerns with the doctors and nurses, and if you need additional emotional support, most hospitals also have an experienced social worker to help you.

Waiting for the Babies to Come Home

If both babies must remain in the hospital after you are discharged, you may feel very empty as you leave for home. After weeks and months spent anticipating a joyful double homecoming, you may now feel cheated, angry, and bitter in addition to feeling concerned for the babies' well-being. Your older children may also be confused and disappointed. If they were unhappy that new babies would be coming, they may feel that they caused something to go wrong. They may also worry that something bad will now happen to you or to them, too.

Try to make time to be with your older children as much as possible, even though you may be physically and emotionally exhausted. Bring older siblings to the hospital for a visit if regulations permit. Older children can view the babies through the nursery windows and at some hospitals may even be

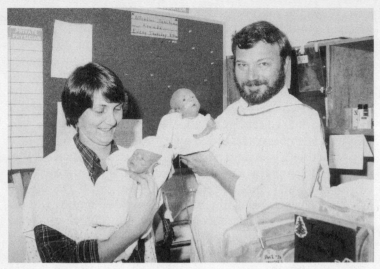

Family photo at three months, the day Steven [left] went home from the hospital

permitted to enter the nursery to touch and handle the babies. Encourage your older children to talk about the babies with you and to learn to recognize distinctive features of each one. For example, if one twin has more hair, you could say, "Jenny is the baby with lots of hair; Karen doesn't have any hair." This helps your older child think of the babies as real people. In addition, you can encourage your older child to make something special, such as drawings or paper dolls, to decorate the babies' incubators or warmers.

This is also a good time to accept help from close friends and relatives. They can prepare meals, take care of the house and the laundry, and even go to the supermarket. This may enable you to spend a little time with your older son or daughter.

Sometimes one baby is able to go home before the other. For some parents, this transition helps ease them into twin parenthood more gradually and gives them a few days, weeks, or months to get better acquainted with the baby who is at home. Making visits to the hospitalized twin may be more difficult with a baby at home to care for, but hospitals will generally try to accommodate your needs by allowing the twin at home to return to the hospital during your visits and under some circumstances will even provide babysitting for your older children. Some hospitals are willing to continue to provide care for the twin who is ready to be discharged until the other is also well enough to go home (for a short period of time, provided that space is still available in the nursery).

When a Baby Dies

Although obstetrical and neonatal (newborn) care is constantly improving, and although excellent medical care is available today, reports indicate that as few as 6 percent to as many as 10 to 15 percent of twins do not survive the pregnancy or the newborn period. Parents need to grieve for the loss of a baby, even if the death occurred in utero, during pregnancy. Mourning for a stillbirth or the death of a newborn is especially hard because the parents never had the opportunity to know their infant and must live with imagined thoughts and lost expectations, not with real memories.

Friends and family may not realize the importance of their support at this time, especially in the case of the loss of one twin. Common words of condolence are, "I'm so sorry, but at least you have another healthy baby." Nobody knows more intimately than the parents that the healthy infant cannot replace the dead twin or eclipse the sense of loss. Parents of twins may need even more support at this time as they try to bond with the surviving baby while mourning the loss of the other.

When twins are born very prematurely, both may be too small to survive. The death of both babies is an ironic twist of

Timothy [left] and Steven [right] on their first birthday

fate for the parents of twins who thought they would have two babies to bring home and who now have none. The mother's body betrays her, too, when her milk comes in, and discomfort from the episiotomy and Caesarean incision during the early weeks are constant physical reminders of her loss.

Touching, holding, and naming a baby who has died is meaningful and helpful. This gives the parents a chance to grieve for a real human being, not just an imagined one. Crying helps parents express their grief, release pent-up emotions, and relieve the hurt. Sharing feelings with one another and with friends and relatives who are sensitive to their needs is an important part of the parents' grieving process. The baby or babies who died will never be forgotten, but time will help heal the wound if the parents accept what has happened to them. Support groups such as S.A.N.D. and the Compassionate Friends (see Appendix I) can be helpful.

Improvements in Medical Care

A discussion of prematurity may one day be unnecessary in a book for expectant and new parents of twins. Medical technology is constantly becoming more sophisticated, and the prognosis is improving for premature and sick newborns, even those with numerous and varied complications. With the greater use of fertility drugs and the increased interest in multiple births, the medical community is focusing more attention on the specialized care required by multiple pregnancies, as well as the unique needs and problems of newborn twins, triplets, and larger multiples. In light of this improving awareness and concern among medical and health professionals, we have every reason to assume that future parents of twins will have increasingly better assurance of bringing home two healthy, full-term babies.

CHAPTER 5

Maternal Nutrition and Health

Good nutrition and a balance of exercise and rest are the ingredients of good health. Staying healthy is essential, both during your twin pregnancy and after the babies' arrival, for your own welfare as well as the babies'. The additional stress on your body during a twin pregnancy requires that you be attentive to your body's needs. This is also true after delivery, due to the greater energy demands on a mother who must care for two infants. Do not neglect yourself, particularly during the busy weeks and months after the birth. Remember that your body needs to restore its own energy supply, and if you are breastfeeding, your body is also nourishing two babies.

Feeling good during the months before and after the birth is easier if you resolve to take care of yourself. As one mother of infant twins and a five-year-old advises, "Make sure you take care of yourself nutritionally, and exercise and get lots of rest because it helps you get through the rough times if you're in good health." Later, by the time your twins are preschoolers, they will be less physically demanding and it will be easier for you to maintain the good habits you have developed.

Nutrition

Good health depends on sound nutrition all of the time—whether or not you are pregnant or breastfeeding. Pregnancy and nursing, because they demand additional calories and nutrients, are discussed in this chapter. If you are bottle-feeding from the start, ask your doctor to help you design a well-balanced postpartum diet suited to your own individual needs.

Pregnancy and Breastfeeding Guidelines

Studies have linked sound nutrition with increased birth weight and a lower incidence of toxemia in twin pregnancies. Doctors and nutritionists agree that a woman expecting twins requires a significantly higher intake of calories. "The last two or three months I was always hungry," one mother recalls, "but as soon as I began to eat, I felt full." You may become uncomfortable toward the end of your pregnancy and may not feel hungry, but do not skip meals.

You may prefer to eat four or five smaller meals per day rather than three large ones. Especially if you have always been in the habit of watching your weight, you may feel like you are cheating when you eat extra meals or snacks between meals. When you are carrying twins, however, the extra calories from these additional meals are extremely important. Try to think of breakfast, lunch, and dinner as the meals you take to nourish your own body and any snacks and extra fluids as food for the babies. This will relieve your guilt feelings each time you open the refrigerator or pantry door and will also encourage you to select healthful, nourishing snacks.

Janet King, associate professor of nutrition at the University of California at Berkeley, stresses that a pregnant woman, whether or not she is expecting twins, should "eat to [satisfy her] appetite, and should choose only high quality foods." King feels that calories in nutritional foods are more beneficial than the empty calories in junk foods (candy, chips, soda pop, pastries). Protein, calcium, iron, and folic acid (folacin) are some of the nutrients that are especially important during pregnancy in general. The foods that are rich in these nutrients also provide other essential vitamins and minerals. Protein builds and repairs all cells in the mother's and the babies' bodies. Calcium is a mineral necessary for the formation of the fetal skeleton and the teeth (which develop in the gums before birth). It helps blood clot and maintains the health of muscles (including the heart) and nerves. Calcium is also stored by the body for release in the breast milk. Iron and folic acid help form red blood cells and protect against anemia, a condition that is frequently associated with multiple pregnancy. Iron from the mother is stored by the baby before birth for use during the early months of life until the iron can be obtained in the baby's diet. "Breast milk as well as cow's milk is low in iron, however, the iron in breast milk is better used by the infant," says King. Because enough iron and folic acid are not always easy to get in the mother's diet alone, they are sometimes prescribed in tablet or capsule form. To avoid constipation, iron is usually limited to 30–60 milligrams daily. Larger doses may be appropriate for women with anemia. Some doctors also prescribe prenatal vitamins; however King cautions pregnant women not to use these as a substitute for good nutritious foods.

Liquids are also necessary to a pregnant woman's diet, whether or not she expects twins. A woman expecting twins should drink at least eight glasses per day (milk, juice, water, soup, and other beverages). Fluids help the cells in the babies' bodies receive nutrients and get rid of waste. In the past, doctors have traditionally recommended limiting salt (because of its sodium content) during pregnancy. Sodium may bring about water retention in the body tissues. Salt, however, is required by the mother's and babies' tissues during pregnancy, says King, so it is important that it be included in the diet. In general, King advises no change in normal salt intake while pregnant (2–3 grams per day). Even in the presence of toxemia, she believes, a decrease could alter a woman's body chemistry and make the problem worse. She notes, however, that an expectant mother with a prior heart condition requiring salt restriction is an exception.

A woman carrying one baby is expected to gain about twenty-four pounds. With twins, the additional fetus, placenta, and amniotic fluid total only about ten pounds. King feels that an ideal weight gain for twin pregnancy is at least forty-five to fifty pounds, accounting for the additional maternal blood and stored fat required for the second baby. Hormonal balance and metabolic rates are not the same for all women, and because every woman's body is different, some may need to gain more than others. For this reason, King advises women not to try to control a weight gain problem with dieting during pregnancy or nursing. Pounds should be put on gradually. After the twentieth week of pregnancy, a sudden gain may indicate water retention in the body tissues and should be followed up by a visit to the doctor. Babies need essential nutrients that cannot be absorbed from the mother's own fat stores, so even an overweight woman needs to eat well during pregnancy, she says, and an underweight woman (weighing less than 85 percent of the recommended body weight appropriate for her height as given in governmental or standard life insurance tables) may need to gain even more than forty-five to fifty pounds and may require a diet that is higher in energy, protein, and other nutrients. With triplets and larger multiples the weight gain should be even greater.

"Mothers of twins who want to nurse should be encouraged to do so," says Sally H. Cohenour, a registered dietitian who has served as research dietitian for the Metabolic Research Unit at the Department of Nutritional Sciences of the University of California at Berkeley. "The mother's goal is to produce breast milk and to reach and maintain her ideal weight," Cohenour continues. "The need for calories is different for each person, however, depending upon the individual's metabolism and activity levels." Cohenour, who has also been a nutrition consultant for the California Department of Health Services and for the California Association for Maternal and Child Health, has prepared a daily food plan (Table 5.1), two tables of nutrient and calorie guidelines (Tables 5.2–3), and two sample menus for adult women pregnant with twins or breastfeeding twins (Table 5.4). This nutrition program is not intended as a rigid dietary regime. If you have specific dietary needs or restrictions, a registered dietitian can help you adapt the program to meet your body's own specific nutritional needs.

Mrs. Cohenour recommends two different food plans for adult breastfeeding mothers of twins, one plan for the first three months and another for after three months. There are two reasons why two plans are needed. During pregnancy, women accumulate stores of fat in their body. These fat stores help provide the extra calories a woman needs to make breast milk. After about three months, some women will have used up all of their extra fat stores from pregnancy and will return to their normal, ideal weight. Other women, however, will need about six months to reach their ideal weight. Once the mother does reach this point, she will need to eat *more* calories to maintain her weight and to produce enough milk for her twins. Also, as babies get older they are larger and need more milk. As the babies grow, their mother must take in more calories and required nutrients to produce more breast milk.

These food plans should meet the needs of most women, but you may want to make minor adjustments to suit your own activity levels better. In addition, for the first two to three months, supplements of iron are usually recommended by physicians for breastfeeding mothers. You can promote good milk production by choosing high-nutrient foods, consuming enough calories, getting enough rest, and drinking enough liquids.

For the first four months, whether they are twins or singletons, babies need only breast milk or formula (plus whatever supplements are prescribed by their pediatrician) to fill all of their nutritional needs. Most pediatricians recommend supplements of vitamin D and fluoride for breastfed babies. Breastfed babies who were born prematurely may also need supplemental iron. Especially in the early months before introducing solids, if you are breastfeeding exclusively (without any formula supplements for the babies) you will need to monitor your babies' weights to be sure they maintain the growth expected of twins, as defined by their pediatrician. If the babies do not maintain these expected growth rates, their need for milk may have exceeded what you are producing at the present time.

The amount of milk a mother can produce depends not only upon her own individual capabilities but also upon her consumption of enough calories, nutrients, and liquids; the amount of rest she is getting; and most important, the amount of sucking stimulation to the breast provided by the babies. Cohenour noted, "If the twins are not maintaining expected growth rates and if you are following the daily food plan, resting, and nursing frequently, your pediatrician will probably recommend formula supplements." Calories required by breastfeeding mothers who supplement their twins with formula must be adjusted for each individual.

The introduction of solid foods to the babies' diet is generally appropriate at four to six months. Usually iron-fortified cereal is the first solid food given to babies. Your pediatrician will offer guidelines on when to introduce solid foods, the appropriate amounts to give, and in which order to offer these new foods. Infants continue to need significant amounts of breast milk or formula during the first year of life. Around one year of age they should receive about 50 to 60 percent of their calories from milk or formula, with the remainder coming from a wide variety of other foods. If you choose to continue breastfeeding your twins after solid foods are started, you should continue with the food plan designated for breastfeeding after three months.

The Daily Food Plan

The daily food plan that follows is designed to meet or nearly meet the current Recommended Dietary Allowances (RDAs) for adult women who are pregnant with or breastfeeding twins. It also reflects the current nutritional guidelines issued jointly by the U.S. Department of Agriculture and the U.S. Department of Health, Education and Welfare (*Nutrition and Your Health: Dietary Guidelines for Americans*).

The plan has five major categories. Foods with comparable

amounts of calories and nutrients are grouped together. The five groups, some with specified subgroups, are as follows:

1. *Protein Foods:*
   Animal protein
   Vegetable protein:
      Beans and Dry Peas
      Nuts and Seeds

2. *Milk and Milk Products** (dairy foods)

3. *Whole Grain Breads and Cereals*

4. *Fruits and Vegetables:*
   High Vitamin C
   Dark Green
   All others

5. *Polyunsaturated Fats and Oils*

In the Daily Food Plan on page 116 you will find a list with suggestions for serving sizes and for the numbers of servings from each food group needed daily. Examples of healthy foods in each of these five major groups and a list of the essential nutrients provided by these foods are given in the Foods and Nutrients list on p. 118. Select any food in each group when you plan your daily menus. Each week try to include a variety of foods from each group. This will help guarantee that you receive a healthy balance of the nutrients you need.

Check your serving sizes with the regular measuring cups you use for cooking. If you have never had to watch your diet carefully before, practice for a couple of days by measuring some of your favorite foods. You will quickly learn what one cup of juice looks like in your glasses or one cup of cereal in your bowl. Then you will be able to estimate the right size servings in the future.

A small kitchen scale for weighing foods (if you have one) will help you when servings are given by weight. If you do not have a food scale, here are some guidelines for estimating

---

*Milk and cheese are also sources of animal proteins.

the weights of various foods. Servings of presliced cheeses are easy to estimate because they are usually packaged in ¾-ounce or 1-ounce slices. Read the package. Meat, chicken, and fish servings are harder to calculate because the bones add weight that you do not want to include in your estimate. Read the labels on the raw packages. About 4 ounces of raw meat (boneless) will equal about 3 ounces when cooked. One pound of hamburger (16 ounces) can be divided into four patties of 4 ounces each. Each patty will weigh about 3 ounces after cooking.

The 500 extra calories per day you will need in order to continue breastfeeding after the first three months can come from any of the foods in the groups listed in the chart on p. 118, or from low-nutrient foods that are not listed (such as jelly). In other words, these extra 500 calories are more important for the additional energy they provide than for their nutritional value. Thus, they do not necessarily have to provide protein, vitamins, or minerals. In addition, these calories do not all have to come from the same source. For example, you could choose a one-ounce serving of nuts or seeds (174 calories), plus another serving of whole grain breads or cereals (124 calories), plus an additional two tablespoons of fats and oils (218 calories).

Use salt in normal amounts when you are cooking at home. Your doctor may want you to take supplements of iron and folacin because the amounts of these nutrients that are present in foods are not adequate for pregnancy. Iron supplements may be necessary for the first two months of breastfeeding; the amount of folacin present in the foods you are eating, however, is sufficient for breastfeeding if you are following the Daily Food Plan.

The liquids you drink while you are pregnant with or breastfeeding twins are important to provide an increase in your bodily fluids and to prevent constipation. Drink at least six to eight glasses of liquids daily in addition to the milk servings given in the sample menus. Liquids include soup and beverages such as milk, fruit juice, and water.

DAILY FOOD PLAN

Food Groups	Pregnant No. Servings/ Size	Breastfeeding First 3 Mos No. Servings/ Size	Breastfeeding After 3 Mos No. Servings/ Size
Protein foods			
Animal protein	(2) 3 oz.	(2) 3 oz.	(2) 4 oz.
Vegetable protein			
Beans and			
dry peas	(1) 1 cup	(1) 1 cup	(1) 1 cup
Nuts and seeds	(1) 1 oz.	(1) 1 oz.	(1) 1 oz.
	or	or	or
	4 tbs.	4 tbs.	4 tbs.
Milk and milk products[a]			
	(6) 1 cup	(5) 1 cup	(6) 1 cup
	or 1 oz.	or 1 oz.	or 1 oz.
	cheese	cheese	cheese
Whole grain breads and cereals			
	(5) 1 slice	(5) 1 slice	(5) 1 slice
	or 1	or 1	or 1
	cup	cup	cup

[a]Vitamin D is an important nutrient during pregnancy and breastfeeding. Milk is usually fortified with vitamin D; other dairy products may not be. For this reason, it is very important that you try to choose milk servings as much as possible. If you have a milk allergy due to a lactose intolerance, ask your doctor for the name of an "aid" that can be added to milk to make it more digestible. Also, you may not be bothered by the partially predigested lactose in yogurt, cheese, or acidophilus milk. If you are allergic to milk proteins, ·ask your physician to recommend a calcium supplement. To reduce calories, choose nonfat or lowfat milk in this food group. Be sure it is fortified with vitamin D.

DAILY FOOD PLAN (continued)

Food Groups	Pregnant No. Servings/ Size	Breastfeeding First 3 Mos No. Servings/ Size	Breastfeeding After 3 Mos No. Servings/ Size
Fruits and vegetables			
	(5) total[b]	(6) total[b]	(6) total[b]
High in vitamin C	(1–2) 1 cup	(2) 1 cup	(2) 1 cup
Dark green	(1–2) 1 cup	(2) 1 cup	(2) 1 cup
All others	(1–2) 1 cup	(2) 1 cup	(2) 1 cup
Polyunsaturated fats and oils			
	(2) 1 tbs.	(3) 1 tbs.	(2) 1 tbs.
Calories from any source			
	0	0	500 per day
Supplements			
Iron	30–60 mg.	30–60 mg. for first two months	0
Folacin	800–1000 mcg.	800–1000 mcg.	0
Liquids in addition to milk			
	(6–8) 8 oz.	(6–8) 8 oz.	(6–8) 8 oz.

[b]At least one serving from each of the three groups.

Adapted by Sally H. Cohenour, R.D., M.S., from the "Daily Food Plan for Adult Women" in Alice White, *The Total Nutrition Guide for Mother and Baby* (New York: Ballantine, 1983), and reprinted by permission of Ballantine Books, a Division of Random House, Inc.

FOODS AND NUTRIENTS IN THE DAILY FOOD PLAN

Foods in This Group	Nutrients in These Foods
PROTEIN FOODS	
Animal Protein	
Poultry (chicken, game hens, turkey); Eggs (3 large = 3 oz.); Beef; Lamb; Pork; Veal; Organ meats (heart, kidneys, liver); Fish (fresh, frozen, canned); Shellfish (crab, lobster, oysters, scallops, shrimp)	High-quality protein; Iron; Zinc; Thiamine; Riboflavin; Niacin; Vitamin B_6; Vitamin B_{12}; Lesser amounts of other vitamins and minerals
Vegetable Protein	
Beans and dry peas ("legumes")	
Dried beans (navy beans, red or kidney beans, pinto beans, garbanzo beans, re-fried beans, lima beans, bean salad, baked beans, bean soup, chili with beans); Soybeans (dried beans or ready-to-eat soybean "nuts"); Tofu (soybean curd—can be used in salad dressings, soups, spreads, and stir-fry dishes; 4 oz. is a standard serving one piece 2½" × 2¾" × 1" or 120 g.); Peas (black-eyed, split, chick—fresh, dried, frozen, or canned); Lentils	Valuable protein but limited in some essential amino acids, so eat with small amounts of animal protein or dairy foods, or eat with complementary plant proteins; Complex carbohydrates; Niacin; Vitamin E; Vitamin B_6; Pantothenic acid; Folacin; Magnesium; Phosphorus; Iron; Zinc; Fiber (not a nutrient, but required for bulk and aids in elimination)
Nuts and seeds	
All nuts (almonds, pecans, cashews, filberts, peanuts, walnuts); All nut butters (cashew butter, peanut butter); Sunflower seeds; Sesame seeds	Valuable protein but limited in some essential amino acids, so eat with small amounts of animal protein or dairy foods, or eat with complementary plant proteins; Iron; Calcium (amount varies with type of nut); Thiamine; Niacin; Vitamin E; Vitamin B_6; Pantothenic acid; Folacin; Magnesium; Phosphorous; Zinc; Mono- and polyunsaturated fats (but no cholesterol)

Milk and milk products (dairy foods)

All milk (regular, skim, lowfat, nonfat, 2%, nonfat dry milk); Buttermilk; Milk shake, frappe; Eggnog; Yogurt; Cottage cheese (1½ cups/serving); Cheese (1 oz.) contains more than 500 mg. calcium/100 g. for these cheeses: American, Cheddar, Colby, Edam, Gouda, Gruyere, Monterey Jack, Muenster, Port du Salut, Provolone, Romano, Swiss, and Tilsit; these cheeses contain less than 500 mg. calcium/100 g., so choose 2-oz. servings: Blue, Brie, Camembert, Feta, Limburger, Mozzarella, and Roquefort

Calcium; High-quality protein; Riboflavin; Vitamin A; Vitamin B_{12}; Vitamin D (if fortified); Phosphorous; Pantothenic acid; Lesser amounts of niacin, folacin, vitamin B_6, magnesium, and zinc

Whole grain breads and cereals

For cooking, choose flours and products made from unrefined whole wheat, corn, rye, or brown rice; also millet, buckwheat, oats, wheat germ, whole wheat berries; Breads (cracked wheat, whole wheat, wheat germ, rye, oatmeal, pumpernickel, cornbread, whole wheat, or rye rolls or biscuits); Bagel of pumpernickel or whole wheat (1); Pita bread (1 slice); Muffins (corn or bran); Tortillas (corn, 2); Crackers (whole wheat, 10 thin or 5 thick; rye, 5; graham, 2 large rectangles; puffed rice cakes, 3; or rice wafers, 6; Pancakes (corn, oat, wheat germ, or whole wheat; 1 medium cake); Waffles (wheat germ, whole wheat; 1 large); Hot cereals (oatmeal, wheat, barley, or rye; 1 cup); Cold cereals (nonsugared wheat flakes, wheat germ, puffed oats, shredded wheat, or 100% bran; 1 cup or 1 oz./serving); Brown rice, bulgur, barley, wild rice (1 cup cooked); Whole wheat macaroni, noodles, or spaghetti (1 cup cooked); Popcorn, unbuttered (3 cups)

Complex carbohydrates; Vitamin B_6; Folacin; Niacin; Riboflavin; Thiamine; Iron; Magnesium; Zinc; Incomplete plant protein; Fiber (not a nutrient, but adds bulk and aids in elimination)

Fruits and vegetables

High in Vitamin C (more than 40 mg. vitamin C per 1 cup serving)

Fruits and juices: cantaloupe, grapefruit, guava, lemons, limes, mango, orange, papaya, and strawberries; Vegetables: broccoli, Brussels sprouts, cauliflower, greens (kale, collard, mustard, turnip), green pepper, sweet red pepper (½ pepper pod), rutabagas, turnips, and kohlrabi

Vitamin C; Fiber; Fruits have simple carbohydrates; Vegetables have complex carbohydrates; Variety of other vitamins and minerals

Dark green

Asparagus; Bok choy (Chinese cabbage); Broccoli; Brussels sprouts; Cabbage; Dark leafy greens (beet, chard, collard, kale, dandelion, mustard, spinach, Swiss chard, turnip); Dark leafy lettuce (red leaf, chicory, endive, escarole, romaine); Scallions; Watercress

Folacin; Vitamin A; Vitamin C; Vitamin E; Vitamin B$_6$; Riboflavin; Pantothenic acid; Calcium (the oxalic acid in these vegetables impairs calcium absorption, not a problem when adequate milk group foods are eaten); Iron; Fiber; Complex carbohydrates; Lesser amounts of zinc, magnesium, and phosphorus

All others

Fruits: apples, apple cider or juice, applesauce, apricots, avocado, bananas (1 med.), blueberries, cherries, cranberries, dates (3), figs (1 cup canned or 2 med. raw), fruit cocktail, grapes, nectar (apricot, peach, or pear), nectarines, melon (honeydew, watermelon, etc.), peaches, pears, pineapple, plums, prunes (5 med. dried or ⅓ cup cooked), raisins (1 oz.), rhubarb, and tangerines; Vegetables: artichoke (1 med.), bamboo shoots, beets, carrots, celery, corn (1 ear), cucumbers, eggplant, green beans, mushrooms, Nori seaweed, okra, onions, parsnips, peas, pea pods, potatoes (1 med. or 1 cup mashed), pumpkin, radishes, sweet potatoes, sprouts, summer/winter squash, tomato and tomato juice, vegetable juice cocktail, yams, and zucchini

Fiber; Fruits have simple carbohydrates; Vegetables have complex carbohydrates; Variety of vitamins and minerals

Polyunsaturated fats and oils	
Soft tub or stick margarine; Oils (cottonseed, corn, safflower, sesame, soybean, and peanut); Oily salad dressings (oil and vinegar, Italian)	Essential fatty acids; Vitamin E; Small amounts of iodine

Adapted by Sally H. Cohenour, R.D., M.S., from the "Daily Food Plan for Adult Women," in Alice White, *The Total Nutrition Guide for Mother and Baby* (New York: Ballantine, 1983), and reprinted by permission of Ballantine Books, a Division of Random House, Inc.

CALORIE AND NUTRIENT GUIDELINES

Requirements for:	Woman 23-50 years	Pregnant adult woman carrying 1 baby	Pregnant adult woman carrying twins	Lactating adult woman, 1 baby	Lactating adult woman, twins, first 3 months	Lactating adult woman, twins, after 3 months
Energy (kcal.)	2,000	2,300	2,525	2,500	2,800	3,500
Protein (g.)	44	74	100	64	74	84
Fat-soluble vitamins						
Vitamin A (mcg. R.E.)	800	1,000	1,200	1,200	1,400	1,600
Vitamin D (mcg.)	5	10	15	10	12.5	15
(I.U.)	200	400	600	400	500	600
Vitamin E (mg. a-TE)	8	10	12	11	12.5	14
Water-soluble vitamins						
Vitamin C (mg.)	60	80	100	100	140	160
Thiamine (mg.)	1.0	1.4	1.8	1.5	2.0	2.0
Riboflavin (mg.)	1.2	1.5	1.8	1.7	2.2	2.2
Niacin (mg. N.E.)	13	15	17	18	18.5	23
Vitamin B_6 (mg.)	2.0	2.6	3.05–3.2	2.5	2.75	3.1
Folacin (mcg. total)	400	800[a]	[a]	500	600	600
Vitamin B_{12} (mcg.)	3.0	4.0	4.5	4.0	4.5	4.5
Minerals						
Calcium (mg.)	800	1,200	1,600	1,200	1,600	1,600
Phosphorus (mg.)	800	1,200	1,600	1,200	1,600	1,600
Magnesium (mg.)	300	450	450–600	450	450–600	450–600
Iron (mg.)	18	[b]	[b]	[b]	[b]	18
Zinc (mg.)	15	20	20–25	25	20–29	25–35
Iodine (mcg.)	150	175	200	200	250	300

[a]Oral supplementation of folacin desirable: 800–1,000 mcg./day reported to meet pregnancy needs. Most physicians continue supplementation during breastfeeding.
[b]Use of 30–60 mg. supplemental iron recommended; upper amount probably recommended for women during and for 2–3 months after pregnancy with twins.

kcal. = kilocalories g. = grams mcg. = micrograms mg. = milligrams
R.E. = retinol equivalents I.U. = international units a-TE = alpha tocopherol
N.E. = niacin equivalents

Twin estimates by Sally H. Cohenour, R.D., M.S., designed and developed for publication in this book. Single baby guidelines from *Recommended Dietary Allowances*, 9th ed. (Washington, D.C.: National Academy of Sciences, 1980).

TWO SAMPLE MENUS FOR ADULT WOMEN PREGNANT WITH OR BREASTFEEDING TWINS

MENU 1

Menu	Pregnancy	Breastfeeding First 3 Months	Breastfeeding After 3 Months**
Breakfast			
Eggs, any style	1	1	2
Bran muffin	2	2	2
Margarine	2 tsp.	2 tsp.	2 tsp.
Honey	0	0	2 tbs.
Milk	1 cup	1 cup	1 cup
Papaya	½	½	½
Orange juice	1 cup	1 cup	1 cup
Lunch			
Bean soup	1 cup	1 cup	1 cup
Rye bread (sandwich)	2 slices	2 slices	2 slices
Margarine	2 tsp.	2 tsp.	3 tsp.
Sliced turkey	2 oz.	2 oz.	2 oz.
Muenster cheese	2 oz.	1 oz.	2 oz.
Milk	1 cup	1 cup	1 cup
Dinner			
Broiled halibut	3 oz.	3 oz.	3 oz.
Salad of Dark leafy lettuce	1 cup	1 cup	1 cup
Oil and vinegar dressing	2 tsp.	1 tbs.	4 tsp.
Brown rice	1 cup	1 cup	1 cup
Broccoli	0	1 cup	1 cup
Margarine for vegetables	0	2 tsp.	1 tbs.
Milk	1 cup	1 cup	1 cup
Blueberries	1 cup	1 cup	1 cup
Snacks			
Boiled egg	0	0	1
Milk	1 cup	1 cup	1 cup
Any type nuts	1 oz.	1 oz.	2 oz.
Apple juice	1 cup	1 cup	1 cup

Note: When following this menu, be sure you are also getting six to eight glasses or cups (8-oz. size) of liquids a day in addition to milk. These liquids can be beverages or soup.

**See note on the following page.

MENU 2

Menu	Pregnancy	Breastfeeding First 3 Months	Breastfeeding After 3 Months**
Breakfast			
Oatmeal	1 cup	1 cup	1 cup
Cracked wheat bread, toasted with	1 slice	1 slice	1 slice
Peanut butter	2 tbs.	2 tbs.	2 tbs.
Jelly	0	0	1 tbs.
Milk	1 cup	1 cup	1 cup
Grapefruit *or*	½ *or*	½ *or*	½ *or*
grapefruit juice	1 cup	1 cup	1 cup
Lunch			
Salad of:			
Dark leafy lettuce	1 cup	1 cup	1 cup
Sunflower seeds	½ oz.	½ oz.	½ oz.
Sliced ham	1 oz.	1 oz.	2 oz.
Sliced chicken	1 oz.	1 oz.	2 oz.
Sliced boiled egg	1	1	1
Garbanzo beans	¼ cup	¼ cup	½ cup
Sliced tomato	½ cup	½ cup	½ cup
Italian salad dressing	4 tsp.	2 tbs.	4 tsp.
Corn muffin with	1	1	1
Margarine	1 tsp.	1 tsp.	1 tsp.

Note: When following this menu, be sure you are also getting six to eight glasses or cups (8-oz. size) of liquids a day in addition to milk. These liquids can be beverages or soup.

**This food plan requires 700 calories more than the plan for the first three months of breastfeeding; about 200 calories come from increased serving sizes of animal protein and from an additional serving of milk or milk products. The remaining 500 extra calories needed can be derived from any food source. The extra 519 calories in this menu (added to the required servings of this food plan) come from 2 tbs. honey (128) at breakfast, an extra 1 tsp. margarine at lunch (36), extra oil and vinegar dressing (2 tsp. extra = 72 calories), 1 tbs. margarine (109) at dinner, and an extra ounce of nuts (174) at snack.

Prepared by Sally H. Cohenour, R.D., M.S.

Menu	Pregnancy	Breastfeeding First 3 Months	Breastfeeding After 3 Months**
Raw celery	½ cup	½ cup	½ cup
Cantaloupe cubes	1 cup	1 cup	1 cup
Milk	1 cup	1 cup	1 cup
Dinner			
Bean salad	¾ cup	¾ cup	1 cup
Game hen (without bones)	3 oz.	3 oz.	4 oz.
Wild rice	1 cup	1 cup	1 cup
Asparagus	0	1 cup	1 cup
Margarine on rice or vegetables	1 tsp.	2 tsp.	1 tsp.
Sliced peaches	1 cup	1 cup	1 cup
Milk	1 cup	1 cup	1 cup
Snacks			
Eggnog	1 cup	0	1 cup
Yogurt	1 cup	1 cup	1 cup
Thin whole wheat crackers	10	10	10
Swiss or Cheddar cheese	1 oz.	1 oz.	2 oz.
Popcorn with	0	0	2 cups
Margarine	0	0	1 tbs.

Note: When following this menu, be sure you are also getting six to eight glasses or cups (8-oz. size) of liquids a day in addition to milk. These liquids can be beverages or soup.

Menu 2 includes several examples of how to make the food plan as versatile as possible. Please note that the required servings in the food plan can be split between two or more foods. The one serving of *nuts and seeds* is divided into ½ serving at breakfast (2 tbs. peanut butter) and ½ serving at lunch (½ oz. sunflower seeds). The 1 cup serving of *beans and dry peas* is divided into ¼ serving at lunch (¼ cup garbanzo beans in the salad) and ¾ serving at dinner (¾ cup bean salad). The 1 cup of *all other fruits and vegetables* is divided into ½ cup sliced tomatoes and ½ cup raw celery. The servings of *fats and oils* can be divided among your meals and snacks. Remember that 1 tbs. equals 3 tsp. (the measuring type you use for baking). So 2 tbs. per day is the same as 6 tsp. per day, and 3 tbs. per day is the same as 9 tsp. per day.

**The 500 extra calories required are included in this sample menu: breakfast—50 calories for jelly; lunch—82 calories for egg and 115 calories for ½ cup garbanzo beans; and snack—101 calories for 1 oz. extra cheese, 46 calories for 2 cups of popcorn, and 102 calories for 1 tbs. margarine.

Prepared by Sally H. Cohenour, R.D., M.S.

Other Health Questions

Alcohol, drugs, and smoking can endanger a developing fetus during pregnancy. In addition, these habits may interfere with proper eating habits. Infants delivered to mothers who smoke often have a low birth weight and may also have major health complications. How much alcohol is too much during pregnancy is not known, so alcohol should be avoided if possible or reduced to a minimum. Heavy drinking can lead to a thiamine deficiency because this nutrient is needed to a greater extent for alcohol metabolism.

In late pregnancy, if a woman is experiencing a series of premature contractions, and this is more common with twins, or if she actually goes into premature labor, her doctor may prescribe alcohol to relax the uterine muscles and possibly forestall the onset of true labor. This treatment must be supervised by a doctor, however, and is not prescribed for women with certain medical conditions or who are taking medication that could be dangerous if combined with the effects of alcohol. Some drugs, such as heroin or morphine, when taken during pregnancy can cause neurological damage to the fetus. *Before taking any drugs or medications, consult your doctor.*

Alcohol and some drugs and medicines, when taken by a nursing mother, will also be found in her breast milk. If you are breastfeeding, be prudent in any social drinking and consult your pediatrician before taking any medications. If you smoke, the nicotine will reach your babies, too. The babies may not appear to react to nicotine, but they may have a sensitivity to it. If you smoke, give up your habit or at least cut back as much as possible.

A recent Food and Drug Administration report cautions pregnant women about the possible dangers of caffeine use. A study done on pregnant laboratory rats who were fed caffeine revealed offspring with birth defects and delayed skeletal development. Caffeine is a stimulant with known drug effects. How it affects a human fetus is not yet known, but it does cross the placenta and does reach the fetus. For this reason, caffeine should be avoided as much as possible. It can be found in coffee, tea, some cola drinks, and some other soft drinks, chocolate, cocoa, and many prescription and nonprescription drugs (including some of the following: decongestants, pain relievers, alertness tablets, and diet pills).

Physical Activity

Taking care of your body's well-being is important all of the time, even when you are not pregnant, breastfeeding, or recovering after delivery, but during and after a multiple pregnancy you have an added responsibility. This section on physical activity with the suggestions and exercises for expectant and new mothers of twins was developed by Mary A. Snyder, a registered physical therapist. Snyder is currently clinical assistant professor in the curriculum of physical therapy at the School of Medicine of the University of California, San Francisco. She has done extensive research on the subject of twin pregnancy and recovery following the delivery of twins. This material is not intended to be used as a recipe that combines specific instructions and generates a specific result. Instead, it is designed to provide useful guidelines to help you understand what is happening to your body during a multiple pregnancy and the postpartum period, to help you prevent some of the problems that could occur (such as disabling back pain), and to steer you on the road to delivery and to postpartum recovery. Every woman's body is unique, so sometimes what feels comfortable to one woman does not feel comfortable to another. Your doctor can help you determine your own safe limits concerning your daily activities and your own need for rest.

During Pregnancy

Body Tone and Posture

Your body is undergoing hormonal and physical changes as it makes room for two babies. Muscles are stretching, ligaments are softening, and joints are becoming more flexible in order to allow for the babies' passage through the bony pelvic opening. This can also make some joints more susceptible to injury, however. Some of the other considerations that may influence your vulnerability to a strain of these structures are your age and number of previous pregnancies, the additional weight of a multiple pregnancy, previous injuries (particularly to the back), your physical condition (including your flexibility and muscle strength before pregnancy and any diseases of your joints, such as rheumatoid arthritis), and the way your clothes and shoes fit. You may be aware of the physical effects of any of these considerations on your own body. If so, keep this in mind when going about your daily activities.

Stand up and look at your profile in the mirror. Your neck should be supporting your head comfortably over your shoulders, and your head and neck should be on the same vertical axis with your trunk. You may be leaning back to keep your balance now that your center of gravity is shifting increasingly forward. This causes a curve or "sway" in your lower back and makes your buttocks appear to be more prominent. As the uterus becomes larger during your multiple pregnancy, you will feel the increasing weight pulling you forward. Some people have this posture even without being pregnant.

An exaggerated lower back curve during pregnancy can strain and weaken the ligaments (loosened temporarily due to the hormonal changes of pregnancy) that hold the spinal joints together, especially if you must suddenly move in another direction. You can help prevent backache by reducing the curve in your lower back and by consciously trying to tip your uterus back into the bowl formed by your pelvis.

Practice the pelvic tilt exercise shown on pages 144–145, by standing sideways in front of a mirror and tilting up your pelvis. The abdominal muscle performing this movement runs alongside the midline of your abdomen, from the pubic bone to the rib cage. The abdominal muscles are stretched by any pregnancy, and this is exaggerated with twins. Women pregnant with twins often develop a separation in the middle of the muscle—just like an open zipper. You may notice a midline bulge like a sausage. The medical term for this is *diastasis recti*. If you notice this kind of separation, try to avoid activities that affect this area. The exercises recommended here for the prenatal period should not aggravate this condition.

Another vulnerable area is the pelvic floor since it will be stretched so much during birth. The pelvic floor is made up of muscles stretching from your pubic bone in front to your tail bone in back. These muscles surround and control the flow of urine, the vagina, and the movement of the bowels. Pelvic floor exercises, also called Kegel exercises, are helpful in maintaining the flexibility of these muscles as well as in increasing your ability to relax during childbirth. The Kegels are described in detail on page 148.

Your knees, ankles, and feet have always supported your entire body weight during every step. The added flexibility in these joints during pregnancy and your steadily increasing weight make good ankle and arch support essential.

How to Stay Comfortable and Avoid Injury

Your muscles often stay tensed when you are under stress. This can be caused by fatigue, emotional distress, work, or the body changes that occur during pregnancy. Muscle tension can make you uncomfortable, especially if it occurs in an area of previous injury. Moving around and changing positions, as already mentioned, may relieve some of the problem. If you sit at a desk at work, try a small back cushion. At least once every hour, stand up and stretch your back by bending gently from side to side, rotating gently to each side as if looking behind you and then stretching your arms over your head.

Constant tension in your neck muscles can pull on your skull and give you a headache. Practice the neck-stretching exercises (page 146–147) frequently. Keeping the neck muscles relaxed and limber will make you more comfortable during your pregnancy.

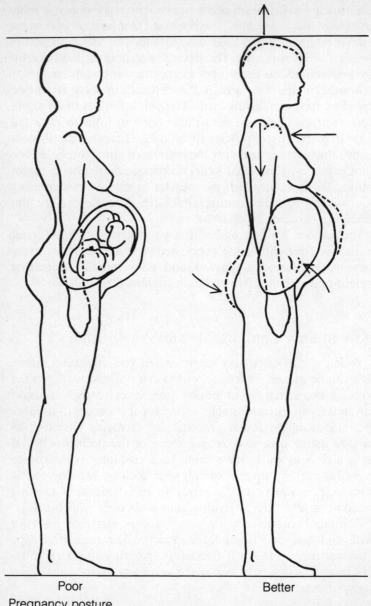

Poor

Better

Pregnancy posture

Vary your position frequently throughout the day and whenever you feel uncomfortable. More than one hour in any single position usually contributes to poor circulation and swelling in the legs, a common complaint during multiple pregnancy. Swelling of the ankles and legs may be greatest during the last few months, particularly with a twin pregnancy. Putting your feet up helps the return of fluid to your central circulation.

At work and when sitting or standing for more than two hours, support pantyhose may help control the swelling. Never wear anything that completely encircles and constricts your legs, such as knee-high hose or thin garters. Avoid crossing your legs at the knee because this compresses the blood vessels behind your knees.

For relief from swelling of the ankles and legs, try the position shown, lying with your back against several pillows to raise your back and with your legs elevated on several firm pillows so that your feet are at the level of your chest. Remember, be sure your neck and head are properly supported. Never lie flat on your back, especially during late pregnancy, because the weight of your abdomen can partially compress a major blood vessel.

Back support is important, even just for reading

Many women complain of backache during a multiple pregnancy. Bending and lifting, if done incorrectly, can aggravate this condition. Your doctor may recommend that you wear a maternity corset when working or walking for a distance if you have a history of back pain or injury. Do *not* wear a corset, however, unless your doctor feels it is necessary. The corset will help your abdominal muscles support your abdomen and back during pregnancy, but it will also weaken your abdominal muscles through disuse. Practice the pelvic tilt exercise (pages 144–145) even if you are regularly wearing a maternity corset. (Corsets are available through maternity stores and through maternity or lingerie departments of some department stores.) Comfortable, stable shoes with low heels will ease the strain on your back and will help maintain stability at the knees by preventing wobbling from side to side. High heels are not only unstable but also throw your center of gravity even farther forward. This forces you to compensate by leaning back, leading to an exaggeration of your lower back curve. Your shoes should have arch support unless you have permanently flat feet.

Here are a few more suggestions that are particularly important during a multiple pregnancy on how to protect your back as you go about your daily activities:

When lifting, even something as light as a towel, either during pregnancy or after the birth of your babies, be sure to bend your knees and keep your trunk upright. You may find your legs getting a little sore at first because you are using muscles you may not have been exercising before, but they will strengthen in a short time.

Keep the load as small and as close to your body as possible. Steady yourself with one hand on stable furniture as you come back to a standing position.

Bending forward is not recommended, particularly during late pregnancy. With twins, the weight of your abdomen can strain your back and may also throw you off balance. Instead of leaning over, keep your trunk upright and bend only your knees (assume a squatting position). When you make beds, work from each side in turn rather than reaching across.

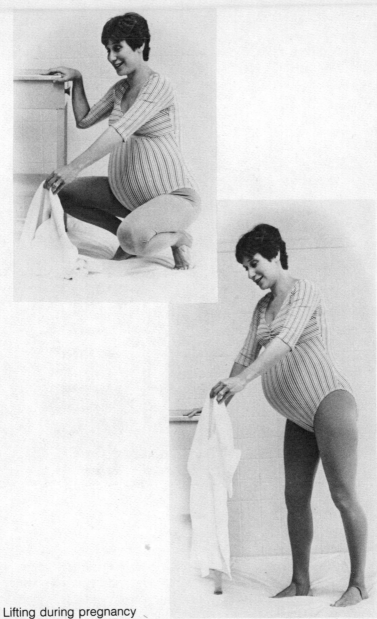

Lifting during pregnancy

Prolonged standing

Sitting (floor or bed)

Finally, do not unload groceries or other heavy packages yourself during the third trimester. Stop sooner if you feel uncomfortable or if your doctor recommends it.

Prolonged standing is not recommended in late pregnancy either, due to the increased strain it puts on your back and circulatory system. If you must be upright for any length of time, put one foot on a low stool or shelf. For example, you could put your feet under the counter or sink when you're working in the kitchen. Be sure to point your feet in the same direction as your work so that you do not twist your body at the waist.

When you are sitting in a chair or a car, it is a good idea to place a small cushion behind your lower back for support. If you can, choose a chair that will bring your knees either level with or higher than your hips. Supporting your elbows on a table, desk, or the arms of a chair will also help reduce the stress on your back.

If you have an older child, you will be sitting on the floor or a bed for reading and play sessions. One way to support your back while doing this is by leaning up against a wall. In late pregnancy, lie on your side and make a play area between the two of you.

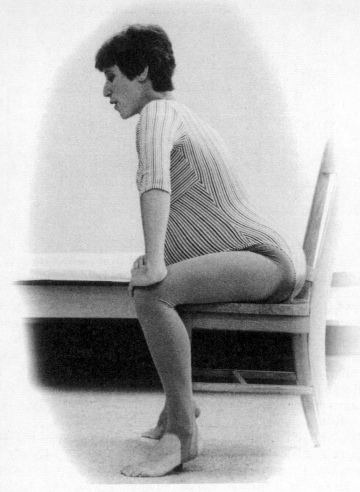

Relief for shortness of breath

Your normal breathing rate during pregnancy may be faster than before, even when you are resting. The rib cage spreads out so that you have a larger lung capacity and enough air for yourself and your babies, even with the pressure on your diaphragm provided by two growing fetuses. As mentioned in

Chapter 2, you may feel short of breath at times. This is particularly common in multiple pregnancies and may be due to the hormonal effects on your respiratory center or to the increased upward pressure on your diaphragm.

For relief from shortness of breath, first, sit down and lean forward with your arms on your knees or on a table. Then breathe in deeply and out slowly through pursed lips. Deep breathing will be important to you throughout your pregnancy, but especially while practicing relaxation. You may learn various additional breathing techniques in your childbirth education class as well as exercises suited to your individual needs.

During your twin pregnancy, lying on your side will be safer and more comfortable than lying on your back. As already mentioned, when you lie flat on your back, the weight of your pregnant uterus may compress the major blood vessel that runs along the back of your abdominal cavity. This may temporarily cut off the blood supply to your babies and hinder the flow of blood to and from your legs. When you lie on your side, the return of blood to the heart is not restricted by the weight of the uterus. This position also permits blood to flow normally through the uterine artery. If you have heartburn you will want to lie on your back, however, in which case you should be propped up by several pillows at at least a thirty-degree angle to the bed.

Getting in and out of bed can seem a formidable challenge, particularly as your multiple pregnancy advances. When you lie down on a bed, sit securely on the edge first and lower yourself to one side using your elbow and opposite hand. Then bring your legs up and gently slide or roll over so you do not fall off. To get out of bed from a side-lying position, bend your knees and gently slide or roll to the edge of the bed, swing your legs over the edge, and use your hands to push up to a sitting position. Stay on the edge of the bed until you have adjusted to the upright position. Remember, take your time. Jumping up too quickly may make you dizzy as the blood rushes away from your head.

When lowering yourself to the floor, use a sturdy piece of

furniture for support, resting one hand on the furniture while lowering yourself slowly to one knee and then the other. Finally, rotate your buttocks to the floor. Once you are seated you can continue to your desired position.

To get up from the floor, roll over to one side and push yourself up to a side-sitting position. Rest one hand on a piece of sturdy furniture, slowly raise yourself to your knees, and then stand on one foot and then the other. Remember, always get up slowly to avoid dizziness.

Sexual Activity

Some women have greater sexual interest during pregnancy than others. During late pregnancy, with the greatly enlarged abdomen of your twin pregnancy, you may be too uncomfortable to be interested in sex. Your breasts and genital area may also be more sensitive now. Your husband may interpret your disinterest as a personal rejection, and he may feel frustrated or hurt. On the other hand, he may also be too tired. Some couples are too concerned about the welfare of the babies or the mother's comfort to consider lovemaking during the last three months. Try to be sensitive to each other's needs and feelings. Even when intercourse is too uncomfortable, especially in late pregnancy, sexual intimacy without actual intercourse may be mutually pleasing and meaningful.

Some physicians are cautious, recommending against intercourse during the last three months of a twin pregnancy because of the possibility of early dilation of the cervix, the onset of premature labor, or introduction of bacteria that could lead to infection. Other doctors prefer to evaluate each woman's situation individually. Your physician will be able to counsel you based on your own pregnancy's history. If the membranes (which surround the fetus and protect it from infection) have ruptured, or if you have vaginal bleeding or spotting, call your doctor and do not have intercourse. If you have no complications, you can probably enjoy the variety of sexual activities that are comfortable for you. A helpful book on this subject for expectant parents is *Making Love During Pregnancy* (1977), by Elisabeth Bing and Libby Colman (listed in Appendix II).

Rest

Once twins have been diagnosed, the doctor may advise you to slow down, nap daily, and avoid rigorous exercise by twenty-four weeks into the pregnancy. Working and traveling may also be curtailed at this point. Because of the extra weight you are carrying with two babies, and because of the additional energy your body must generate to nourish twins, you will probably become tired toward the end of the pregnancy. Do not push yourself. Your body needs more rest now, so do not fight this natural urge. If a pelvic exam reveals that your cervix has begun to dilate prematurely, as is often the case with twins, your doctor may advise you to spend the remainder of your waiting in bed.

Although the benefits have not been conclusively proved, many doctors believe that bed rest during the last trimester carries little risk to the patient and may discourage the onset of premature labor by relieving the constant weight on the cervix. Each woman's pregnancy, however, needs to be considered individually. When bed rest is prescribed, the mother is usually told to remain in bed in her own home, but in some cases the doctor may recommend hospitalization. If confined to bed, you may be bored and uncomfortable. Call your local mothers of twins club for moral support. They will also help you find mothers of twins who can boost your spirits and can pass along their own successful time-killing hints or those of other mothers who have shared your experience.

Exercise

Aerobic exercise, such as swimming, jogging, or bicycling, or the currently popular dance-related exercises, increases muscle endurance and the efficiency of your heart and lungs. All of these types of exercise, however, may be too strenuous as your twin pregnancy progresses. The exercise you get as part of your daily activities is safer and easier on your body. In recent years, medical and health professionals have been researching whether exercise is advisable during pregnancy. In general, studies have indicated that a woman who is in good physical health and who exercises regularly need not be restricted during the first half of her pregnancy unless her physician advises against it. The increased demands on the body during the second half of a multiple pregnancy, particularly on the circulatory system, generally call for at least a decrease in the intensity and duration of exercise at that stage. Your own doctor and childbirth instructor can help you develop guidelines that correspond to your own needs and limitations.

Sometimes an expectant mother of twins who is able to jog comfortably throughout the first three months may be surprised to find climbing stairs is like climbing a mountain during the last half of her multiple pregnancy. Whenever you feel uncomfortable, whether you are climbing stairs, shopping at the department store, or working at a desk, take rests frequently. Slow down as you perform each activity, and change your position (as mentioned earlier) whenever possible. Stop what you are doing if your discomfort persists. Do not push yourself. Let your body be your guide.

If you have the equipment and are in the habit of regularly monitoring your own heart rate, you may have noticed that it has increased even when you are just resting. The resting pulse normally increases between 15 and 40 percent during a single pregnancy and may increase even more during the last few months of a twin pregnancy. Do not be alarmed if this happens to you. Your blood pressure may also go down a bit during pregnancy, contributing to the dizziness you feel when you try to get out of bed too quickly.

Your own physician can advise you of any medical reasons specific to your twin pregnancy that may warrant restricting your exercise. Various conditions of the body or daily habits are known to affect the way your body and the bodies of your babies respond to exercise. These conditions and habits include heart disease, anemia, smoking, excessive alcohol intake, and chronic inactivity.

A variety of activities are appropriate for pregnancy, but this is not the time to take up a new sport. For example, wait until next year to learn how to cross-country ski. Nonjarring exercise, such as walking, is better than jogging as you gain weight. Swimming is an excellent form of exercise since it supports the weight of the uterus. Be sure to stretch your muscles and joints before exercise and to cool down afterward by doing a slower exercise. This helps prepare the muscles and circulatory system. Finish with a session of relaxation in a side-lying position (see page 153).

Apart from the overall conditioning exercise you get from your normal everyday activities while you're pregnant, a daily routine of prenatal exercises can help you through pregnancy, childbirth, and postpartum recovery with more energy, strength, and flexibility. Below is an exercise program designed specifically for twin pregnancies.

Exercise Program for Twin Pregnancy

Relax and breathe between exercises.

Group I:
Perform these exercises by incorporating them into your normal daily activities. Repeat all of the exercises in this group several times a day as you sit at your desk, watch television, or lie in bed. Practice them for a couple of weeks until you have full control, and then continue to make them a part of your daily routine.

The Kegel exercises are an especially important part of the exercise program because they help to maintain the muscle tone of the pelvic floor. This area is particularly vulnerable during a twin pregnancy due to the additional weight and pressure of two fetuses. Kegels can be performed frequently throughout the day.

Pelvic tilt I *Pages 144–145*
Chin tuck *Page 146*
Neck stretch *Page 147*
Slow Kegels *Page 148*
Push-in/Pull-out Kegels *Page 148*

Group II:
Perform these exercises several times daily. The exercises in this group are particularly useful whenever you are sitting or lying down with your feet up. They become even more important if you are confined to bed—and the chances of this happening are greatly increased with a twin pregnancy—because they help pump out some of the fluid that may be building up in your legs.

Buttocks exercise *Page 148*
Thigh-knee exercise *Page 148*
Ankle circles *Page 149*

Group III:
Perform these exercises once or twice daily.
Although all of the exercises in this group are helpful, the relaxation exercises are especially important. Relaxation is essential in order to reduce muscle tension, which is greater

during pregnancy—especially multiple pregnancy. Relaxation exercises provide a much-needed relief from the stress and tension of your busy daily routine. Even if your doctor prescribes bed rest, do not assume that this is a replacement for the relaxation exercises described in this program.

Pelvic tilt II *Page 150*
Leg stretch I *Page 151*
Arm circles I *Page 152*
Relaxation exercises *Pages 153–154*

Developed by Mary A. Snyder, R.P.T., M.S.

Caution: Do not *bounce* when you stretch. Not only may this strain a muscle or ligament, but the muscle may reflexively pull in the opposite direction. *Avoid double straight-leg raises and full sit-ups with your legs out straight.* Both of these are supposed to exercise your abdominal muscles, but they also use other muscles (the "hip flexors") that pull on the lower back joints. The double straight-leg raises demand that you lie on your back and lift both legs straight up. This can create excessive stress to your back and is difficult to do even without the increased load of pregnancy. The full sit-up with legs straight does use the upper abdominal muscles as you begin to curl up to a sitting position. Studies have shown, however, that beyond about a forty-five-degree angle, the rest of the sit-up is performed by the hip flexor muscles. This pulls on your spine and does not strengthen your abdominals.

Do not bend forward at the waist when standing because the strain on your back increases dramatically with each additional degree of forward bending. Avoid such exercises as "windmills" (bending to reach for the toes).

PELVIC TILT I

Pelvic tilt—to maintain strength
of abdominal muscles and stretch
or maintain flexibility of the lower back.

1. Begin by standing against a
   wall with your knees relaxed.

2. Place your hand behind your
   lower back and feel the hollow
   of the curve.

3. Now attempt to flatten your
   spine against the wall by using
   your abdominal muscles to pull
   up on your pelvis and by
   tightening your buttocks and
   pulling them underneath you.
   At the same time, pull your
   shoulders back to the wall.

4. Continue to breathe and
   hold this pelvic tilt for at least
   five seconds. Try to hold it
   for longer periods of time
   without a wall to guide you.
   Do this at least once
   every hour.

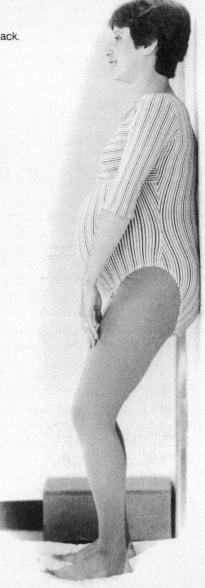

CHIN TUCK

To stretch and relax neck muscles.

1. Fold your hands behind your neck just under your head.
2. Pull in your chin and stretch your neck up with your hands.
3. Relax and repeat.

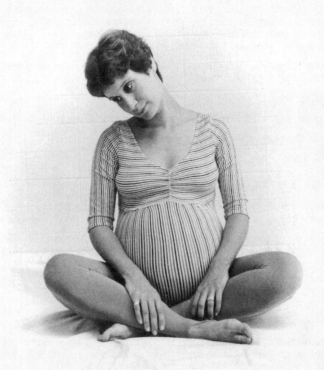

NECK STRETCH

To stretch and relax neck muscles.

1. Bend your head forward and then to one side (in front of your right shoulder).

2. Breathe deeply and remain in that position as your neck muscle relaxes.

3. Repeat to your left side.

SLOW KEGELS AND PUSH-IN/PULL-OUT KEGELS

Kegel exercises—to maintain strength and control of the pelvic muscles.

You can identify the pelvic floor muscles this way: sit on the toilet with your legs spread apart. Stop and start the flow of urine without moving your legs. The pelvic floor muscles allow you to control urination. (You will also be using some of your abdominal muscles.)

Breathe normally as you perform these exercises. You can do them when standing, sitting, or lying down.

Slow Kegels

1. Tighten the pelvic floor muscles as you did to stop the urine.

2. Hold this position for a slow count of three.

3. Relax and repeat.

Push-in/Pull-out Kegels

1. Imagine that your entire pelvic floor is an elevator. Pull the pelvic floor slowly up into your pelvis—your imaginary elevator should rise slowly.

2. Push out or bear down as if you were trying to speed up the flow of urine—your imaginary elevator should descend slowly.

BUTTOCKS EXERCISE

To maintain strength of the buttock muscles and to help your circulatory system pump fluid out of the legs. You can do these exercises standing, sitting, or lying down.

1. Squeeze your buttocks together and hold for a count of three.

2. Relax and repeat five times.

THIGH-KNEE EXERCISE

To maintain strength of the thigh muscle and to help your circulatory system pump fluid out of the legs.

1. Sit on the floor or bed with your legs out straight, and tighten the muscle on the front of one thigh so that the back of your knee pushes down.

2. Relax and repeat with alternate legs, five times for each leg.

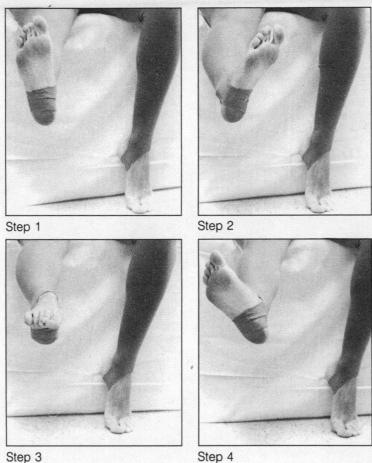

Step 1

Step 2

Step 3

Step 4

ANKLE CIRCLES

For ankle flexibility and to help your circulatory system pump fluid out of the legs.

1. Sit in a chair or lie on your back on the floor or on a bed. (During pregnancy, perform this exercise while sitting. Do not lie on your back.)

2. Bend one foot up toward your head.

3. Trace a circle in the air by pointing your foot first toward the right, then down, then to the left, and then back up toward your head.

4. Continue making circles, repeating five times with each foot.

PELVIC TILT II

1. Get on your hands and knees.
2. Relax and breathe deeply.
3. Push your back up like an angry cat.
4. Continue to breathe and hold that position while you count to five.
5. Progress to a count of ten.
6. Relax.

LEG STRETCH I

To stretch the muscles behind and inside your thighs.

Do not bounce during pregnancy as this could tear a muscle. You can, however, rock gently as you stretch.

1. Sit on a firm surface with your legs straight in front of you forming a "V." You will feel a stretch on the inside of your thighs and behind your knees.

2. Stretch forward gently and relax the leg muscles. You will feel a slow lengthening inside your thighs and behind your knees.

3. Relax and return to an upright position.

4. Repeat.

ARM CIRCLES I

To strengthen your upper back.

1. Sit cross-legged ("Indian style," with your ankles crossed). You may feel some tightness around your hips and inner thighs. Try to relax your legs in this position rather than force them down.

2. Raise your arms out to the side at shoulder height.

3. Trace small circles in the air forward and backward.

4. Relax.

Position for pregnancy

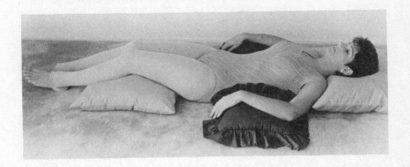

Position for postpartum

RELAXATION EXERCISES

To help you relax all muscles for tension relief.

Relaxation is a conscious process of muscle awareness; thus it is different from sleep. If you are relaxed, you will be able to fall asleep more easily. When you do relaxation exercises you will be tensing and then relaxing each muscle group so that you can feel the difference more easily. Once you know what muscle relaxation feels like, you will be able to take inventory of all of your body's muscles once a day. Allot at least fifteen minutes. Do not rush or you will not be able to relax completely. Contract and relax each muscle group as outlined below. (You may prefer to have someone else read the instructions slowly and quietly to you until you remember the routine.)

Relaxation exercises should be done in a room that is warm but not hot.

Position for pregnancy: Lie on your side on a firm bed with two pillows to support you, one between your knees and one to support your head and neck. Alternate the side you lie on each time you do relaxation exercises.

Position for postpartum: Lie on your back on a firm bed with two pillows under your knees, one under your neck and head, and one to support each forearm.

The exercises are done as follows:

1. Let yourself feel heavy, fully supported by the bed. Your breathing should be slow and rhythmic.

2. Make a fist with one hand. Then slowly tense your entire arm, working up from your fist to your shoulder until the arm is rigid. Feel the tension. Now let go. Let your arm lie motionless on the bed. Think about how your arm feels when it is relaxed. (Use your available arm for this exercise if you are in the side-lying position of pregnancy. If you are in the postpartum back-lying position, repeat with your other arm.)

3. Tense one leg, thinking of each part of your leg until it is very tight. Now let it relax completely and go limp. (Use your available leg for this exercise if you are in the side-lying position of pregnancy. If you are in the postpartum back-lying position, repeat with your other leg.)

4. Close your eyes. Keep your breathing slow and rhythmic. Think back to your arm(s) and leg(s). Are they relaxed? The muscle softens and lengthens as it relaxes.

5. Squeeze your buttocks together. Then relax. Pull your abdomen in. Then release it. Pinch your shoulder blades back toward your spine. Then let go. Pull your shoulders forward. Then relax. Raise your shoulders toward your ears. Then relax.

6. Check your breathing. Mentally review all of the areas just described. Repeat tensing and relaxing any area that does not feel limp and relaxed.

7. Press your head against the pillow. Feel the tension. Now let go and let the pillow support the weight of your head. Close your eyes tightly and clench your jaw. Hold this position and then let go. Raise your eyebrows and then let go. Swallow and relax.

8. Mentally review all of the muscle groups. They should feel heavy and restful. All muscle tension should be gone. Lie still and enjoy the sensation of relaxed muscles. You may have to repeat these exercises several times before you are completely relaxed.

9. When you get up after your rest, sit up slowly and stretch as you would after a good night's sleep. This helps your blood circulation.

After Delivery

Body Tone and Posture

Good posture and body mechanics are still essential as your body readjusts to an appropriate posture without the extra weight of a multiple pregnancy. Stand up and look at your profile in the mirror, just as you did when you were pregnant. Depending on the length of time that has passed since delivery and on your individual rate of recovery, you may still have a midriff bulge. Getting back to your normal figure or shape takes longer following a twin birth. Pull your abdomen in and tuck your buttocks under. This is the same pelvic tilt you did while you were pregnant, but it is easier to do now. Practice finding that posture several times daily until your body becomes accustomed to good posture again. If you are breastfeeding your twins, your breasts will be heavier than if you were only nursing one baby. The weight of your breasts will tend to pull your shoulders and neck forward, causing pressure on the blood circulation and nerves of your arms. A well-constructed nursing bra with wide straps will help support the weight of your breasts, enabling you to maintain an upright posture.

How to Stay Comfortable and Avoid Injury

The suggestions for protecting your back during pregnancy still apply. Follow the same steps when lifting or bending, and for nursing, follow the guidelines pertaining to sitting. Bend your knees, not your back, when picking up the babies (or your older children), the laundry basket, or toys. Keep the load close to your body while standing up. Elevate one foot when standing for a long time. Support your back when sitting to nurse, when playing with children, or when driving. Sit on a bed or sofa to nurse, and prop your arms and the babies on pillows while breastfeeding (especially when you are feeding both babies at the same time) to avoid excessive

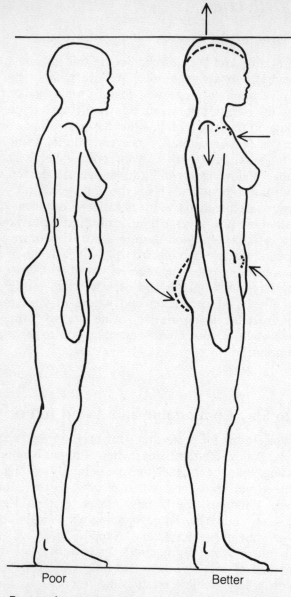

Poor   Better

Posture for postpartum

Postpartum lifting

stress on your shoulders. Practice some of the same loosening up exercises (Groups I and II) given under "Exercise Program for Twin Pregnancy" as often as every hour if possible (these can be done anywhere), and follow the steps for the relaxation exercises (pages 153–154) once or twice a day.

If either one or both of your twins was born vaginally and you had an episiotomy, the stitches may feel uncomfortable for a few weeks. Inspect yourself with a mirror to monitor the healing process. Report any signs of inflammation to your physician. Bowel movements can be performed normally without danger of interrupting the healing process. You may feel more comfortable if you put your feet on a footstool during a bowel movement. Avoid sitting on the toilet for long periods of time or straining that can cause stretching of the sensitive, soft hemorrhoidal tissues.

Following a C-section, deep breathing may be uncomfortable and may cause you to cough. Do the breathing exercises (described later in this chapter) every hour if possible for the first few days. As after any surgery, you need to take care of your lungs to prevent pneumonia. While you are recovering from the anesthesia, hold a pillow against your abdomen to support the incision while you breathe deeply and cough a couple of times. To minimize discomfort while breastfeeding, sit on a bed and place a pillow on your lap. You may have to nurse one baby at a time at first if your incision is too uncomfortable. Ask your older children to sit beside you rather than on your lap. Your incision will need two to three weeks to heal, but it may be tender for a month or more. Report any signs of inflammation to your physician. You may have some discomfort from gas and slowed digestion. Try lying on your side for relief. Getting out of bed or up from a sofa may also be uncomfortable at first. Begin by bending your knees, rolling to your side, and pushing up with your arms (just as you did when you were pregnant). Sit for a minute. Then swing your legs over the side of the bed or sofa. Take a deep breath. When you feel steady, stand slowly with someone to assist you.

Sexual Activity

Your physician can advise you on how much time to allow your body to recover before resuming sexual intercourse. The appropriate amount of time to wait will depend upon the circumstances of your delivery and your body's physical condition. In general, wait as you would following a single birth until vaginal bleeding and discharge has stopped, the episiotomy (vaginal delivery) or abdominal incision (Caesarean delivery) has healed, and you are feeling comfortable enough to resume sexual activity. Discuss this with your doctor when you are released from the hospital.

If you had a vaginal delivery, the soft tissues of the vagina and pelvic floor have been stretched to their limit not once but twice and need time to rest and recover. If you had an episiotomy, the incision may be uncomfortable for a month or so. The hormonal depletion that occurs after birth (vaginal or Caesarean), especially among women who are breastfeeding, causes the vagina to shrink. The vaginal wall becomes thinner and less elastic, and vaginal lubrication may occur more slowly and sparely. These conditions are only temporary and begin to normalize as your body returns to its prepregnant hormonal balance. Following a Caesarean section, your incision may be tender for several weeks or even months. This may make some lovemaking positions uncomfortable. When resuming sexual activity, communicate your feelings to one another. Begin slowly. If you are uncomfortable, find another position that is satisfying to both of you. If you have persistent pain or discomfort or renewed bleeding after you resume intercourse, consult your physician.

Breastfeeding twins may delay the return of menstruation for many months (frequently for longer than with a singleton) but that does not necessarily mean you are not ovulating. You can get pregnant while breastfeeding, therefore, so do not rely on breastfeeding for birth control. Discuss appropriate birth control methods with your physician.

Rest

In the weeks that follow delivery, whether you are nursing or not, your body needs more rest. Attending to two babies' feedings interrupts your night sleep, so a nap during the day is advisable for as many weeks as you feel you need it. The best time to nap is when the babies are sleeping. Try to get the babies on the same feeding and sleeping schedule to guarantee yourself time to rest each day. Ideas on how to do this are discussed in Chapter 12, "The First Year," in the section on feeding and sleeping during the first three months.

Exercise

Your uterus is shrinking back to its size before pregnancy. Your abdominal muscles have been stretched to their limit, and you may even have had surgery. Your stretched and weakened muscles and ligaments may need several weeks to recover, and they may feel sore as you begin exercising. Below are two lists of postpartum exercises especially designed for new mothers of twins. One is to be used for recovery from a vaginal delivery, the other after a Caesarean birth. If you delivered one twin vaginally and one by C-section, do the exercises given in the Caesarean list.

Following a C-section, the thigh-knee exercise, buttocks exercise, and ankle circles should be done frequently right from the beginning. Continue with the exercise progression as you feel ready. You will feel sore at first as you retrain your muscles, but strengthening these muscles provides for a smoother recovery. Begin slowly and build up stamina. Do not push yourself.

Once you are comfortably able to complete several repetitions of the postpartum exercises designed for either vaginal or Caesarean delivery, you will be ready to resume normal activity.

Exercise Program Following a Vaginal Delivery of Twins

Relax and breathe between exercises.

Group I:
Perform these exercises several times a day. They can be incorporated into your normal daily activities. Kegel exercises can be performed with greater frequency. They are especially important after delivery as you strengthen the pelvic floor.

Pelvic tilt I or III *Pages 144–145 and 164*
Slow Kegels *Page 148*
Pull-in/Push-out Kegels *Page 148*
Buttocks exercise *Page 148*
Thigh-knee exercise *Page 148*
Ankle circles *Page 149*
Diaphragmatic breathing exercises *Page 168*
Chest expansion breathing exercises *Page 169*

Group II:
Perform these exercises once or twice a day in addition to those in Group I. Begin with two repetitions of the first six exercises and progress as you feel able.

Do one sequence of the relaxation exercises. These continue to be helpful in reducing tension as you regain your strength and energy and begin the demanding job of caring for two babies.

Chin tuck *Page 146*
Neck stretch *Page 147*
Leg stretch I and II *Pages 151 and 165*
Arm circles I *Page 152*
Knees-to-chest exercise *Page 167*
Curl-ups II and III *Page 171* (You may have to begin with Curl-ups I, *Page 170*)
Relaxation exercises *Pages 153–154*

Group III:
Progress to this group when you are able to do ten of each of the exercises in Group II easily. Begin with two to five of the following exercises:

Developed by Mary A. Snyder, R.P.T., M.S.

Exercise Program Following a Caesarean Delivery of Twins

Relax and breathe between exercises.

Group I:
Perform these exercises several times daily. You can begin with Group I while you are still confined to bed after surgery. Kegel exercises remain important as you strengthen the pelvic floor, which was weakened during your pregnancy by the weight of two fetuses. Relaxation exercises also continue to be helpful because they reduce tension as you regain your strength and energy and begin the demanding job of caring for two babies. Do one sequence of the relaxation exercises.

When you feel comfortable with the exercises in Group I, progress to Group II.

Group II:
Perform these exercises daily in addition to those in Group I. Begin with one or two repetitions and progress as you feel able. Do one sequence of the relaxation exercises.

Group III:

Progress to this stage when you are able to do ten of the previous exercises easily. Begin with two to five repetitions of the following:

Pelvic tilt IV   *Page 164*
Arm circles II   *Page 166*

Group IV:

Begin these exercises when you feel you are able.

Leg stretch I and II   *Pages 151 and 165*
Knees-to-chest exercise   *Page 167*
Curl-ups II and III   *Page 171* (You may have to begin with
   Curl-ups I,   *Page 170.*)

Developed by Mary A. Snyder, R.P.T., M.S.

PELVIC TILT III

1. Lie on your back with your knees bent.

2. Roll your pelvis back until your lower back is flat. Check with your hand to be sure that the space is gone.

3. Hold for a count of three.

4. Relax.

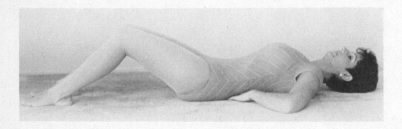

PELVIC TILT IV

1. Lie on your back with your knees bent and roll your pelvis back until your lower back is flat (as in Pelvic Tilt III). Breathe.

2. Maintain the pelvic tilt as you slide your legs down straight. (Remember to maintain the tilt. You will not be able to straighten your legs to a completely horizontal position.)

3. Slide your legs back up to the original position and repeat the exercise.

LEG STRETCH II

1. Sit on a firm surface with your legs straight in front of you forming a "V."

2. Reach smoothly for your left foot, keeping your knees straight. Relax. Return to an upright sitting position.

3. Repeat, reaching for your right foot. Continue the exercise, alternating sides.

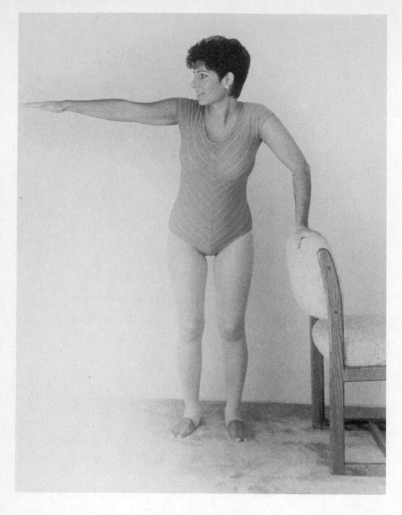

ARM CIRCLES II

1. Lean forward while standing and support yourself with one hand on a table, counter, or back of a chair.

2. Straighten the other arm to the side and do small circles forward and backward.

3. Repeat to the other side.

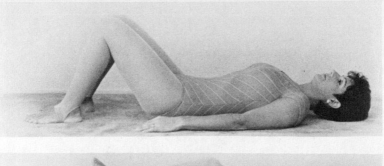

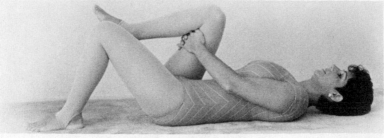

KNEES-TO-CHEST EXERCISE

To stretch your lower back.

1. Lie on your back with your knees bent.

2. Lift one knee to your chest. Hook your lower arm under the knee to pull it close to you.

3. Return your foot to the floor.

4. Repeat with the other leg.

5. Bring both knees to your chest and return to the starting position.

6. Repeat the entire sequence.

BREATHING EXERCISES

To help you control your breathing and maintain your lung capacity. You can do these exercises while sitting or lying down.

Diaphragmatic breathing exercises

1. Put your hand on your upper abdomen, just under your rib cage. Push out your upper abdomen while taking a breath. Feel how this area pushes your hand out as you inhale.

2. Exhale slowly and feel your abdomen pull in.

3. Relax and breathe normally.

4. Repeat the sequence.

Chest expansion breathing exercises

1. Put your hands on your rib cage.

2. Inhale and feel this area push outward on your hands.

3. Exhale slowly, and feel your rib cage pull in.

4. Relax and breathe normally.

5. Repeat the sequence.

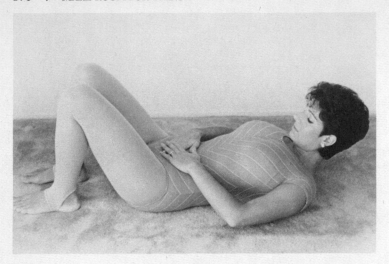

CURL-UPS I

To strengthen your abdominal muscles.

Before beginning this exercise, check for a gap between the two vertical bands of your abdominal muscles. Do this by lying on your back on a firm surface and curling your chin to your chest. If you are able to fit three or more fingers into the gap, do only Curl-ups I. Do not progress to Curl-ups II and III until the separation has narrowed to less than a three-finger width.

1. Lie on your back on a firm surface with your knees bent.

2. Cross your arms over your abdomen to support the muscles.

3. Lift your head off the floor, tucking in your chin.

4. Return your head to the floor.

5. Relax and repeat.

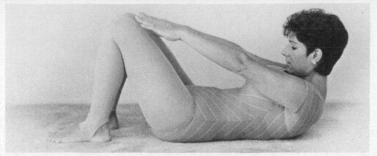

CURL-UPS II

1. Lie on your back on a firm surface with your knees bent.

2. Tilt your pelvis back, flattening your lower back to the floor, and extend your arms forward.

3. Tuck in your chin, and while breathing out, lift and reach forward until your shoulder blades are off the floor. Only go as far as is comfortable at first, even if you are only able to raise your head.

4. Return smoothly to the floor. Do not drop down.

5. Relax and go directly to the next exercise, Curl-ups III.

CURL-UPS III

1. Lie on your back on a firm surface with your knees bent.

2. Tilt your pelvis back and extend your arms forward to the left of your knees. Lift your right shoulder diagonally toward the left. Return smoothly and relax.

3. Tilt your pelvis and extend your arms forward to the right of your knees. Lift your left shoulder diagonally toward the right.

4. Return smoothly to the floor.

5. Relax and repeat the entire sequence of Curl-ups II and III (if you can do it comfortably a second time).

MODIFIED CURL-UPS

1. Lie on your back on a bed in a semireclining position with pillows to prop your back and with your knees bent, feet flat on the bed.

2. Take a deep breath.

3. Stretch your arms forward, tuck in your chin, and exhale as you begin to curl up. (Just begin to curl up. Do not sit up all the way.)

4. Return to your starting position.

5. Relax and repeat.

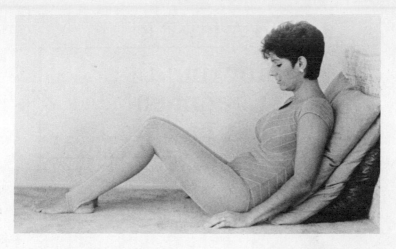

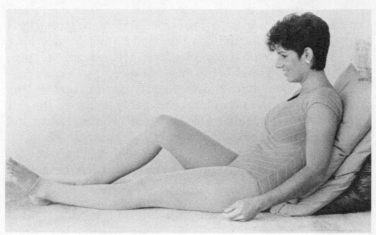

ALTERNATE LEG-STRAIGHTENING

For mild abdominal strengthening and to stretch hip and thigh muscles.

1. Lie on your back on a bed in a semireclining position with pillows to prop your back and with your knees bent, feet flat on the bed.

2. Slide the heel of one foot down the bed and back up to a bent-knee position again.

3. Repeat with the other leg. Continue with alternate legs.

CHAPTER 6

Stocking Up: Equipment and Layette

The cost of providing for twins can be very high, especially if you are expecting for the first time and do not already have any equipment. With early diagnosis it is possible to plan ahead, but even if your twins were unexpected you can benefit financially from more educated and thoughtful buying. The items discussed in this chapter are primarily limited to the first year or two. The quantities of these items you will need and how to use them most effectively and economically with twins are also suggested. Once these major expenses are behind you, you will probably be able to plan for the normal necessities as they arise, anticipating future needs and budgeting ahead for them. Toys are not discussed here because the selection is too great and depends on individual taste.

Buying Suggestions

For parents of twins even more than for parents of singletons, thoughtful purchasing becomes essential in order to minimize costs. Develop a budget for the necessary expenses, plan carefully before buying, and borrow or buy used equipment when-

When triplets arrive . . .

ever possible. Mothers of twins clubs exchanges and sales, garage sales, classified ads, and flea markets or swap meets often yield terrific buys. Hand-me-downs are also helpful. Cut expenses by buying new items at discount drug or department stores, where you can usually find name-brand merchandise at lower prices. The coupons sent out by manufacturers of baby products can also reduce costs. If you subscribe to a baby magazine (some are free for the first six to eight months), you may be on a mailing list to receive these money-saving coupons on such items as disposable diapers, baby lotion, powder, wipes, and baby food. Some department and children's clothing stores have special discounts if you are buying for twins; be sure to ask. Your pediatrician or clinic may even have a special rate for well-baby health care.

Always keep in mind your children's health and safety before buying any product, large or small. Contact the Consumer Product Safety Commission (see Appendix I) for required or recommended safety features on products you purchase, whether new or used. Throughout this chapter are lists with safety and convenience considerations. These are merely suggestions, and following them does not give you a fool-proof safety guarantee. These guidelines are offered solely to encourage you to give careful thought to safety as well as comfort and cost before choosing products for your children.

Essential Baby Equipment

Although most major expenses fall in this category, you do not need two of everything. If your twins arrive unexpectedly, you may not have the luxury to shop around, but some of the equipment may not be necessary immediately. Be sure the equipment you select meets current safety standards and does not present your children with potential dangers (as in the case of some older models of cribs and car seats). With all equipment, *never leave a baby unattended and always follow the manufacturer's instructions for safe assembly, installation, and use.* Information on equipment that you purchase secondhand is generally available by writing to the manufacturer.

Car Seats and Other Approved Auto Safety Restraint Systems

The first pieces of equipment you will need are two car safety seats *designed for infants and approved for use in an automobile—* not regular infant seats, which are not safe for use in the car. Standard car safety belts (lap and shoulder) do not provide adequate protection for children under age four or under forty pounds. Car beds do not offer the maximum protection afforded by car seats. Since January 1, 1981, the U.S. government has required that car seats be crash-tested by the manufacturer before they can be federally approved. Check the label on the seat for the manufacturing date. If you have or are purchasing seats manufactured before that date, find out first whether they meet current safety standards by writing the manufacturer. Be sure to give the correct model number. Even before your babies get home they will need protection in the car as you depart from the hospital. Infants and children are *not* safe in an automobile when carried in the arms of an adult, even if the adult is fastened into lap and shoulder belts.

Although today's car seats come in various fashion colors with many available options, the most important consideration should always be safety. Will the car seats or child restraint systems you select give your children the maximum protection, and will they fit properly in your car? You can choose from numerous styles and brands designed for infants and children of various ages and weights. Infant safety seats have harnesses and are designed for babies between nine and twelve months and weighing less than twenty pounds. Some seats are convertible and can be adjusted to accommodate babies from birth to age four or up to forty pounds. For children between twenty and forty pounds, there are two basic designs—seats or restraints either with harnesses or with protective shields. These are forward-facing and are intended for one to four year olds, up to forty pounds. New booster seats now available for three to six year olds raise the child's eye level and position the child so that the car's shoulder belt properly crosses the chest rather than the face. *Never leave infants or children in an unattended automobile, even if the motor is off.*

Car seats or restraint systems are safest when used in the back seat. Safety seats should be in a backward-facing position for newborns and infants who cannot sit up unsupported or who weigh less than twenty pounds. A rolled-up receiving blanket can be used to provide a protective cushion around a baby's head and shoulders, giving a newborn additional support. Convertible seats should be used only in the positions recommended by the manufacturer for a safe degree of tilt. Most convertible or toddler seats must be used with a top tether strap. In order to protect a child, this strap must either be bolted into the shelf of the rear window for back-seat use (some newer cars have predrilled holes for attaching the strap), or it must be attached to the safety belt in the back seat for front-seat use. If you have a compact car, be sure the safety seats you choose will fit in your car. Check that lap belts are long enough to pass properly through or around the car seat. Some stores will let you try out the seat in your own car before purchase. Rental or loaner car seats are available through some hospitals or through county health departments or private organizations in some states. Consult Appendix I for information on where to write for materials concerning automobile safety. The National Organization of Mothers of Twins Clubs has also done research on this subject.

Safety Checklist:

---

1. Sturdy construction to withstand the force of a collision.

2. Held in place by car's safety belt through or around the car seat or restraint system.

3. Has a protective shield covering the body, or has its own lap and shoulder safety belts to distribute the force of deceleration and collision, thereby reducing the impact on any single part of the body.

4. Well padded with a high back to minimize possibility of whiplash injury.

Cribs

For the first month or so, the babies do not need to be in full-size cribs. Until you have cribs, bassinettes, cradles, or even boxes or laundry baskets may be adequate. During the early weeks twins may get comfort from sleeping together, seeking out the warmth of one another's body and often reassuming their fetal positions. Although even two babies sharing a crib can inadvertently poke fingers or toes in one another's eyes, nose, or mouth, one mother of quadruplets frequently put all four babies in the same crib together during the early weeks. "We didn't have a separate space for each

baby yet because we thought we were only expecting triplets, and even providing for three was a financial strain."

Later, as they get older, twins will feel more secure if they each have a specific crib to call home. Cribs will probably be the most expensive baby equipment you will need to buy. They can be found in various colors, shapes, and styles, but safety and durability must be your foremost concern in making your selection. Used or hand-me-down types can help cut costs dramatically, but they should meet the same current governmental safety regulations required for standard size new cribs bought at a store. In addition, look for convenience features that will add to the babies' comfort as well as your own.

Safety Checklist:

1. Spindles or slats to be no more than 2⅜ inches apart. Use bumper pads for additional protection.

2. No rough edges.

3. Head and foot boards without pointed or sharp decorations or designs where an infant's head could become caught or lodged and no beads or knobs that a baby could detach from the crib and later swallow or choke on.

4. Lead-free, nontoxic paint. (The paint on new cribs must be nontoxic to meet current safety regulations. Some older cribs may have paint that contains lead. Babies like to chew on the railings and head and foot boards of their cribs. The lead in any paint scrapings that are swallowed could cause severe illness. Even with lead-free paint, babies should not teethe on paint, and side rails should have a protective covering for this reason.)

5. Teething rails to prevent teething on side rails. (Teething rails must be in good condition. If damaged, they can cut a baby's mouth.)

6. Two or more height adjustments. (Frame and mattress can be placed in the highest position for newborns, but once babies can stand, it must be at lowest position and drop sides should be kept in highest position. Cribs are outgrown and unsafe when sides are less than three-fourths the child's height.)

7. Sturdy steel bars to stabilize sides. (Bars must be tightened from time to time.)

8. Sturdy locks and latches on dropside. (Must be safe from accidental release.)

9. Well-constructed, using good-quality parts (including hardware, frame, and wood).

10. Snug-fitting mattress that provides good support, is flame resistant, washable, and wet-proof. *Caution:* Do not use thin plastic (such as dry cleaner bags) to cover mattress. An infant can easily rip the plastic and use it to cover his or her head or mouth, causing suffocation.

Strollers

Specially designed twin strollers are available in many styles, but they can be expensive. Many families save money by buying a used model. The two most familiar types are face-to-face and tandem (with two forward-facing seats like a two-seater bicycle). Twin strollers can be purchased or ordered at local baby equipment stores or from a catalog or mail order house. Face-to-face models are narrow enough to fit through standard doorways and may or may not be collapsible. Once the twins are old enough to sit up, they can entertain one another. For older babies, this type of stroller can also double as a feeding or play table when away from home by taping a cafeteria-style tray across the middle to hold finger foods or toys.

Tandem strollers are also narrow enough for doorways, give both children a forward view, and may or may not be collapsible. Some models have a front seat that can face either forward or backward, converting the stroller to a face-to-face type.

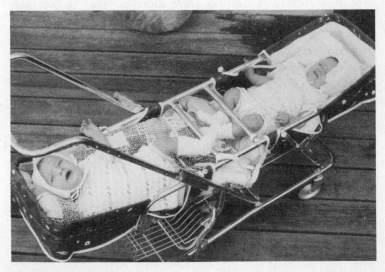

Face-to-face stroller

Tandem triplet stroller, also available as a twin stroller

Side-by-side twin strollers were more popular in our parents' generation than they are today. Most have a heavier and wider construction, which makes them less portable, but most of these traditional models are collapsible. They are also too wide to pass through a standard doorway.

A more recent concept is the double umbrella stroller, which looks like two side-by-side umbrella strollers but is permanently linked. When collapsed, it is more convenient to carry than two umbrella strollers, and when in use it is narrow enough to pass through most doorways. Two single umbrella strollers also can be joined side-by-side with an inexpensive adapter clip that can be removed to pass through narrow spaces. The clip is available at most baby equipment stores. Mothers of twins surveyed by the National Organization of Mothers of Twins Clubs (NOMOTC) complained, however, that two umbrella strollers fastened together are hard to push and that the clips often break, causing both the inconvenience and the expense of frequent replacement.

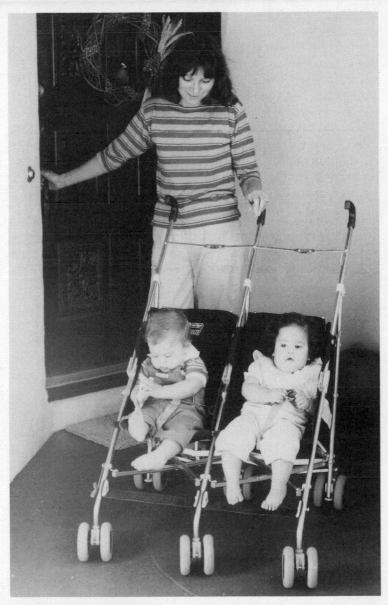

Double umbrella stroller

Another new twin stroller is known as the "little wheeler limousine." This double stroller has a two-position handle, and each of its two seats will face forward or backward. It has the lightweight construction of an umbrella stroller, but the seats are positioned end to end rather than side by side. The stroller can be folded flat for storage. Several types of strollers can be modified by the manufacturer for use with triplets. These can be specially ordered through local baby equipment stores. If you are unable to find or order the twin or triplet stroller you want, contact the National Organization of Mothers of Twins Clubs for information on how and where to order (see Appendix I).

Safety Checklist:

1. Well-padded seat and backrest (or bed) to support back and head if stroller hits a bump or tips backward.

2. Backrest—straight or nearly straight for firm support.

3. Good parking brake.

4. No dangerous hardware (no sharp, pointed, or loose parts; no small detachable elements that could be put into the mouth; and no parts where fingers or toes could be caught).

5. Safety latch to prevent collapse. (The latch must be safe from accidental release and must be protected so a child's fingers and toes cannot be trapped or injured.)

6. Safety belt.

7. Wide wheel base and wheels with a large diameter.

Infant Seats

With twins as with singletons, infant seats are an indispensable item for the early months, providing a comfortable place for young babies who are not yet able to sit up on their own.

A few models are also designed for safe use in a car, meeting federal automobile safety standards. *Do not use an infant seat in a car unless the manufacturer's guidelines specifically provide for its use as a car safety seat.*

Infant seats can be adjusted to various positions for a baby's comfort, and they give support to a baby's head and back. Although an occasional infant may not like the seat, most babies sit cheerfully, enjoying the opportunity to watch a mobile or to observe people and scenery. Various styles and prices are available, but many of the less expensive models seem adequate, especially since these items are outgrown so quickly and do not need the same kind of durability required by car seats or cribs. Seats can be made more comfortable when lined with a blanket, quilt, or infant seat cover.

Safety Checklist:

1. Seat belt or harness. (These should be used at all times.)

2. Well-padded and with a high back to support infant's head.

3. Broad, nonskid base to prevent tipping or falling.

High Chairs and Cantilevered Seats

High chairs are not necessary immediately, but plan ahead for this cost because you will need to have two, and they can be expensive. Secondhand chairs in good condition can save money. Various styles and features are available. Many newer models have an extra-large tray that can be used as a play table. This is a very useful feature, but for families with a small kitchen, two high chairs with these large trays may take up too much space. Some high chairs can be moved around on wheels, and some have a tray with an easy-to-release, child-proof catch that can be unfastened by an adult using only one hand. Collapsible chairs are especially useful for families who travel.

Safety Checklist:

1. T-shaped safety-belt. (A belt between legs is joined to seat belt and both should be used at all times. The belt should not be attached to the tray.)

2. Well-padded seat and back to support baby's back and head.

3. Safety latch to prevent collapse. (The latch must be safe from accidental release and must be protected so a child's fingers and toes cannot be trapped or injured.)

4. Brakes (on models with wheels).

5. No dangerous hardware. (No sharp, pointed, or loose parts, no small detachable elements that could be put into the mouth, no places where fingers could be caught.)

6. Sturdy frame and broad base to prevent tipping.

7. Tray that locks securely in place and cannot be unlocked by a child.

8. Slip-resistant seat. (If the seat is slippery, attach rough-surface adhesive tape to it.)

Caution: Never allow a child to stand up in a high chair.

As their babies get older, some parents of twins prefer the new, convenient cantilevered seats that are designed to clip onto and hang from the table, enabling the baby to sit at the table with the rest of the family. With some models, the infant's own body weight holds the seat in place; with others the seat is secured to the table by a clamp. These seats are smaller than standard high chairs and occupy less kitchen space. Some can even be folded to make them more compact for traveling. A cantilevered baby seat should not be used, however, until a baby is old enough to sit up unsupported. It should have a T-shaped safety belt to protect an infant or toddler from slipping out from below and should be safe from accidental collapse. Molded plastic seats are more durable than fabric types, which can unravel or rip. Babies should not be left unsupervised, especially as they get older and are able to climb out of their seats onto the table. Check for dangerous hardware, and be sure that the seats are assembled correctly.

Gates

Gates prevent babies' access to stairways or other danger areas, or they can be used to keep infants in a child-proofed playroom. With not one but two babies to supervise, gates are especially helpful. The traditional "safety gates" have an accordionlike construction. These are potentially dangerous, as a baby's head can be caught or squeezed when the gate expands or contracts to close or open. Some are installed directly into door frames using metal hardware. Others are adjustable and need no hardware to be secured in place. Adjustable pressure gates that have vinyl-coated wire mesh are generally safer than the accordion style when properly installed.

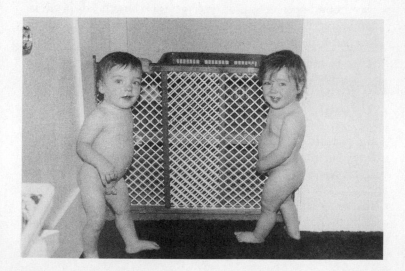

A variation on the traditional gate is the optional corral play yard, an expandable continuous gate that can be used to keep children in (like a playpen) or out (such as around a diaper can). Corrals are available in various sizes and can be useful for picnics or trips. Those that are constructed like the traditional "safety gates," however, present the same potential danger to babies, and they should never be used when babies are unsupervised. Gates and corrals are *not* safe for babies who can climb and should not be used when the babies are unsupervised.

Safety Checklist:

---

1. Secure, childproof latch (if gate is expandable).

2. Sturdy frame.

3. No dangerous hardware. (No sharp, pointed, or loose parts, no small detachable pieces that could be put into the mouth.)

Caution: Accordion-style expandable gates and corrals can cause strangulation. Children should *never* be allowed to play around open accordion-style gates because heads or necks can become trapped, cutting off the oxygen supply. Hands or feet can become caught, and fingers or toes can be severed.

Training Seats, "Potty" Chairs, and Training Pants

Some parents can successfully teach their twins to use the big toilet right from the start. Others find it easier to use either a training seat that attaches to the large toilet or a small separate "potty" chair. Children often make their preference clear and each twin may have a different preference. Various styles of seats and chairs are available; some even convert to a regular chair or a step stool. Be sure the style you buy is easy to keep clean. When you do begin toilet training, your twins will also need to have training pants—up to two dozen pairs (twelve pairs for each) at the beginning, and less (about five pairs for each) as your children learn to keep themselves clean and dry. If possible, try to borrow the extras needed at the beginning because they will only be needed for a short time.

Both training seats and "potty" chairs should be free of any dangerous hardware. Training seats should fasten securely to the toilet. "Potty" chairs should have a pot that is easily removable by a child. Training pants should be loose-fitting, so that the child can put them on and take them off unassisted and should have an extra-thick center panel, for maximum absorption.

Optional Baby Equipment

Playpen

A playpen can be useful even with a singleton when you are distracted, such as when answering the telephone and can be especially useful with twins when changing one baby's diaper. Infants are more likely to accept the confinement of a playpen if introduced to it at an early age. Two babies can occupy the same playpen and may be happier together than when separated, but they must not be left unsupervised. In the early months, twins can watch a mobile or can even study one another's arms moving. Two playpens may be useful in a two-story house or to separate babies for safety reasons as they get older. Toys such as pounding benches, wood spoons, pots and pans, or anything heavy could be used by one baby to harm the other and should never be put in a shared playpen. The strings or cords on mobiles or toys that hang from the sides of a playpen (or crib) should be shorter than twelve inches. Babies can also fall out of a playpen by climbing on blocks or other large toys.

Those who favor playpens are pleased with the security they provide by confining babies to a safe, child-proof area. Opponents feel that playpens become a crutch if used by parents as a babysitting device and that parents often leave their babies for too long without attention and without the opportunity to explore their environment.

Traditional wood models are heavier and less portable than the newer vinyl types, but wood is less vulnerable to damage because it cannot be punctured or torn. The vinyl kind have nylon mesh sides and come with padding of various thicknesses and in a choice of materials of various durabilities. The sides of vinyl/mesh playpens (or portable cribs) must be locked securely in their upright position when the playpen (or portable crib) is in use. A baby could become trapped in the folds of mesh and suffocate if one side is left in a lowered position.

Safety Checklist:

1. Slats no more than 2⅜ inches apart (wood playpens).

2. Lead-free, nontoxic varnish or paint (wood playpens).

3. No rough edges (wood models).

4. Tightly woven mesh on sides (vinyl playpens) smaller than the tiny buttons on infant clothing.

5. Thick, durable padding for floor of playpen such as foam or a heavy blanket or quilt.

6. No dangerous hardware (no sharp, pointed, or loose parts; no small detachable beads or other elements that could be put into the mouth; no place where fingers could be caught).

7. A sturdy floor to prevent collapse (on playpens with legs).

Carriages

Twins can occupy a single standard-size baby carriage for the first two or three months but will gradually be too crowded to sleep comfortably. They will soon begin to awaken each other even if their heads are at opposite ends. Special carriages, built wider to accommodate two babies, are heavy and cumbersome and are too wide for standard doorways. Another narrower style is designed with two canopies so that the babies' heads can be at opposite ends. A twin carriage must be specially ordered in most stores. Carriages are primarily designed for families who regularly take long walks and who can afford an unessential major expenditure.

The *safety features* for carriages are the same as for strollers, except: (1) harnesses may have to be purchased separately for use once babies are old enough to sit up; and (2) canopy must lock into position when in use and lower to rear when not in use.

Baby Bathtub

For their own safety, infant twins should be bathed separately until they are old enough to sit up unsupported. An infant bathtub is convenient when bathing young twins who cannot sit up, but even a large dishpan will do. You can use the kitchen sink or the regular tub with only two or three inches of water, but this is more uncomfortable for you and the babies. By about six to eight months the twins will probably be strong enough to sit up in the big tub for a true bath. If you do buy a special infant tub for the early months, one is all you will need for twins since the babies will have to be bathed individually.

Many types of baby bathtubs are on the market. A "bathinette" that can be stored in the bathroom or kitchen resembles a changing table with a flip-lid concealing a fillable tub. After the bath, water drains out through a rubber hose into a bucket or the sink or tub. A bathinette is large and awkward to store, but it is very convenient at bath time.

Inflatable tubs are useful for small babies and are easy to pack for traveling, but they are too small and inadequate as babies get older. Another advertised tub is molded to fit conveniently into a kitchen sink and will even fit a two-sided sink. A baby bathtub can be placed inside a regular tub or on the kitchen counter. You can also use a cloth-covered piece of thick plywood to cover the entire full-sized tub, providing an entire work space to lay out towels, wash cloths, and clothing changes.

Safety Checklist:

---

1. Designed (or accompanied by an attachment) to keep a baby's head above water at all times.

2. Sturdy and skid-proof.

3. Tip-proof and noncollapsible. (Inflatable tubs should be watertight and airtight. Check before use.)

Swings

Many a fussy or colicky baby has been rhythmically coaxed into sleep in a swing. One twin can be soothed in the swing while the other is fed, changed, or bathed. Or, with two swings, both babies can be calmed while their parents have supper or while mom or dad is attending to the older children. An occasional baby does not like a swing, but for most families of twins, one swing can be a real benefit, and two can definitely make life easier for the first three or four months. As with most baby equipment, swings are available in various price ranges, depending on the optional features. Some have automatic settings and will operate for about an hour; some come with an additional attachable cradle that can be used for a young baby. Others feature a combination swing and infant carrier, a padded seat, or a posture-molded reclining swing. Each of these options brings up the cost. The standard wind-up variety is adequate and is most economical.

Safety Checklist:

---

1. No dangerous hardware. (No sharp, pointed, or loose parts; no small detachable beads or other pieces that could be put into the mouth; and no parts where fingers or toes could be caught.)

2. Sturdy, tip-proof construction.

3. Good support for infant's head and back.

Changing Tables

Since you can only change one baby at a time, one changing surface is sufficient. If you live in a two-story house, however, you may prefer to have a changing area on each floor. Changing tables are available in many styles, from basic functional types to wood spindle, wicker, or even ultra-modern molded plexiglass in a variety of decorator colors. Some children's dressers have a built-in top with elevated sides that is designed for changing a baby. A bathinette can also serve as a changing table. Many manufacturers also make a portable changing pad. Some changers fold into a carrying case; others consist of a pad inside a molded plastic tray designed to fit over the crib rails or rest across a crib. Portable changers can be placed on a dresser, bed, or even used directly on the floor. They are also good for travel and for your budget. Be sure all surfaces are covered with a durable, washable (or wipable) pad. If you do not have a changing table or pad, be sure to keep launderable "lap pads" handy to put under babies' wet or messy bottoms during changes (see "Layette," later in this chapter).

Safety Checklist:

---

1. Safety belt (to prevent baby from falling).

2. Sturdy construction.

3. Tip-proof and noncollapsible.

4. Safe storage for diaper pins, wipes, lotions, and oint-ments (away from reach of babies).

Jumpers and Walkers

Many jumpers are designed to hang from the top of a door frame. The baby is placed in a harness or seat connected to the door frame by a long spring. The device is adjusted so that the baby's feet touch the floor. He or she can bounce to strengthen the legs and to burn off excess energy. Two jumpers can be fun for twins at about four to five months or one jumper can help entertain one twin while the other is getting a diaper change. An infant who can pull up to a standing position is ready for a walker. Until the time a baby begins to walk without support, a walker provides the mobility to move in new directions otherwise out of reach. Quiet infants, however, may have little interest in this kind of exploration, preferring to sit in one place.

Once twins figure out how to make their walkers move, they need to be watched carefully at all times, since they are now able to act as a team when attacking house plants, getting

trapped in furniture-laden corners, gliding over precipices, or falling down unprotected stairs. Walkers are useful for teaching babies how to use and exercise their legs even before they are able to walk. Standard models are reasonably priced. Additional features that increase the cost are extra seat padding or a built-in jumping feature. A large play tray, which can also double as a feeding surface, is standard on most models. Be sure the walker has brakes if you use it as a play table or feeding chair.

For *safety*, jumpers and walkers should have no dangerous hardware (no sharp, pointed, or loose parts, no small detachable elements that could be put into the mouth, and no exposed coil springs or other parts that could catch fingers or toes). Jumpers must provide good support (so that the baby cannot tip over, fall, or climb out). Walkers and walker-jumpers must have good stability (a wheel base that is wider and longer than the frame of the walker itself) and be tip-proof and noncollapsible while in use.

Caution: Never use either walkers or jumpers near open stairwells, fireplaces, swimming pools, or areas that have not been child-proofed.

Front-pack and Back-pack Carriers

Front packs can be used with newborn twins; back packs become useful when the babies are about four to five months old. Packs are good items to borrow from friends if possible, and are especially useful for hiking, or for going to the supermarket when putting both babies in the shopping cart leaves no room for groceries. Shopping may be easier with one twin in a pack and the other sitting up in the cart or lying in an infant seat that is placed in the deepest part of the shopping cart. (Do *not* leave a baby in the cart unattended.) Special double packs are even designed to carry both infants at once, either with both in front or with one in front and one in back. (Write to the National Organization of Mothers of Twins Clubs [NOMOTC] or the Parents of Multiple Births Association of

Canada [POMBA] for more information on double packs.) The twins' combined weight may exceed the comfort range very quickly, however, and the babies' excessive or unequally distributed weight could cause you back injury or could cause you to fall by throwing you off balance. Packs should be completely machine-washable or should have a machine-washable panel for under the baby's face.

Safety Checklist:

1. Pack can safely accommodate the baby's size, with enough depth to support the baby's back, leg openings small enough to prevent the baby from slipping out but big enough to avoid chafing the baby's legs.

2. Good support for the infant's head.

3. Safety strap.

4. Soft padding for around the infant's face and head.

5. Sturdy material with strong stitching and heavy-duty snaps.

6. Sturdy, lightweight frame (back pack).

7. No joints that may close and pinch or cut (back pack).

Caution: Do not use a pack if you have a history of back problems or back injuries.

Toddler Harnesses

Harnesses, which were relatively unpopular for almost two decades, are now gaining popularity once again—especially with parents of twins who must watch two active toddlers at the same time. Each twin can be buckled into a chest harness which is attached to a leash that the parent holds. Some parents feel that harnesses are too restrictive. Says one mother of two year olds, "My twins are not dogs, and I think it's an insult to a child to be connected to his mother by a leash." But an increasing number of parents swear by the harnesses, especially when traveling or when in public places among crowds of people. "Sometimes people tease me about it, but I feel strongly about using harnesses for our two-year-old boys," maintains one busy mom. "The threat to children in our society is greater than it has ever been. My children are always running in opposite directions. I want to know where my kids are when we are out at all times, especially at the shopping mall or on a family outing or trip.''

As an alternative to chest harnesses, several companies are advertising a wrist cuff system with two cuffs, one for the parent and one for the child, connected by a leash. This system frees the parent's hands for other activities. Using two cuffs—a double cuff—can accommodate twins, with the parent (or one of the twins) wearing a cuff that is attached to two leashes which connect separately to each twin.

Here are some *safety tips* for harnesses and cuffs: A harness or cuff system should be designed with sturdy, non-abrasive strapping and no dangerous buckles, zippers, or other hardware. It should be secure enough that a child cannot remove it but an adult can do so without difficulty. Most harnesses have zippers in the back so that a child cannot unzip them. Twins, however, can unfasten one another's harnesses so you will have to monitor your twins carefully. A momentary distraction for you may be enough time for your children to make their getaway. Never leave a child unsupervised in a harness or cuff, especially if the leash is trailing behind the child. The leash could become caught, disabling or injuring the child. And, never use a harness as a safety restraint system in an automobile.

Household Equipment

Washer/Dryer

With twins, having a washer and dryer in your own home can save a lot of time and hassle if space and budget permit. At the beginning, if you are not washing diapers, you may not be doing a bulk of laundry. This comes later, as the children wear larger and larger sizes. You will be doing frequent loads in the early months, however, in order to keep up with the babies' needs. Your time is precious, so having to park yourselves in the laundromat for indefinite periods can be frustrating and difficult, too, if you must take two babies with you. A washer and dryer, even if only a small portable, will make life with twins easier.

Caution: Be sure that babies cannot open the doors to these appliances and become injured or trapped inside. With gas dryers, keep access to the pilot light securely closed.

Freezer

A freezer (even a small one) can be very useful by the time the twins are on solid foods. The large quantities of homemade baby foods, milk or formula, and even family meals made from double recipes can be prepared ahead and frozen.

Caution: Keep freezer doors locked so that a baby cannot get inside and become trapped.

Layette

Diapers

When deciding how to handle the diaper situation with twins, consider which are the easiest to use, the greatest timesavers, and the most cost-effective. Your three choices are: (1) cloth diapers laundered at home (approximately six to eight dozen for twins at the beginning when laundering every other day); (2) disposable diapers (about 180–200 per week to start); or (3) commercial diaper service (approximately 190–200 per week).

Laundering Diapers at Home

Laundering your own diapers can be a tiresome chore with twins, especially during the first few months. Unless you have your own washer and dryer, you will probably spend more money at the laundromat than you would if you were using disposables or a diaper service. The six to eight dozen suggested above includes "burpers." Prefolded diapers are easier to fasten and to keep neatly stacked when clean. Stretch diapers shrink to an hourglass shape to conform to the shape of a baby's bottom, but because of their shape, they are not practical for use as burpers. Day/night or overnight diapers are heavier and more expensive and are rather bulky for newborns, but they may come in handy as your babies grow and also become bigger wetters. Park pins out of reach of babies during diaper changes if you use cloth diapers, and put your hand between a baby's body and the diaper while you pin the diaper.

Disposable Diapers

Disposable diapers are very easy to use, with their self-adhesive strips that bind front to back. Many now have elastic that fits the contour of a baby's legs to prevent leaking. Purchasing disposables by the carton is more economical. Discount drug, toy, or baby equipment stores usually have the lowest prices. Disposables cost more but are popular because they require no pins or rubberized pants and because they eliminate the need to handle the wet or messy part of a diaper. Disposables make diaper changes quicker, but they are not useful as burpers. Keep two dozen cloth diapers for this purpose. When considering the total cost, remember to add the expense of the plastic trash bags and the service charges for the extra trash or garbage cans you will need if you pay your own garbage bills. The convenience factor of disposables may outweigh the higher cost with twins.

Diaper Service

Commercial diaper service, where available, may be the most practical choice with twins considering the babies' comfort and the actual dollars saved. Some services expect you to rinse soiled diapers before putting them into the can; others do not. Although a diaper service may seem expensive with only one baby, with twins you reap the benefits. Most charge a flat rate for weekly delivery plus a nominal incremental amount for each ten diapers ordered. The flat delivery rate usually remains the same with twins as with a single baby, and because the incremental rate is so reasonable, the total cost of service for twins is only a few dollars more per month.

As part of the service most companies furnish diapers, cans, deodorant, and can liners. Some also include a free subscription to a national baby magazine as a courtesy to their customers for the duration of service. In addition, some have special diapers for tiny premature newborns and training pants for toddlers. If you use a diaper service, be careful with the diapers you use. You will be charged for any that are lost or damaged (such as if your dog bites a hole in the center). With this in mind, keep disposable diapers on hand for outings or vacations. While on vacation, you can usually postpone service without charge until you return.

Clothing and Bedding

Twins do not need twice as much clothing and bedding as a single baby, especially if you have your own washer. Primarily because you will be doing the laundry more frequently, you can probably manage comfortably with about one and a half times the necessities for a single baby. Most full-term twins will wear the newborn size at birth. Twins are frequently born early or have a low birth weight, however, and they may need the smaller "Preemie size." Preemie clothing is available at most baby specialty stores.

Use the lists below as a guideline for how much to buy if you have your own washer. If you do your laundry at a laundromat, add two or more of each item (one more per baby) and you will not have to go there as often. Wash all new garments and bed and bath linens before use. Detergent can be very harsh to your babies' sensitive skin, so use a gentle soap (except with sleepwear if detergent is recommended by the manufacturer to retain flame-resistant properties).

Suggested Clothing Checklist

Numbers given are totals for two babies.

Cotton gowns	10–12
Cotton T-shirts (side snaps) (as undershirts in winter or to be worn alone in summer)	10–12
Receiving blankets	6–8
Stretch terry sleepers	6–8
Blanket sleepers (winter)	2–4
Pram suits and/or snow suits (depending on climate and season)	2–4
Sweaters	2–4
Sacque sets (summer)	4–6 (optional)
Booties (winter) (under gowns or kimonos)	4 pairs
Hats or bonnets (depending on season)	4
"Rubber pants" of rubberized nylon or vinyl (snap-ons because they can be opened up to hang dry after washing)	12 pairs (necessary with cloth diapers, optional with disposables)

Suggested Bedding Checklist

Fitted crib sheets	6 or more
Bassinette and "port-a-crib" sheets (For each bassinette or portable crib, you will need two sheets, more if you do not use a lap pad under a baby's bottom and a diaper under a baby's head. Use bassinette sheets for baby baskets, "port-a-beds" or car beds, and carriages. King-size pillowcases also fit some portable crib mattresses.)	4–6
Waterproof flannelized lap pads (to protect sheets from wetting, and for under a baby's bottom during diaper changes)	6–8 (optional)
Quilted or flannelized mattress pads for cribs	6 (optional)
Heavy crib blankets (or comforters, or infant "sleeping bag" with zipper)	4
Crib bumper pads	2 sets (1 set for each crib)

Bath Linens (Optional)

Infant bath linens are made of a soft, absorbent terry cloth. Hooded towels keep a baby's head warm after a bath. Terry buntings (zipper bags with hood and sleeves), if you can find them, also keep a baby warm and dry. Regular towels and washcloths can be used if you do not have the kind designed for infants. You will probably need six towels and six washcloths total for your twins.

Small Articles and Toiletries

Suggested Small Articles and Toiletries Checklist

Bottles (with sealing rings and covers)	12–16 if bottle feeding; 4–6 (optional) if breastfeeding
Nipples	12–16 if bottle feeding; 4–6 (optional) if breastfeeding
Formula	enough to make 12–14 of the 4-ounce bottles per day (Once open or prepared, formula must be refrigerated and can only be kept up to 48 hours.)
Sterilizer	(optional if you have another large pot or a dishwasher)
Bottle brush	1
Nursing pads (disposable or washable), if breastfeeding	(optional)
Breast cream, if breastfeeding	(optional)
Breast pump, if breastfeeding	(optional)
Pacifiers	2 for each baby (optional)

Caution: Pacifiers are not safe unless they have a shield or guard large enough that the entire pacifier cannot be drawn into the child's mouth and must have at least two ventilation holes to allow breathing even if the pacifier is swallowed. Also, never tie a ribbon or cord to the pacifier. The cord could cause strangulation.

Feeding spoon	1 or more (Both babies can be fed from the same spoon.)
Feeding dish	1 or more (One multi-sectioned, hot water–heated or electric dish can be helpful.)

Bibs	10–12
Baby food grinder	(optional)
Premoistened wipes	
Ointment for diaper rash (Ask your pediatrician for recommended type.)	
Baby lotion or oil	
Baby powder (for use after baths and for diaper changes)	
Pins	6 pairs (only for cloth diapers)
Cotton balls, tissues	
Diaper cans	2 per changing area with cloth diapers (one for diapers, one for disposable wipes, tissues), 1 per changing area with disposable diapers
Baby rectal thermometer	1
Baby soap	
Baby shampoo	
Baby nail scissors	
Large tote bag (for outings and traveling)	
Camera and film (to capture special moments)	

CHAPTER 7

Feeding:
Breast or Bottle?

When you found out that you were having twins, you may not have realized that breastfeeding twins is even possible. Indeed, it is not only possible but many mothers have successfully nursed more than one baby with little or no supplementation. Whether to breastfeed or bottle feed, however, is a highly personal, if not emotional decision. Surely every experienced mother, whether or not she has twins, has an opinion on the subject. The suggestions given in this chapter are not intended to promote any specific method but are designed to give you the information you need to make your own choice. Your decision should be based on what feels most comfortable for you and what works for your babies.

Some women nurse their twins because they feel strongly that breast milk is the best diet for their babies; others feel formula is an excellent substitute. Some women's maternal instincts are heightened by breastfeeding; others like the freedom offered by bottle feeding. Some highly allergic infants cannot tolerate anything but breast milk; others struggle so vigorously at the breast that a mother may not have the energy or desire to force the issue. Bottles become a necessity at least part of the time for the children of working mothers, but some women express or pump their own milk to leave in bottles for their twins. Bottle feeding is the obvious answer for

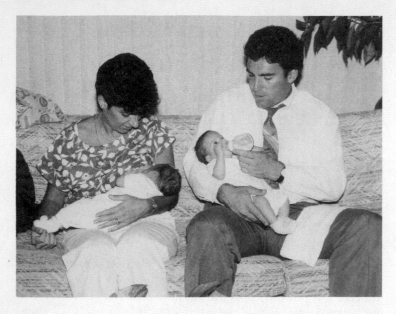

adopted twins. But if highly motivated, an adoptive mother can breastfeed with the help of supplements. La Leche League (See Appendix I) has information on this.

Feeding two infants demands a lot more energy and patience than feeding a singleton, and finding the most comfortable feeding arrangement for all three of you may take time. There is no single right way to do it. Family and friends may try to be helpful, making suggestions or well-intentioned criticisms. This can be frustrating and annoying. What works best for you is what is most important. Use your own judgment; you know your babies better than anyone else does. With patience, perseverance, and flexibility, you will be able to weather the initial weeks of confusion and inconvenience. Whether you choose to feed your twins "on demand" or "on schedule," together or separately, breast milk or formula, if you feel good about the method you are using, your babies will thrive.

General Questions About Feeding

Feeding Methods

Whether to feed your twins together or separately is a question of comfort and convenience. Try both ways to find your (and the babies') preference. The hospital is a good place to experiment, and the nurses there can help you find a comfortable system. Feeding twins seems complicated at first, whether you nurse or give bottles, but after you get accustomed to a routine, it becomes easier and more enjoyable. You can feed your babies either on demand, whenever they seem hungry, or on a schedule. Mothers of twins who nurse may prefer demand feedings because a fussy baby gets comfort as well as milk from the breast. With twins on demand, however, you may be feeding babies all day long. For this reason, other women prefer to feed their twins on a schedule.

Judi Linney in her book *Multiple Births* (1983) reports on her own study of eighty-four breastfeeding mothers conducted in England in the late 1970s. Linney found that 60 percent breastfed on a schedule, 36 percent nursed on demand, and 4 percent used a combination of both methods. For scheduled feedings, your own pediatrician can advise you how often to feed your babies. Even on a schedule, sometimes one or both infants may be decidedly hungrier than usual (especially nursed babies) and will want more frequent feedings. Enforcing the schedule on those days will only make you and the babies miserable. When only one twin wakes up for a feeding, the second can be awakened either immediately to be fed simultaneously or within a half hour to be fed separately.

Burping Techniques

Most babies cry, arch their backs, pull their legs up to the chest, or pull away from the nipple if they have an air bubble. Sometimes, however, a baby who needs to burp acts suddenly frantic. First-time parents may mistake this behavior for hunger. If allowed to continue feeding, the baby may be temporarily soothed by the milk, but the air bubble must eventually come up and may bring the additional milk up with it. Breastfed babies generally take in less air than those on bottles. Bottle-fed infants usually take their milk more quickly than those who are nursed. Because milk flows so rapidly from a bottle, a baby does not have to suck as hard on a bottle as on the breast and may gulp a lot of air. For this reason, give bottle-fed infants a chance to burp at the halfway point and again at the end of the bottle. Some infants need more time to burp than others, and they should not be rushed.

With twins, burping one baby while the other is feeding, or burping two babies at once is quite a trick. Sometimes the bubble will come up if you lie the baby face down on your lap

Three burping positions

or on the bed next to you. Gentle pats on the back often help. For some infants, however, this brings milk up, too. The inclined position of an infant seat often brings up a bubble while keeping the milk down. Many babies protest loudly unless they are held. Shoulder-burping one twin while feeding the other is not easy but it is possible. Remember never to pull an infant up by the arm, however. This puts excessive stress on the baby's shoulder. If you support the babies with pillows as you feed them, slide your free hand under the pillow and lift the baby, pillow and all, to your shoulder. Then, while holding the baby, let the pillow slip away and pat the baby's back. Never try to shoulder-burp your twins at the same time as you cannot give adequate support to both. By the time the babies are old enough to sit up they are generally able to burp themselves.

Monitoring Feedings

Keep track of your twins' feedings by making a chart for each twin like the one shown below. You can also monitor their health and hygiene this way. This will be especially helpful when you have questions for the pediatrician. Use the chart below, or The National Organization of Mothers of Twins Clubs sells a wipe-off board called a Twice Upon a Time Schedule.

SAMPLE CARE CHART

Baby's Name:

Breastfeeding
No. of minutes

Starting breast

Supplement?
  How much?

Bottle Feeding
No. of ounces

Wet Diapers

Bowel Movement

Bath

Vitamins

Medication

Additional Notes

Time (AM/PM)	1	2	3	4	5	6	7	8	9	10	11	12

Adapted from Donald M. Keith, M.B.A., Sheryl McInnes, and Louis G. Keith, M.D., eds. *Breastfeeding Twins, Triplets, and Quadruplets* (Chicago: The Center for Study of Multiple Birth, 1982), and reprinted with permission of The Center for Study of Multiple Birth.

Breastfeeding

Deciding Whether to Breastfeed

The female body was designed with two breasts, perhaps in order to nurse two babies. Evidence of women feeding multiple babies dates back to ancient Greco-Roman times, when nursing mothers would sell their surplus milk at the market. Often these women, called wet nurses, were hired to breastfeed the babies of others who were either unable (for whatever reason) or unwilling (it was generally unfashionable in urban societies, particularly among the wealthy) to nurse their own babies. Wet nurses frequently provided milk for babies of more than one family at a time. The idea of breastfeeding other peoples' babies as a livelihood may seem strange or distasteful to us, but knowing that historically women have successfully been able to nurse more than one infant is reassuring to those with more than one of their own.

Mothers of multiples today have proved that women can indeed successfully breastfeed more than one baby. Some mothers of twins nurse their babies for many months without the use of any formula supplements or solids. Even if you are petite you can produce enough milk for twins, and you need not be buxom. The amount of milk your body can produce has nothing to do with your physical stature or breast size. Despite your physiological capability to nurse two babies, psychologically you may feel uncomfortable or awkward about it, especially about the idea of nursing the twins simultaneously.

"Friends who happened to visit me at feeding time always joked about my nursing two at once," began one woman. "I tried to take this in stride, which was not easy at first. I was convinced that breast milk was the healthiest source of nutrition I could give my babies, and I was determined to continue nursing. After a while I became so accustomed to feeding two that it felt completely natural, and I didn't mind being teased any more."

Some mothers are even able to nurse triplets or more successfully. One mother of quadruplets announced proudly, "I breastfed all four girls, two at a time, for three months with no supplements at all. The nurses at the hospital thought I was crazy."

If your twins are in intensive care and are too small or weak to nurse, the commitment to breastfeeding may be harder to make. Many women with premature babies who wish to nurse express or pump their milk directly into sterilized bottles either at the hospital or at home. Many physicians believe that mother's milk is the best diet for these babies once they are large enough to take oral feedings. Breast milk from the nearest milk bank is often given if the mother does not leave bottles of her own milk. Recent studies have shown, however, that the milk produced by a woman who delivers prematurely has a nutrient content and balance that is different than that of a woman who delivers at term and that is better suited to the needs of a premature infant. For this reason, if you do want to breastfeed, by giving your premature babies your own milk, you are not only maintaining your milk supply but you are also reassuring yourself that you are doing something to help your babies.

Information About Nursing

During the first few weeks you may feel more fatigued as a result of breastfeeding, particularly because you are feeding two babies. Your body burns extra calories producing milk. At the beginning, when you are still recuperating from the stress of childbirth, you may be more aware of this energy depletion. Do not become discouraged. If you have the desire and the perseverance, nursing generally gets easier and more relaxing. With encouragement from others, breastfeeding can be a pleasurable experience right from the start. The hospital staff may be able to give you the reassurance you need. "The nurses were very supportive when I wanted to nurse the babies," said one new mother. "They helped me sit up and were delighted that I chose to nurse." You can also get encouragement from mothers of twins who have successfully nursed. Contact your local mothers of twins club or La Leche League for names. Reading can also help. *Breastfeeding Twins, Triplets, and Quadruplets* (1982), edited by Donald M. Keith, M.B.A., Sheryl McInnes, and Louis G. Keith, M.D., and La Leche League's booklet, "Mothering Multiples," by Karen Kerkhoff Gromada, are two useful resources. (See Appendix I for a complete list of organizations and publications concerned with breastfeeding.)

Colostrum

The breasts begin to make milk three to five days after delivery. Until that time, they produce a small quantity of a clear, thick, yellowish liquid called colostrum, which then becomes mixed in the milk for the next month or so. Colostrum, a substance rich in amino acids (the "building blocks" of protein), vitamins A and E, and antibodies, protects babies for many months until their bodies are more developed and are better able to fight disease.

Milk Supply

When the milk comes in, it may be very plentiful, although unlike cow's milk, it has a bluish-white, watery appearance. The breasts may become engorged at first and may be too full and hard for a baby to grasp the nipple. One of the nurses at the hospital can show you how to express a small amount of milk manually in order to make the nipple more pliable. (See also "Expressing, Pumping, and Storing Milk," later in this chapter.) Soon your body will adapt to the feeding needs of your twins by regulating the amount of milk produced for each feeding according to the quantity your babies consume and your body's own energy level. When you are well rested and relaxed you will have more milk than when you are fatigued, tense, or upset, so the milk is usually most abundant in the morning and least at the end of the day. In addition, the more frequently you nurse, the more milk you will have.

"Let-Down" Reflex

After a minute or two with one or both infants sucking at the breast, the milk will involuntarily "let down" and will begin to flow (or even to spray) more heavily. The sucking triggers the release of the hormone oxytocin into your system, causing the milk to "let down." Both sides will let down at the same time, so nursing both babies at once is most efficient. If only one of your babies is nursing, cover the other breast with a milk cup, a nursing pad, or a diaper to catch the milk. After a few months of nursing, your breasts will probably no longer leak when only one twin is feeding.

Nutrition for Nursing Babies

Breast milk offers babies a perfectly balanced diet and is also the most digestible form of milk for human babies. It has both proteins and amino acids, as well as water to flush out any unneeded proteins and salt. Human milk is much lower in saturated fats than is cow's milk, and the sugar content, which is about two times that found in cow's milk, is digestible lactose rather than galactose or glucose. In addition, lactose helps the infant's body absorb necessary proteins and creates a comfortable acidic state in the infant's intestines that is unfavorable to the growth of harmful bacteria.

Breast milk is rich in fat-soluble vitamins, which can be stored by the body, particularly A and E, and also contains water-soluble vitamins that must be replaced daily, such as the B complex and C, and a small amount of D, which is synthesized by the body when exposed to sunlight. (Supplements of vitamin D may be advisable; consult your physician.) Although nursed infants get less calcium and phosphorous than those on formula, they do not lose these minerals through excretion as do formula-fed babies.

Iron content is low and may not be sufficient for the babies' needs, so the pediatrician may recommend that other sources of iron be introduced into a baby's diet. Fluoride is often given as a supplement to nursed babies if the mother does not drink fluoridated water. Iodine is also transmitted through the breast milk. As a result, it may be dangerous for a nursing mother to undergo diagnostic tests using radioactive iodine because of the potential damage to a baby's thyroid gland.

Are the Babies Getting Enough?

Nursing mothers of twins often wonder whether their babies are gaining enough. At the beginning, babies normally nurse between eight and twelve times a day. In general, they are doing fine if they have six to eight soaking wet diapers in a twenty-four-hour period, and if they are each gaining approximately a pound per month, but check with your pediatrician. Growth spurts often cause babies to nurse more frequently in order to meet their increasing nutritional needs. More frequent nursing for up to a week can usually build up the milk supply of the mother of twins to meet the demand adequately. Growth spurts most frequently occur in the early weeks and around six weeks, three months, and six months, but may also occur at other times.

Plugged Ducts and Breast Infections

General care of the breasts and nipples is described in Chapter 4, "Labor, Delivery, and Postpartum," in the section on postpartum care of the breasts. When milk builds up in the breasts for a period of time and is not removed by a nursing baby or by expressing or pumping, the risk of a plugged duct or breast infection becomes greater. Sometimes this is caused by general engorgement or by a brassiere that is too tight. Milk buildup in one or more of the breast sinuses behind a duct often forms a large, red, and painful lump. If this condition develops, nurse one of the babies on the affected side (even if it is between feedings) or express some milk to relieve the buildup. Fatigue, tension, poor nutrition, or missed feedings often aggravate this problem. If you develop a red, sensitive, or hot area on either breast, keep the affected breast as empty as possible through nursing or expressing milk, apply warm, moist compresses, get a lot of rest, and contact your obstetrician immediately. Be sure to follow your doctor's instructions. If he or she prescribes an antibiotic, ask for one that is safe for your nursing babies, too.

Logistics of Nursing

Whether and When to Offer Supplements

Some mothers of twins feel a strong commitment to breastfeeding as a total experience and do not wish to offer any other supplements. For these women, nursing is emotionally fulfilling, establishing a warm bond between mother and babies. The body's natural lactating hormones actually promote a mother's protective feelings toward her baby. Some women have breast discomfort or even develop a headache as a result of missed feedings. In addition, some babies have an allergic response to formula or juice.

Other nursing mothers of twins do offer formula supplements to their babies for a variety of reasons. Some give a "chaser" of formula after a feeding if the babies still seem hungry. Others alternate bottle and breast, feeding one baby with the breast and one with a bottle and then switching for the next feeding. Working mothers may have to supplement breastfeedings during the middle of the day. If you plan to use formula supplements, ask your pediatrician to help you select the best kind of formula for your babies and to tell you how much to offer at each feeding.

Positions for Simultaneous Nursing

During the early weeks, total feeding time needed to nurse twins separately can range from ten to as many as fifteen hours per day, according to one researcher's estimate. Simultaneous feeding can cut this time in half. Finding a comfortable position for simultaneous nursing may require experimentation. Pillows can help prop up the babies to breast height, especially when they are very young. Four positions for simultaneous nursing, are:

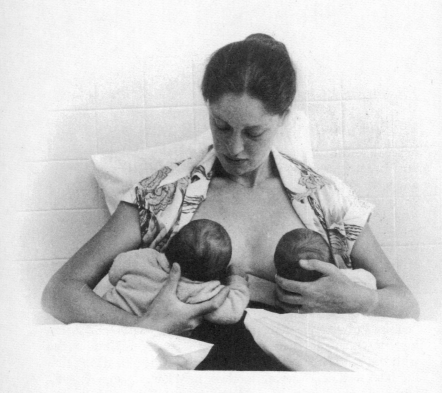

Football hold. Put one baby's head at each breast with their bodies under your arms, their feet toward your back.

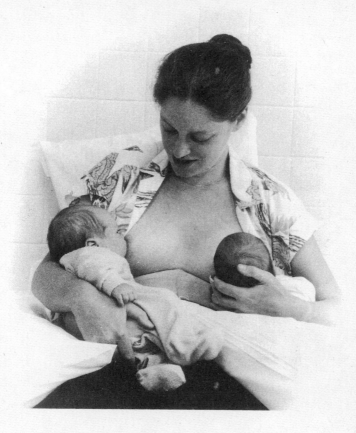

Parallel hold. Put one baby in the conventional nursing position across your lap and the other with head at the other breast and feet under your arm.

Crisscross hold. Place both babies across your lap in the conventional nursing position, with one infant at each breast so that their bodies cross one another.

Front "V." This is similar to the crisscross hold. Put one baby's head at each breast, facing each other, with their bottoms seated on your thighs. Cradle each in one arm with your hand cupped around each baby's buttocks. (*Note:* Be sure to hold the babies securely at your breasts. Do not lean forward to reach the babies as this could cause discomfort or injury to your back.) This position may not afford you good eye-to-eye contact with young babies, but older babies who want to sit up may prefer this position.

Favorite Breast

If you nurse both babies together at a single feeding, try to alternate sides at each feeding in the early weeks. This is especially important if one baby is a more vigorous eater than the other in order to establish an ample milk supply in both breasts. Later each may develop a preference for a specific breast. Indulging this preference is fine, but since one baby may be a bigger eater than the other, do not be surprised if one of your breasts becomes temporarily larger than the other. Each of your breasts will adjust the milk supply to meet the demand and will be larger than normal during the weeks or months you are nursing. Your breasts will return to their former size and relative proportion after you wean the babies, but they may lose some of their former skin tone.

Expressing and Pumping Milk

You may want to express or pump your breast milk to be given to the babies in bottles, particularly if you have premature babies who cannot yet nurse at the breast, if you are a working mother, or if you will be away from your babies. You can express milk either by hand or with the help of a pump. Expressing milk is not always easy at first, especially if you are under stress. You will become more adept with practice.

If you are expressing milk correctly, you will feel neither pain nor discomfort, nor will you feel sexually stimulated Be gen-

Expressing milk

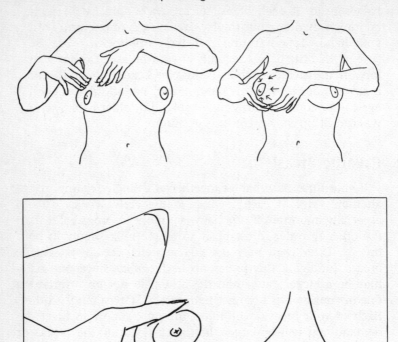

tle so that you do not bruise the breast tissue. If you are unable to express much milk, try at another time of the day, but not right before nursing because you do not want to deplete your milk supply at feeding time.

How to Express Milk

---

1. Always wash your hands with soap before expressing milk.

2. Relax, close your eyes, and take slow deep breaths for a minute or two.

3. Massage cach breast gently, working toward the areola (the dark area that encircles the nipple) and the nipple.

4. Using one hand, place your thumb at the upper edge of the areola (above the nipple) and your index finger at the lower edge (below the nipple).

5. First press your thumb and index finger inward and then gently squeeze them together while holding a sterilized baby bottle to catch the milk that will begin to be expressed in slow drops and then in steady squirts.

6. Repeat this procedure, rotating your fingers around the areola to reach all milk ducts.

7. If both breasts are full, alternate every few minutes.

Adapted from Donald M. Keith, M.B.A., Sheryl McInnes, and Louis G. Keith, M.D., eds., *Breastfeeding Twins, Triplets, and Quadruplets* (Chicago: The Center for Study of Multiple Birth, 1982), and reprinted with permission of The Center for Study of Multiple Birth.

Some women prefer to use a breast pump. Before using a pump, however, always sterilize all equipment that will come in contact with the milk. Be sure to follow the directions for safe and proper use. Try to find the best kind of pump for your own needs. La Leche League has information on individual pumps. (See Appendix I for the organization's address or check your phone directory for a group in your area).

Manual pumps are inexpensive and can be purchased at a baby equipment store, or at a maternity store. Some types of manual pumps are slow and difficult to use. If not used correctly, they can bruise or damage the breast tissue or nipples. Other types are safer and easier to use. The rubber suction bulb on some manual types cannot be sterilized, and milk may be contaminated if it runs into the rubber bulb.

Battery-operated pumps are also now available at many of the same places that sell the manual variety. Some types are as inexpensive as a manual pump. The gentle, pulsing pressure of a battery-operated pump may be ideal for some women but not strong enough for others.

An electric pump can be an invaluable aid, particularly if you want to maintain your milk supply for premature or sick newborns who must temporarily remain in the hospital. If you are too ill to nurse or if you are on medication that the pediatrician feels could be harmful to the babies, you may not be able to give your milk to the babies, but you can continue expressing or pumping milk to maintain your supply until it is safe for you to resume nursing. Electric pumps are very expensive to buy, but you can rent one from a hospital or milk bank, from some drug stores, or you can find out where and how to rent one by contacting a La Leche League group. To avoid breast injury, discontinue pumping after the milk stops dripping from the breast.

Storing and Warming Milk

Breast milk must be refrigerated immediately and can be kept for twenty-four hours in the refrigerator or stored in the freezer under certain circumstances. The milk must be flash-frozen in a deep freezer to prevent the growth of harmful bacteria. Freezer compartments of refrigerators that do not have dual temperature gauges may not be cold enough. Milk stored in a deep freezer will keep for several months. Always put a date and amount (number of ounces) on the bottle before freezing, and be sure to leave room for expansion at the top of each bottle. Containers of frozen milk should be defrosted quickly in several changes of cold and then increasingly warmer water.

Many pediatricians recommend against warming milk (or formula) in a microwave oven because scalding accidents have occurred. The internal temperature of the bottle is difficult to control, and although the outside of the bottle is cool, the contents may be hot enough to burn an infant's mouth. Also, a sealed bottle could explode if heated for too long in a microwave.

Before offering a warmed bottle to a baby, cover it, shake it well to distribute the heat more evenly, and test it by shaking a drop or two from the nipple onto the inside of your wrist. The temperature should be warm but not hot enough to burn your wrist. Because breast milk has not been to a dairy to be homogenized, it will separate (fat content at the top) once refrigerated or frozen. Shake the bottle well after warming.

Do not leave milk to thaw at room temperature, and never refreeze it. To avoid contamination, never remove the milk from the sterile plastic bottle or plastic nurser bag in which it was stored. In addition, plastic nurser bags are too thin to prevent the escape of nutrients and these bags must be protected by an outer plastic bag or container. Glass bottles are not recommended for freezing because they are more likely to break.

Weaning from the Breast

When to wean your babies is a personal decision—either yours or the babies'. Sometimes a mother decides to give up nursing if she is returning to work or if she is going to be away from her babies for an extended period. Sometimes only one baby loses interest; sometimes both. Do not wean the babies abruptly. If you plan to wean your babies before they are able to take a cup, introduce bottles from time to time before you begin weaning. This will help your children adapt easily. Abrupt weaning can be uncomfortable for you and can also present a greater risk of breast infection. Begin by gradually leaving out one nursing at a time. Wait a week or two before cutting out the next. When you do stop breastfeeding, do not give up the time you spend cuddling or holding your babies. Hold young babies while giving them their bottles. Spend extra time hugging or reading to older babies. If one twin loses interest in nursing before the other, you can wean only the disinterested one by following the same steps.

The Advantages of Breastfeeding

1. Breast milk is always pure, is always at the right temperature, and is a totally natural product intended for human babies.

2. Breastfed babies seem to acquire fewer food allergies and to have greater resistance to illnesses.

3. Breastfeeding offers a greater opportunity to cuddle and hold both babies at once than bottle feeding does.

4. Breastfed twins can enjoy one another's closeness and companionship while nursing.

5. Unless you give supplements, you do not need to prepare formula or bottles or to carry all of that paraphernalia with you when you go out with the babies.

6. Breastfeeding can eliminate the cost of formula, bottles, nipples, etc. (though you may be spending a little more for your own foods in order to keep up with the additional calories you need to consume while nursing twins).

Bottle Feeding

Information on bottle feeding can be useful, even if you are nursing, for those occasions when a bottle may be necessary.

Formula

If you want to bottle feed your twins, or if you have decided to wean them, your doctor will help you select the formula best suited to your children's needs. Today you no longer have to make your own formula from scratch; numerous brands are available. Most have a cow's milk base, but some are derived from soy. Soy formulas are designed primarily for allergic babies or for those with a family history of allergies. Goat's milk is also available in some areas for highly allergic babies. You can purchase most formulas in three forms: the expensive prepared form ("ready-to-pour"); the less expensive concentrate; or the powder, which is least costly. Both the concentrate and the powder must be mixed with boiled water. The ready-to-pour type is convenient when going out with the babies, and it is available in disposable bottles (to which a standard nipple and sealing ring can be attached) or in cans (which require a can opener). Once open or prepared, formula must be kept in the refrigerator, where it can be safely stored up to forty-eight hours.

Bottles and Nipples

Disposable bottles have become very popular in recent years and can be a great convenience with twins because they eliminate the need to be washing bottles constantly. A specially designed flexible plastic bag is attached to a hard plastic outer "nurser." Formula is poured into the sterile inner bag, which collapses as the baby drinks, preventing him or her from gulping too much air. Standard glass or plastic bottles are available in four-ounce and eight-ounce sizes. The smaller ones are handier for the first few months, when babies take a maximum of around four ounces at a feeding. Later you will need the larger eight-ounce size. Buy the plastic kind, as they do not break when dropped. The colored or decorated styles, however, make it difficult to see how many ounces a baby has taken.

Many doctors today feel that standard bottles can be safely cleaned in a dishwasher, but some physicians still recommend sterilizing bottles, especially with newborns or premature babies. Sterilizers, available at stores that carry baby equipment, have a wire rack on the bottom that holds the bottles in an inverted position. The loaded sterilizer is filled with a few inches of water and then put to boil. A large pot (to accommodate bottles that are eight inches high) will also work. Nipples are boiled separately.

Standard nipples have a single hole perforated in the top through which the milk flows freely. These are best suited to young babies who have not yet developed a strong sucking reflex. One mother suggests, "Buy nipples designed for milk, water, or orange juice which are color-coded so you will not confuse them. The orange juice nipples have a 'cross-cut' perforation. This way the pulp can pass through without clogging the nipple." Cross-cut nipples do not drip when inverted, and they create a slower flow so that babies are not constantly taking in air. Some brands of disposable bottles have a nipple designed expressly to fit the accompanying nurser. Some nipples are specially designed to conform to the shape of the palate. Because babies have different feeding styles, you may have to experiment with the various available products. Each of your twins may even have different preferences.

Preparing Bottles

Follow the directions on the can when preparing bottles. Make only enough bottles for one day at a time, and store them covered in the refrigerator. Bottles can be warmed in a container of hot tap water, preventing the overheating that often occurs on the stove. Two changes of water will warm a bottle in about five minutes. Many pediatricians now recommend against using a microwave oven to heat bottles. (See the section on "Expressing, Pumping, and Storing Milk" earlier in this chapter.) Most babies prefer to drink warmed formula; those with more sensitive stomachs can become very uncomfortable and gassy from a cold bottle.

Bottle-Feeding Positions

Babies need the love, warmth, and attention they get from physical contact. Try to hold your twins as much as possible when you are feeding them. When you must prop bottles, a baby can be placed on his or her side with the bottle wedged between two rolled diapers or blankets. Bottle holders can also be purchased at baby equipment stores or at some department stores. *Never leave your babies alone with propped bottles because they could choke.* You can feed the twins separately, or you can alternately hold one and prop a bottle for the other. When feeding the twins together, holding both infants and bottles at the same time is difficult. Pages 232 and 233 show a few positions for you to try, or you may be able to devise another position that is more comfortable for you and your babies. Be sure that your back is supported.

BOTTLE-FEEDING POSITIONS

Leg "V." Sit on a bed with your back against a wall and make a "V" with your legs. Place the babies inside the "V" with their heads side by side on a pillow, their legs pointing toward you. Drape two pillows across your upper legs to use as arm rests for your elbows as you hold both bottles. (This position enables good eye-to-eye contact with both babies.)

Two-sider. Sit on a sofa or bed with the babies in their infant seats or on pillows on either side of you and against your body if possible. Hold up the two bottles, one in each hand. The babies will be able to watch you feed them. (You can also sit on the floor with your back against a sofa or low chair. The seat of the sofa serves as an arm rest for your elbows while you hold bottles.)

Cradle and Side. Rest one of your elbows on the arm of a sofa and cradle one baby in the crook of that arm while supporting the bottle with that same hand. Place the other

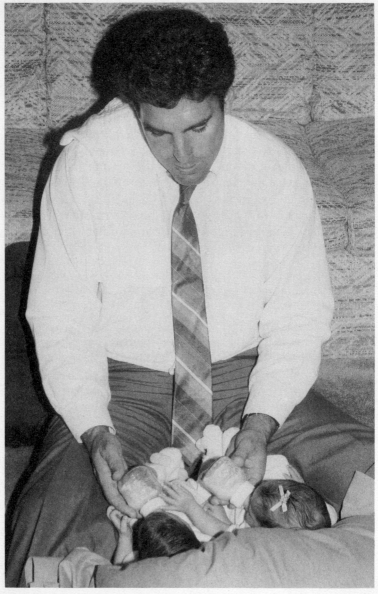

Leg "V"

Two-sider

Cradle and side

baby on a pillow or in an infant seat against your body on the side of your free hand. This hand can then hold the second baby's bottle, or the bottle can be propped. At the next feeding, switch babies. (This method gives you the opportunity to hold one baby at each feeding.)

Once babies are old enough to hold their own bottles, you may be able to hold them both on your lap while they drink.

How Much Formula at Each Feeding?

Your twins may have different appetites and feeding habits. Your pediatrician will tell you the appropriate amount of formula to feed each baby. An infant will usually drink most of the formula before becoming disinterested. Do not coax a baby to take more. This can cause discomfort or gassiness and may set up an unnatural pattern for overeating. In general, however, if a baby regularly rejects more than two ounces or still seems very hungry, it is time to consult with the doctor to reconsider the appropriate feeding amount.

Sleeping with a Bottle

As the twins get older, they may insist on taking bottles to bed with them. The sugar content in the formula, milk, or juice that collects in their mouths as they begin to doze can cause tooth decay. A bottle of water or a pacifier are better choices. (See Chapter 6 for a safety caution on pacifiers under "Small Articles and Toiletries.")

Weaning

Convincing your babies to give up their bottles can be an ongoing battle. Some babies become very attached to a bottle for security and may need lots of extra affection and cuddling as they learn to give it up. If your twins do not lose interest in their bottles by themselves, replace each feeding gradually (one per week) with a cup of milk or juice and a hug. After the children are off the habit, throw away or hide the bottles to avoid regression.

One mother had a very creative solution: "For breaking them of their bottles, I let them drink from the bottle with no top." If you use this method, use only plastic bottles; never try it with glass. Be sure that the rim is smooth and without sharp or rough edges. The bedtime bottle is usually hardest for babies (and parents) to give up. Without this calming effect you may need to rock, cuddle, or sing to your twins, or even to sit in their room for a while before they will go to sleep. They will probably adjust within a couple of weeks.

Bottles to Supplement Feedings

On particularly warm days, bottle-fed babies and even those who are breastfed may need additional fluids between feedings. Babies can take bottles of purified water, or as they get older they can even have diluted fruit juice. Purified water can be purchased at the supermarket. Ask your pediatrician about juices—when to offer them and what kind.

The old practice of sweetening the water to make it taste better is not advisable. This encourages a baby to develop a reliance on sugar, a habit that may later be harmful to the baby's teeth. (Dipping a pacifier in a sweetener is also not recommended for these same reasons.) Sugar, corn syrup, or even honey have traditionally been used as sweeteners for a baby's bottle. Honey (even after purification), however, is now known to be a source of spores that can cause infant botulism. Governmental agencies and honey producers have joined together to recommend against offering honey to infants. An infant's immature digestive and immune systems have not yet developed a resistance to the spores, although adults and older children can safely consume honey. *Do not give honey to infants under a year.*

The Advantages of Bottle Feeding

1. Bottle feeding is less fatiguing for many women than breastfeeding because the body of a nursing mother must expend a lot of energy to produce the amount of milk necessary to feed two babies.

2. A baby on formula may not demand feedings as frequently. Formula is digested more slowly so the baby does not get hungry as quickly.

3. Someone else other than their mother can feed the babies (especially in the early weeks when the twins need night feedings, or if their mother is working).

4. Bottle feeding can be done anywhere.

CHAPTER 8

 The Mother's Role

In most families of twins, as with families of singletons, everything revolves around mother—at least at the beginning. But the time and energy demands on a mother of twins are far greater than those facing a mother of a singleton. In addition, although fathers of twins usually recognize the need to help at home, most are working during the day, so the moms are on their own most of the time. In your own family you probably play many roles simultaneously. You are provider and protector to not just one but two babies, giving them love, feeding them, comforting them, and keeping them clean. You have very little time for yourself, yet during these few moments the older children turn to you for love, praise, and reassurance. Somehow you find the time to read to them, play with them, and even discipline them. In addition, you manage the household, juggling many tasks, such as preparing the meals, doing the laundry, cleaning the house, and doing the grocery shopping.

All of these responsibilities on a day-to-day basis cause a great deal of stress, especially in the early months when you are spending long hours caring for your infant twins and also losing sleep getting up at night with two babies. Yet, despite or perhaps because of the additional demands on a mother of twins, you can find great joy, satisfaction, and pride in yourself and your family. "With twins it is a woman's own state of mind that can make it easy or hard," says one experienced mom. A positive attitude and a strong sense of self-determination are the keys to your success as a mother in general and more particularly in caring for twins.

At Home

Managing the Family

The Twins

Lack of time is the greatest enemy of a new mother of twins. "It's hard to find enough time to give as much as your heart would like," complained one woman, "time for the twins, for the older children, for your husband, and finally for yourself." At the beginning, your twins will probably still be on separate schedules. You will spend most of your day feeding and changing babies, with little time in between for anything or anyone else. This is more difficult for some mothers than for others. "I didn't truly enjoy the first year," confessed one. "It was mostly maintenance and not too much pleasure." Another, however, "loved [the closeness of] mothering them the first year."

As the twins grow, they will adjust to your schedule and you to theirs. The work may not decrease, but as you begin to get more sleep, you will be able to do more in a shorter period of time. During the busy toddler stage, you will need a burst of energy to keep up with two active little people. This is frustrating for some mothers. "Two was the hardest age," volunteered a woman whose twins are now eight. "As they gained independence and became more mobile, [each went in the opposite direction and] I lost control." For others, however, this stage is much easier, as reflected in this woman's comment. "I felt as if I had a new lease on life."

By the time the twins are preschoolers, they will be even more independent, going to the toilet without your help,

eating sandwiches neatly at the table, and even beginning to dress themselves and one another. "Taking care of my twins is not so physically demanding anymore," noted a woman with four year olds. "Now I am more like a combination teacher-policeman, helping them learn and settling their quarrels."

The Older Children

It may be more difficult to meet the emotionally demanding requests of an older child or children than the primarily physical needs of infant twins, particularly during the early months. After the birth of twins, older siblings must compete with not just one but two babies for your attention. Trying to carve out another little wedge of time from your already frantic schedule may not be easy, and you may feel selfish and possessive of your time. As one mother admitted, "I feel that I cannot find enough time for my older child because [on the rare occasion] when both babies are napping I want time for myself."

As the babies get older, their big brother or sister may be better able to accept them as part of the family, but by the time the twins are toddlers, the older children need you to provide other kinds of reassurance. Sometimes you must be a peacemaker as the children compete for territory. The potential for mischief, both separately and as a team, is decidedly greater with twins than with a singleton. One mother with two-year-old twins at home noted, "Our five-and-a-half-year-old doesn't like the twins to interfere with his toys or his friends." At other times, you will be needed to soothe your older child's hurt feelings. One mom had to come to the rescue when "the twins ripped up David's new book."

Some mothers feel guilty and worry that they give more attention to the twins than to their older children. "I wanted my older son to know I loved him just as much as his baby brother and sister. I gave him lots of extra time and love because I always thought he'd feel cheated that he didn't have a twin, too." Just by being with your older children you reassure them that they are loved, and this helps regenerate the self-confidence they may have lost when the twins arrived. (See also Chapter 10, "Siblings: Older and Younger.")

When a new baby comes along after the twins, you assume new roles. At first, you must protect the baby from the innocent roughhousing of not one but two curious older children. Later, once the baby-turned-toddler can invade their world, the twins may team up against the little one and may require your constant supervision. One woman believes that her twin boys "pick fights with their little sister just to get my attention." The twins may even quarrel more often with one another as an attention-getting device. You have probably had little opportunity to give individual attention to the twins. They will get even less of your time now. Although they have the security of each other's company, they need you, too. Spend as much time with them as you can—with the two of them together if you cannot find time now for each alone.

Your Husband

As a new mother of twins, you may have trouble switching roles from the babies' caretaker by day to your husband's friend and lover when he is home in the evenings and on weekends. It is hard to be cheerful at the end of a long and exhausting day. On weekends you are both involved in child care and household responsibilities, and you may be too tired to have time for one another. This makes it difficult to reestablish an intimate husband–wife relationship.

At first, many new mothers of twins are too fatigued or tense to be very interested in lovemaking, and fathers who help at home during the early months may be equally tired. "The most difficult part for my husband and me was to have a close marriage relationship when we were exhausted a lot," says the mother of eighteen-month-old girls and a five-year-old. "It was difficult not to see each other just as another body with demands." After quadruplets arrived, one woman recalls, "My husband and I had to 'make a date' on the calendar to make love."

Sometimes a man, particularly if he is not at home with the family during the day, does not understand the reason for his wife's lack of interest and fatigue and may feel personally rejected. Dad may need reassurance that you do love him and that he is important to you. After a few months, when you regain your energy and strength and the babies adopt a single, dependable schedule, your intimate relationship will also gradually return to normal.

Yourself

The early weeks and months may be far more hectic and fatiguing than for the new mother of a singleton, but the situation does improve. Over two-thirds of the mothers of twins questioned for this book felt their lives were under control again by the time their twins reached six months, most by three months. Almost all of them reported that the twins' arrival had made major changes in their life-style, but most had adapted successfully, and as one put it, "I have gotten faster with practice in what needs to be done." Mothers felt the experience was gratifying despite the additional effort required to care for twins. "I love having twins; it's been one of my most exciting times," said one. And another affirmed, "They are dearer and more fun every day."

Even in their moments of frustration, mothers recognized that having twins is a very special opportunity. This feeling was best captured by a woman who already had three children when her twins arrived, "Keep in mind that at times you may wish there were two of you, but never only one of them."

Nevertheless, many mothers felt housebound. "I felt better if I could find twenty minutes of quiet time a day for myself, though that wasn't always easy to do," recalled one mother of four year olds. "You do need to think of yourself, too," remarked another woman. Try to find a few minutes for yourself each day when you can relax. Reading, sewing, taking a long bath, or listening to your favorite radio station while the children are napping can help you unwind. A phone call or a short visit from a friend can also be special.

Managing the Household

Finding time during the early months—even just for phone calls, the laundry, or your own meals—is not easy. Fortunately, slowly but steadily, things get easier. Once you have developed a rough schedule, you can choose the most convenient block of time during the day to take care of household necessities. "But remember," says one mom, "it is more important to have happy babies than a clean house." Do not expect to get everything done at once. With baby twins to keep you busy, you quickly learn "how to do anything with interruptions," adds another mom.

For the first three months, do only what is absolutely essential. "Limit housework to one major task per day," advises a third woman. As soon as you have had breakfast, wash and put away the dishes so they will not pile up by lunch time. Then straighten beds and cribs and put away any clothing or toys. A large bag is useful for collecting all miscellaneous things that need to be put away. Plan a project for each day, one that can be done little by little whenever you have a few free minutes. For example, when you feel a bit energetic or if both babies happen to be taking a long nap at the same time, vacuum or dust, but only where it is really needed.

The biggest household challenge with twins after the first year is cleaning up messes—food everywhere after meals, toys scattered throughout the house, and constant clothing changes due to food spills. Food messes need immediate attention, but as far as toys are concerned, cleanup need not be done more than once or twice a day if toddlers and preschoolers are limited to only one or two play areas (such as their bedroom and a play room). Outdoor play in good weather helps children get fresh air and burn off pent-up energy while the house stays neat.

Twins definitely get dirtier and into more mischief than one child alone, and you must always be on your toes to keep up with them. Said one woman, "I felt more organized before they started changing their own clothes, moving around so much, and making so many messes." Some mothers find it is easier to pick up toys throughout the day as needed. Others prefer to do one major cleanup when the twins are napping and another in the evening after they go to bed. As the children get older, teach them to pick up after themselves. This takes time and patience, and you must work along with them at the beginning, giving encouragement and praise when they cooperate.

Laundry can be done either at a specified time of the day or whenever you have a few minutes. With baby twins, you can expect at least one full washload per day of just clothes, bedding, and towels, plus another load if you do your own diapers. Check the washing instructions in baby clothes before laundering. A fabric softener in the rinse cycle or in the dryer prevents harsh static electricity, and vinegar used in the final rinse helps neutralize the urine in their diapers. Children need fewer clothing changes as they get older and are toilet-trained, but the sizes they wear get larger, keeping washloads at least as large as before. By the time the children are three or four, they can help you by putting away their own clothes.

Try to simplify meal preparation, especially during the first few weeks. This can be done without developing a junk food habit. Plan easy-to-prepare menus of single-dish dinners, such as a meaty casserole complete with vegetables and rice or noodles, a summer julienne salad, or a big pot of meat and vegetable soup for winter. Welcome any friends, neighbors, or relatives who offer to bring you a home-cooked meal; they can even cuddle the babies for you while you enjoy the dinner. On the days you must cook, double the recipe and refrigerate or freeze leftovers of these hot meals for another evening's supper. Spaghetti sauce, stews, or soups often taste even better the second time around. Good advice from one mom is to "prepare dinner in the morning when you have more energy."

Cleanup is easier if you use paper plates and cups. They can save a lot of time at a minimal cost. Ask dad to handle the cleanup when you use regular dishes, or leave the scraped dishes, cups, and utensils soaking in a dishpan of hot sudsy water until you have time to attend to them. Take dishes directly from the table to the dishwasher, if you have one. Dishes can be stored in the machine whether clean or dirty, and your kitchen looks and feels neat.

Going to the supermarket is faster and easier without two babies, who can become tired and impatient very quickly. If you must take them with you, shop quickly and for as few items as you can. Toddler twins may love the supermarket, but they can be a hazard, pulling cans and boxes down from all directions. One mother found it hard to remain calm when "one of my twins took a container of yogurt from the dairy case. She handed it to her twin who poured it over his head and all the other food in the cart." Preschool twins can help you with your shopping by fetching such things as cereal or bread, but they can also be demanding, begging for a favorite soda pop, candy, or gum. One helpful suggestion is offered by a woman with three and a half year olds. "I usually let the twins pick out one nutritional snack when we first get to the store so that they will be happy and not ask for junk at the checkout line." One mom prefers to "use the phone for errands whenever possible."

Planning Activities Outside of the House

With the Children

You may feel housebound with baby twins since you must get two babies ready every time you want to go out. Still, mothers of twins recognize the need to get out of the house on a regular basis, as summed up here: "I took the children shopping, to the park, or to a friend's house. The change of scenery and the chance to see others made me feel like a person again." Some mothers worry that their twins need more time apart from one another. "I would like to do more things with each child separately, which takes much more planning and arranging." Others stress the need to get away periodically with the older children, too. One mother of twins with an older son age five says, "I tried to continue life as usual by taking him with me alone to the store and to his swimming lessons."

The advice for the first year offered by a mother of six-and-a-half-year-old boys is to "get out of the house every day even if only for a short walk." Another whose boys are now five remembers taking regular "walks in the morning and afternoon around the neighborhood, and walking to parks and exploring things." Yet even for women like these who enjoy full-time motherhood, getting out of the house with two babies, especially during the first year, presents a challenge, as one mother admitted. "My main difficulty has been doing things on time, either by the clock or before the babies fall apart. I generally start a whole lot earlier doing whatever has to be done so I'll be ready on time."

"Because of the twins," said a woman with eighteen-month-old boys and an eight-year-old daughter, "I have learned to organize and make use of my time." She now also has a six-week-old baby. "I took the twins on many hikes from three months on, and camping at eleven months," recalls another organized mom. "I'm far from an energetic person," she says, "but the need to get out was great."

Play groups, "kindergym," swim programs, and cooperative preschools all provide opportunities for moms to participate in organized activities together with their twins. "Play group helped me get ideas on childrearing from other mothers," acknowledges one mom. "The twins got to meet and be friends with other children their age."

Without the Children

Time away from the children gives you a chance to clear your mind. This is just as important when the twins get older as during the hectic first year. One mother of two-month-old twins and an older son revealed, "For me, the most difficult part is the constant attention that twins and a two and a half year old require. The intensity exhausts me emotionally. I have to take time out for me." Similarly, a woman whose twins are now six complained, "I never have had enough time for myself."

Most of the mothers interviewed wished they had gone out more without the children. Remembering how it was during the first year, one said she was "worried too much that as the mother I should do all their caretaking."

A divorced mother felt this need to an even greater extent, recalling, "Because my obstetrician is a twin, he was very understanding. When the twins first came home from the hospital, he stressed the need for extra help and the importance of getting out. I only wish I had listened." Another woman urged, "Get out once a week for a few hours. Your husband can babysit. It's good for both of you." Yet another mother was more specific, "Take a class once or twice a week, and join a mothers of twins club."

The first few times you go out after the birth of your twins, feeling good about yourself and your appearance is especially important to your morale. Buy or borrow something new to wear, even though you probably still have weight to lose. You will feel rejuvenated no matter how insignificant or inexpensive an item it is. Find a necklace, a hat, or shoes, or get a new haircut if you are not yet able to get into your old size. Even a small change in your appearance will boost your morale.

Getting out alone with your husband is also important because the stress of the day-to-day routine and two babies crying or children underfoot may make it impossible for you to enjoy each other's company while at home. These ventures out together are not only relaxing and enjoyable but are necessary to the continued happiness of your marriage. "You need special time alone with your husband," insists one mother of a two year old and five-month-old twins. "Don't forget you were lovers and friends before you were parents."

Single Mothers

Single mothers are at the greatest disadvantage during the first year, a time when most mothers of twins rely heavily on their husbands for help. One woman with two older children and two-month-old twins worried she would not get through the first few months. "My mother helped for three to four weeks, but after that I was completely worn out and screaming for help." If you cannot bring the help to you, bring yourself to the help, as another woman did. "For the second and third months, the twins and I stayed with my mother."

Faced with the initial burden of caring for twins, some single mothers resorted to short-cuts they later regretted. "I should not have given in, even when I was so tired," reflected the divorced mother of two year olds. "I should never have let the twins sleep in my bed," another woman added. One woman did not feel twins made life any more difficult. "I expected to have children, and having twins was not a problem," she began, "but I never thought I'd have to raise my children by myself, and it's been lonely." The hardest time of the day for her was at six o'clock at night, when "you're tired and you're alone with two screaming children. There's no one to come home to tell you you've done a good job or to take over for you for a few minutes." Fortunately for most single mothers, caring for the twins became easier in time.

Some women had exhusbands who remained involved with their children's care. "Their father does enjoy them during his visit," noted one woman who was on her own from the time the twins were born. "He frequently gives them their bottles," she adds. Coparenting is an answer for some separated or divorced couples. The twins may alternately spend time with mom and then with dad, or mom and dad may alternately occupy the kids' permanent home. Shared custody, however, does not work in every situation. One mother of two-year-old girls felt, "Children can grow up with divided loyalties in two warring households. I believe that children need a single place to call home and a parent who does not continually move in and out of the children's life."

How much a separation or divorce affects twins in particular may be difficult to assess. "I think the major impact is that it strengthens the twin bond, but I don't know if that's good or bad," reflected one woman. "The fact that my twins have each other creates a temporary sense of security, but I wonder whether this will lead to an abnormal dependency later on." When asked how she would handle her twins' questions about the divorce, one mom replied, "I hope that it will be like sex education. I'll answer their questions honestly when they decide to ask." Another woman said that she would "explain that divorce is a grown-up's problem and that it is not caused by children."

Although it was not easy, most single mothers of twins managed to take care of their families quite well, despite the lack of a partner to share in the responsibilities of the household.

"My husband left me when I was three months pregnant, so I'm pretty much on my own now," said one woman. "I plan to go back to work full time when the babies are four months old. I know we'll all be okay."

"The babies went everywhere with me during the week and I didn't even have a car," recalled the divorced mother of twins age four and an older daughter. Even so, almost all of the single mothers interviewed strongly advised new mothers to get help at whatever expense. Despite the difficulties of raising twins alone, most described the experience of twin motherhood in glowing terms, as reflected in this comment, "I enjoy every moment and developmental change."

Working Mothers

Perhaps the hardest part of the day for a working mother of twins is when she gets home from work. The children's demands are greatest when mom first walks in the door. They have been waiting all day for this reunion. You, however, are tired and need a few minutes to wind down and to re-energize before you can face a half-hour of constant activity and two children competing for your attention. "Sometimes I have to restrain myself from flying off the handle," admits a nurse who is the mother of five-year-old girls. "I'm always so excited to see the girls when I pick them up at day care, but as soon as we get home, the whining and fighting begins and I just can't take it. I wish I could come home and sit down and read to them for a half-hour, but usually they are hungry and I have to begin cooking dinner right away."

Feeding the children as quickly as possible when you get home seems to be a good way to settle them down and reduce tension. During dinner, if they are old enough, your children can tell you about the day's activities. Take a small snack for yourself, such as cheese and crackers, to satisfy your own appetite temporarily. Dinnertime for mom and dad can then come later and be a more relaxing way to share the day's experiences. After the children's supper, a bath or quiet time before bed is a good way to end their day. With toddlers and preschoolers, let each twin select a favorite book that mommy (or daddy) can read to both.

Finding time for all of the household chores, the laundry, and the marketing requires ingenuity. Some errands can be done over lunch hour, such as shopping for household items, or a trip to the bank or post office. Other tasks can be saved for weekends, such as cleaning the house or going to the laundro-mat. Weekends can also provide time to prepare dinners in advance in large quantities that can be divided into one-night portions and then refrigerated or frozen. Food for the children can be stored in separate containers, and if the twins are still babies, their supper can be pureed before storing. "If you have your own washer and dryer, after you change the children for bed, toss the day's laundry into the machine," suggests one mother. "While you have your own dinner, the dirty clothes are getting clean. After your dinner the clothes go into the dryer. Then, first thing in the morning you can fold and put them away." Some working mothers prefer doing the laundry every two to three days. For others, doing it daily cuts back on the quantities to be folded and put away. "I always find it easier to spend ten minutes every morning and night than a half-hour every third day," says one mom.

The supermarket is usually crowded on the weekends, but for most working mothers, this is an unpleasant but necessary weekend activity. Shopping on weekday evenings reduces the time you can spend at home with your children. "During the week I stop at the supermarket only when I have to," says a woman with preschool twins and an older son. "On week-ends I do my 'big shop' and buy the staples we need for the coming week." One working couple even makes a trip to the supermarket a regular weekend excursion with their toddler twins. "My husband and I each take half of the shopping list. We each put one twin in our separate shopping carts," says mom. "The girls love it, and I think we actually shop faster together than I could if I went by myself. The girls learn a lot from watching other people and from identifying foods they have never seen before, and they each get a half-hour alone with just one of us."

The working mothers of twins interviewed for this book had positive feelings about how their jobs affected their own emotional state. They did not feel that the well-being of their children was being jeopardized either. Additional financial responsibilities imposed by the arrival of twins forced some to seek employment; others decided to enter the work force without pressing financial need. Those who took jobs to help support the family seemed to accept this role without resentment and did not seem to worry about the children's abilities to respond to another caretaker. The six-month-old twins of one woman "have been with a sitter five to seven days a week since they were two months old, and when I work the P.M. shift or when I go to the grocery store, my husband takes care of them—about sixteen hours a week."

Among the women who chose to work for personal reasons other than financial need, some felt more secure with the decision than others. One mother had what she called "the continual problems of a working mother—guilt and the search for quality day care." Another woman who returned to her job when the twins were two and a half months old "was able to nurse the babies two times a day until they were five and a half months old." She had no regrets and felt that her "return to work has been a plus. The time I spend with the twins is quality, happy time for all of us. It has eliminated the confined feeling of full-time motherhood and is important to my personal self-esteem."

Some women who might have preferred to stay home with their twins for an extended period returned to work because they were afraid to be away from a career for too long. After four years at home with her twin daughters, a lawyer returning to work three days a week noted, "Having twins and watching them grow is a uniquely special experience, but I am afraid to pass up the opportunity to return to work. It's rare for an attorney to find a part-time position," she admitted, "and even if this job isn't right on a permanent basis, I am in touch with what is happening in my profession. Even so," she confessed, "I feel physically and emotionally drained much of the time during the three days [a week] I am at work and during the two days I am with my kids now, and that makes me feel guilty." For another professional woman her regular business trips away from home made life complicated. "Not only do I hate having to be away from the children, but my husband also works long hours and if I must go away unexpectedly, arranging childcare for infant twins as well as a preschooler is very difficult."

Managing the children's activities is also difficult for the working mother of twins. "To get to work on time I have to get up at 5:30 so that I can feed both babies and get them dressed and to day care," says a secretary. For other mothers, arranging their twins' leisure activities and not the essentials becomes a pressing concern. "When they were little, I enrolled the children in a baby swim class," recalls one woman. "The babysitter couldn't take care of both children at once in the pool, so every Tuesday I went late to work wet and soggy and I worked an extra hour at the end of the day." However, other women were more informal about arranging these kinds of extra activities for their children. "As twins they will always have to make some compromises," reflected a part-time secretary whose four-year-old son and daughter spent most of their early years at home with a babysitter. "At four, they appear to be as normal and happy as other children their age—and maybe are even better off because they have a sense of continuity. They have played with the neighborhood children, and they have been at the same preschool for two years, and this gives them a sense of stability. Their daily routine is predictable, not changing all of the time, so they have always felt very secure."

For most working mothers of twins, life at home is more hectic than for moms of singletons, and requires more creative solutions to the familiar problems of working parents. However, most of the working mothers of twins who were interviewed seemed to be comfortable with their dual roles and felt they were able to handle job responsibilities effectively and still find enough time to meet their children's physical and emotional needs. Those interviewed for this book agreed that a positive attitude is the key to successfully juggling the responsibilities of a job, the household, and the childrearing. Many felt that as working mothers they could make a more valuable contribution to the family than if they remained home. This was accomplished either because the woman's salary helped reduce the family's financial burdens, and/or because the job gave her a greater sense of self-worth and a more positive self image, thus enabling her to improve the quality of the time she spent at home. Although having twins occasionally also made finding childcare more complicated, especially during the twins' infancy, most women admitted that even an inconvenience such as this did not deter them from taking a job or returning to work.

Getting Help

The overwhelming advice from experienced mothers of twins is to get as much help at home as you can, particularly during the first three to six weeks. "My husband took time off when the twins were born, and for one week he helped with shopping and laundry and care of our three-year-old," remembers a grateful mother. A woman whose twins are still under a year insists, "The best help is from my husband, who cares for the babies about 50 percent of the time. He does as much or more than I do."

Although you may not want others to do the baby care during the first few weeks, friends or relatives who offer their help can answer the phone, do the laundry, prepare dinner, or go to the supermarket. If you are bottle feeding, you might also appreciate having a friend's help at feeding time, as did a woman whose "neighbor came to help with most feedings for five and a half months."

An extra pair of hands can even be useful at bath time or when taking the babies to the doctor. Teenagers can be a great help after school during the fussy couple of hours before supper or even just as a relief for you after a long day. One mother of five "tried to have a teen come every afternoon for one to three hours so that I could leave or do something with the older boys or even be alone."

When twins are born, relatives and friends will often go out of their way to be helpful. Make a list of things others could do to help you. If recruiting volunteers makes you uncomfortable, ask a relative or friend to do this for you. Ask your helper to plan a baby shower—before or after delivery. Instead of gifts, guests can sign up to help with one of the tasks listed below:

Dinner	Housecleaning
Laundry	Baths
Grocery shopping	Feedings
Errands	Visits to the pediatrician

Add to the list or change it according to your own needs. One mother of quadruplets "kept a calendar of who was available to help on which days and at which hours." Twinline, in Berkeley, California, has a helpful packet of materials for new families of twins called *Rx Packet for Twin Families* (see Appendix I for the organization's address). Your local mothers of twins club may also have printed material with suggestions on how to get help.

If space permits, ask a willing friend or relative to stay with you during the early weeks to help with the daily routine and to assist with night feedings. If you are nursing, you need your rest to maintain milk production. Your helper can change the babies before and after the middle-of-the-night feeding and can burp them so that you are able to get some sleep. If you are bottle feeding and have a helper to give bottles, you can actually sleep through the night feeding. Assistance at home is particularly valuable to unprepared mothers whose twins arrive unexpectedly. "I don't know what I would have done without help so I could get rest and adjust to the surprise," reflected one woman who asked her mother to move in for the first month.

Getting out of the house without the children depends on your finding someone who is willing to care for twins and who is capable of handling the job. If you go out only occasionally, even if you cannot afford a babysitter, "make some sort of arrangement with family or a friend for free time," one mother emphasizes. One couple had a unique arrangement for their triplets during the first few months. They sent the babies home with different friends, relatives, or members of their church each weekend. "From five-thirty on Saturday night until five-thirty on Sunday night my husband and I could spend time with our older son, could go out together, or could even make love," she recalls. During the week if both you and your husband are working, you will have to look for a more permanent, regular child care arrangement. The sections that follow offer ideas for both part-time and full-time care. Although these sections discuss many of the same concerns parents of singletons have in choosing child care, with twins the additional cost of some of these arrangements may also be a consideration. In addition, convenience may be a more important issue with twins, and the presence of other children to encourage group play may be a lower priority with twins than with singletons.

Cooperative and "Shared Care"

Membership in a babysitting cooperative lets you get out alone or with each of the twins separately without the cost of a babysitter. Every co-op has its own rules, but essentially the principle is the same for all. You leave your children at the home of a member. The hours are tabulated upon your return, and you owe the co-op the equivalent number of hours of babysitting in your home. Co-ops seem to work best for women who do not need full-time child care, whose time is flexible, and who enjoy taking care of additional children. You alone can decide whether you are ready to take on the responsibility for extra children.

Some play groups are also designed for child care, with one or two parents babysitting all members' children at each meeting on a rotating basis. This kind of arrangement usually works better with toddlers than with infants. If you have a close friend who wants to exchange babysitting on an informal basis, you may not even need a co-op or a play group. For mothers of twins, however, it may be difficult to find a friend who wants to share child care, especially for twins under age two. As you know, handling the needs of two babies is not easy, especially while caring for other children.

Day Care Centers

A day care center may be an advantage if you are working, because you can leave your twins there all day. Many centers, however, will not take infants. Although day care may be a good choice for toddlers, who need to socialize and interact with other children, it may not be the ideal arrangement for infants. Some additional points for a family of twins to consider are these:

1. A day care center can be expensive for twins. Although some have "sibling discounts," centers generally charge a flat rate per child and may be more expensive than a babysitter in your own home.

2. You must have your twins dressed, packed with a day's supply of bottles, diapers, and change of clothing, and at the day care center before you can leave for work, school, or wherever you are going. (With not just one but two babies this can be very time-consuming.)

3. Many centers have rules prohibiting the care of sick children. Even if your children are not very ill or if only one of the twins is ill you must make other arrangements, and this can be difficult to do or extremely expensive.

Babysitters

Another option is a babysitter to care for your twins in your own home. The best way to find a capable, reliable, and trustworthy babysitter is by asking friends for recommendations. You can also read the work-wanted ads, post an ad at your church or synagogue or at the local high school, place an ad in a local newspaper, or call a child care resource and referral center or reputable babysitting agency. Ask for local references when interviewing prospective sitters. Give your sitter a trial visit when you are home. Observe how the sitter handles your children. Chances are he or she has never cared for twins, and you may be able to offer some valuable tips and short-cuts. Sitters' prices vary. You will probably have to pay a higher rate for the care of twins than for a single baby. Some charge whatever the market will bear, so ask around before you agree on a wage.

You will have to find adult sitters during the school year. Look for someone young and highly motivated, or find a mature person who has already raised a family. In either case, be sure the sitter has enough energy and enthusiasm to care for infant or toddler twins. Another mother who brings her infant or toddler with her may also be a good choice because she is more aware of safety concerns with infants and young children. A housekeeper can even be a babysitter if you stress child care as the most important part of the job. Teenage babysitters will be less expensive for after school, weekends, and during the summer months, but many teenagers do not have the mature judgment and patience to care for young twins. You may want to use two teenagers together, particularly if you also have an older child who is still in diapers, but this can be very expensive.

Live-in Help

A live-in babysitter is a luxury available only to those families of twins who have the money and the space. A salary, paid weekly or monthly, is generally provided, as well as lodging and food. Salaries vary according to the individual. After the arrival of twins if your home still has ample space but you have a limited budget, you may be able to find a student or young working person who is willing to exchange babysitting for room and board. Search for live-in help by contacting a reputable babysitting agency or by reading or placing an ad in the classified section of your local newspaper. A round-the-clock maternity nurse can be hired to live in during the early weeks at considerable expense.

A "baby nurse" can usually be located through a babysitting agency or by word of mouth and may or may not be registered or licensed. Most are booked for months in advance, however, and many will not care for twins or will charge extra. They generally charge by each twenty-four-hour period and will live in your home, taking a few hours off in the middle of the day. Nurses will care for the mother and babies and will help get the babies on a comfortable schedule. They may even do the laundry and help with older children, but most will not cook or do any kind of housecleaning or shopping.

CHAPTER 9

The Father's Role

A father plays a special and important role in the twin family. Although a father's help at home is generally appreciated by a mother of singletons, the help offered by a father of twins is not only welcomed but needed, especially during the early months. As one man maintains, "With one baby you can avoid helping, but with two you have to help." Undoubtedly there are still some expectant fathers for whom twins means merely handing out a second cigar at the office. These men are in for a rude awakening—at two, three, four, and five o'clock in the morning. On the other hand, those who willingly involve themselves in the preparations for the babies' arrival feel more comfortable helping with their children's care. Perhaps the greatest gift of love parents can give to one another and to their twins is to work together and share responsibilities.

During Pregnancy

Experienced fathers urge those whose wives are expecting twins to complete all household projects as much as possible in advance and to arrange a more flexible schedule at work for the first few weeks after the babies are born. One man suggests, "Make a resolution to help with the everyday activities as much as you can once the twins come home." Another reminds, "These children are just as much your responsibility as they are your wife's."

The concept of shared responsibility is a relatively new one for parents of singletons as well as for parents of twins. Mutual support is the key to successful pregnancy, childbirth, and childrearing, especially for parents of twins in light of the greater emotional, physical and financial pressures brought on by a multiple birth. Expectant mothers openly talk to their husbands about the sensations of pregnancy, from the minor discomforts to the joys of feeling the babies kicking. Dads are no longer relegated to the waiting room at the hospital but are encouraged to accompany their wives in the labor and delivery rooms to watch the birth of their twins. Even the Caesarean delivery room is open to fathers at many hospitals.

One father of twins who is a registered nurse and works in the newborn nursery insists, "The father should be at the birth. . . . Men have the same abilities to bond with their babies as women do." Thus, despite their greater potential for complications, twin births are increasingly becoming a two-parent affair.

Labor and Delivery

Surveyed fathers responded to the delivery of their twins with a variety of emotions. Some reacted on the basis of earlier expectations for a single birth. One man with an older son announced upon the arrival of his boy-girl twins, "I got the girl I wanted so much." A first-time father at the birth of his twin boys was disappointed and admitted, "I expected one to be a girl." Others were overjoyed by the arrival of twins. "They were perfect, healthy, normal, and beautiful!" Or incredulous at the wonders of a multiple birth. "I couldn't believe it! I was happy as hell!" Still others were overwhelmed by the experience. One remembered being "speechless—amazed

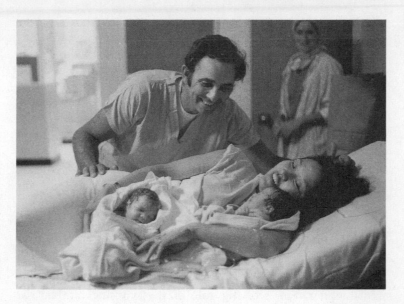

at the miracle of life!" Yet another was overcome by emotion after witnessing the unexpected birth of his identical boys and recalled, "I wept." One father of five, when asked his advice for the delivery room replied, "Take a double Scotch on the rocks!"

Even if you have just shared a healthy and joyful multiple birth experience, initial jubilation may lead to a period of despondency and concern as you try to reorganize and re-shape your thoughts about family and home. You may have little opportunity to get to know the babies during the early hours when mother and babies begin developing rapport and communication through nursing or other early physical contact.

As one father freely admits, "I was feeling left out because there was little I could do in terms of nourishing the children since Carol was breastfeeding. I think my feelings were com-mon for men whose wives were breastfeeding." Others were relieved that they did not have to help. As one recalls, "I was apprehensive. I had never been around any babies before, let alone twins." One father of triplets said he felt shoved aside. "When the triplets arrived they almost broke up our marriage."

A father's feelings of helplessness or inadequacy during the initial hours after a multiple birth are very natural and can lead to a sense of alienation or can temporarily cause a man to withdraw from his wife and the babies. This period of self-examination is usually brief for those who have these feelings. For others, the transition from expectant to new father of twins is accomplished easily with never a backward glance. For nearly all of the fathers interviewed, an overall feeling of joy and relief outweighed any concerns.

Helping at Home

Today's father is no longer universally regarded as the sole breadwinner. The growing role of the working mother has both enabled and required fathers to become active partici- pants in the management of the household and child care. Not only is it now considered okay for a father to help with household duties, but your involvement is a sign of pride in your family and home. And given the additional pressures of raising twins, your help at home will help forge a stronger bond with your wife and children.

Many companies, organizations, and offices now offer "pa- ternity leave," which entitles a father to take a specified period of time off work, sometimes with pay and sometimes without. Inquire about the availability of paternity leave and benefits where you work. In some two-income families, parents of twins may be able to devise a job-sharing arrangement. If you and your wife have flexible work situations, you may be able to plan your job hours so that one of you is always at home. This gives each of you an opportunity to enjoy the children without feeling housebound and to maintain a career at the same time.

Even with the increasing flexibility of parental roles today, mom is usually the one who cares for the children, and if only one parent is working it is usually dad. At-home fathers are still a rare breed, and fathers of twins in this role are even less common. Fathers of twins who are homemakers not only do exist, however, but they are generally good at the job. One man, whose wife works as a nurse, cares for his two older children, the two-year-old twins, and now watches the new baby, too. Yet no matter how able a father of twins may be at managing the household and child care, he needs his wife's support and participation just as much as an at-home mother needs help from her husband.

In most cases, however, if either parent stays home to take care of the kids, it is mom. If your wife takes care of the children, you can help with the twins' morning and evening feedings or meal times, can assist with baths before bed, and can read bedtime stories to the older child or children. You can both share these jobs if each of you is working. You can also help with the household chores—the laundry, shopping, vacuuming, dishwashing, even the cooking. Your participation will not only help get an essential job done but will also relieve tensions at home and will help win your wife's confidence in you as a caring husband and parent.

Child Care

Most of the fathers of twins surveyed for this book recognized and willingly accepted the added responsibilities that typically accompany the birth of twins. The ultimate father not only accepted responsibility but even enjoyed the opportunity to participate in the care of his children during the first year. "Fathers need to find ways to incorporate themselves in the activities of daily care of their children," insisted one man with four-year-old boys. From the very beginning, "fathers should try to take the first week off to be with their wife and babies, and they should (along with the mother) hold, bathe, and clothe their babies," he added.

Few of the fathers of twins in the study were home during the day on weekdays, but according to their wives, they still

found time to spend an average of twenty-four hours per week helping at home during the first year. The number of hours was considerably higher for the early months and tapered off as the twins neared their first birthday and life at home became less frantic. A majority of the men said they regularly changed diapers, and among those whose wives were not exclusively breastfeeding, most assisted by giving bottles to their children, even if only occasionally. More than half said that at one time or another they had given the twins their regular bath, and many said they even took their children on outings alone. On the whole, fathers in the study had fun playing with their twins as well as watching them and observing the interaction between them.

Managing the Household

Despite the demands on your time, with infant twins at home you can help by doing a few loads of laundry in the evening even if you work a long day. Sorting, folding, and putting away the clean clothes may take only a half-hour of uninterrupted time, but just a half-hour will considerably lighten the daily work load of household chores after twins arrive. Particularly during the first year or two, when you and your wife will be more tired and your time alone together will be at a premium, you will both appreciate having a few free minutes. Sharing responsibilities helps both of you feel more relaxed and relieves tension.

Doing the grocery shopping is one of the hardest chores for new parents of twins. Taking two tiny babies to the supermarket is both difficult to coordinate and exhausting. In the evening or on weekends when both you and your wife are at home, you can do the shopping while she watches the children or you can even use the grocery shopping as an opportunity to get out alone with your older child or children. Later, as the twins get older, you can take them with you to the supermarket to give mom a little time to catch her breath.

Cleaning the house is rarely an enjoyable task, either for mothers or for fathers. Following a multiple birth, you can help by vacuuming, dusting, or other household cleaning, or by straightening or picking up clothing, papers, or toys. Go around the house periodically collecting all unclaimed items in a paper bag to be sorted at a more convenient moment. If you are too tired after a long day at work, you can at least help by keeping your own things in order. A messy house aggravates tempers; a neat house, even if it is not spotless, helps give the whole family a sense of order and organization.

Prepare meals (and do the after-dinner cleanup) if you are handy in the kitchen. If your wife is busy tending to babies or toddlers, you can be busy in the kitchen creating a tasty concoction. If your cooking talents are limited to pouring a cup of coffee, just doing the dishes is a terrific help.

Single Fathers

Few single fathers responded to the survey for this book. Those who were willing to discuss their separation or divorce were those who were actively participating in their children's care. "We separated when the boys were two and a half," began one man's story. "Karen and I wanted to promote togetherness and independence in our children. In our coparenting agreement," he continued, "it is written that we would each have times alone with each of the twins as well as with both together." In this situation, father as well as mother were still an integral part of the children's life. "I would urge all separated parents of twins to share custody and maintain contact," felt a father who had been separated for almost two years. Another noted, "I have a very real bond with my boys. If I lost the opportunity to care for them, I would feel like a very important part of my life was missing."

Twins may come to rely more heavily upon one another when their parents separate or divorce, as seen in one set of identicals. "Our separation has caused the twins to become more dependent on each other's presence. Theirs is the only permanent, stable relationship they have ever had." As far as the long-range affects on his children, one insightful man observed, "With divorce or separation, you go through a grieving process. Until the adults can come to a place of acceptance, you can't expect the children to. Even so," he added, "children of divorce always harbor the unfounded hope their parents will get back together."

Family Relations

The arrival of twins can tip the comfortable but fragile family balance, as fathers themselves acknowledged. Those interviewed spoke of less free time and less energy to be with wife and family, more work at home, and less sleep, all of which often aggravated tension. During the early weeks, one father became angry at his wife because he was constantly being awakened at night. He finally realized, however, that "when you have twins there is no choice but to get up and help." Once he had accepted this responsibility, he "enjoyed the twins much more and actually felt no more 'stress' about getting up in the middle of the night." Most men made a concerted effort to offer their wives moral support in whatever way they could. For example, one man recommended, "Read [the section on twins in] the breastfeeding book so that you can be a resource and a support person when your mate is having difficulty."

As with fathers of singletons, for many fathers of twins, an important source of concern was the relationship with their older children. The two older sons of one man "craved more attention" when their fraternal twin brothers arrived, and the father was frustrated because he could not give the older boys enough time. A man with a four-and-a-half-year-old boy and two-year-old twins noticed a change in his attitude toward his older son. "I often expect him to be older than he is." Many fathers, however, reported no change in the relationship with their older children after the twins were born. One man with boy-girl twins said his older daughter "has always been 'daddy's girl,' " and she will always retain this special place of importance. For a number of fathers, rapport with their older children actually improved after the arrival of twins. "I feel closer to my daughter now," admitted one man whose little girl was two and a half when her identical twin brothers were born.

One man was sensitive to the demands on his wife of caring for two babies. When asked to offer helpful hints for new and expectant fathers of twins, he advised fathers, "Do not expect your wife to go right back to work." With two sons ages twelve and two as well as infant twins, another man counseled, "Hire a babysitter at least once a month, and take your wife out." Most fathers of twins acknowledged that their wives incurred more of the responsibilities, as one man made

clear, "There is no question that the demands are much greater on the mother, particularly if she is breastfeeding."

Many men were frustrated because their wives were too tired in the early months following a multiple birth to reestablish an intimate marital relationship, but most recognized that the situation would improve with patience and time. Said one, "Expect the maximum of a kiss in the early months." Another father, however, expressed his own anxieties, "I worried that if we were too sexually active we might have another set of twins." Most agreed that the investment of time and energy at home gave them great satisfaction and gave their wives support that helped foster a strong family and marital bond. As one father of twins so aptly summed it all up, "My wife and I are not able to spend as much time 'doing our own things' anymore, and that causes tension. But I believe that the stress [of raising twins] has forged our marriage, made it stronger, and given us a strong purpose."

CHAPTER 10

Siblings: Older and Younger

One of the greatest concerns of expectant and new parents of twins is how their older child or children will adapt to not just one but two new babies. Parents with older twins often worry about how a younger sibling will adjust to the attention focused on twins. Your older singleton's response to new baby twins depends on many considerations, including the child's age, personality, the sex of the babies, and the number of other children in the family.

A younger sibling's adjustment often depends on whether or not the twins look alike, whether they are of the same sex as the younger child, the age difference, the family's attitude about twinship, and the personalities of the children. The interrelationship of all of these factors and the outside influences, such as parental attitudes and home environment, can all affect the child's response and adaptability. If you have more than one older or younger child, consider how you can help each in a way that is appropriate to the child's age and stage of development.

Being a sibling of twins can be lonely, particularly for a child who was mommy's and daddy's only child before the twins arrived. Siblings of twins may yearn to be part of a twosome—like the twins, and like mommy and daddy. One study reports on a four year old who was frequently trying to separate her younger twin sisters. Unconsciously, she wanted to design her own twin relationship with one twin and to exclude the other. At times, she searched for other types of twin substitutes or for another mother figure who did not also have to care for twin rivals. For a singleton with siblings who are twins, normal jealousy can be intensified. Address problems as they arise. Do not ignore signs of anger or frustration. They may not go away and may become more deep-seated.

The comments and advice of experienced parents of twins in this chapter are designed to help you offer your singletons a warm and lasting bond of trust and love. Consider your child's feelings and fears, and select those suggestions that you think will be most helpful to your own family. If you are still worried about your singleton's adjustment, speak to your pediatrician for guidance or referral.

Older Siblings

Orientation

Sit down together and discuss the subject of twins before the birth if you know you are expecting two babies. Let your child know what to expect. With toddlers and preschoolers, the reality of twins may not be fully conveyed until two babies come home. Older children who can understand the concept will adjust to the idea more comfortably if given a little time. Provide an opportunity for questions, and try to answer directly and honestly. Your child will follow your example; if you feel comfortable about the arrival of the twins, your older son or daughter will probably feel comfortable about it, too.

Toddlers and Preschoolers

A toddler may scarcely even notice mommy's growing abdomen and may be too young to grasp the idea of one baby, not to mention two in mommy's tummy. One sixteen-month-old boy "seemed too young to comprehend the twins' arrival," according to his mother. A father remembers, "Our daughter was only fifteen months when the twins were born, and she thinks they are supposed to be there." Preparing your toddler for twins can be frustrating. Says another woman, "I pointed to my tummy, said 'baby,' and hoped for the best." Spend time talking to your toddler about babies. Your child will love to read stories about them and what they do and will happily watch the babies you see when you are out together.

Preschoolers of two and a half and older are usually interested in the arrival of a new baby. Even a two and a half year old, however, may not be able to connect the idea of a real baby with the kicks felt when touching mommy's tummy. Two babies do not seem to be of more consequence than one to a child at this age, yet he or she will be quick to point out on a daily basis how mommy's lap is getting smaller. One mother explained to her three and a half year old "how special she was to be having two babies that she could help mommy look after."

Mom's hospital stay can be frightening to some young children, particularly those who have not been separated from their mothers for any period of time. One preschooler saw a photo of a mother lion wrestling with her two cubs. He gave his teacher the following interpretation: "The babies are killing the mommy lion," he said, and he worried that the same thing would happen to his own mommy while she was at the hospital with the two babies. Reassure your preschool child ahead of time by taking a family tour of the hospital a month or more before the due date. If mom is confined to bed, dad can take the kids on the tour. Seeing where mommy is going helps eliminate the child's fears of imagined monsters.

A three or four year old can understand that two babies are special and will want to be involved in all of the planning. One woman took her four-year-old daughter with her to the obstetrician for a prenatal checkup to listen to the babies' heartbeats. After the babies' birth, in order to make her daughter feel special, "we gave her a special shirt that said 'New Big

Sister' to wear to preschool, and we went through her baby book and baby pictures and told stories about when she was a baby."

Let your preschooler help get the babies' room ready, by putting baby clothes into dresser drawers, or filling the changing table with diapers. As the babies' room is readied, particularly if this involves a room or crib-to-bed change for your older one, the concept of the impending arrival of two babies will become more real.

Let your singleton help you select a few new toys at the store to give to the babies. Then let your older child pick out something for himself or herself, too. Be sure to tell your child that the babies will be too small at first to play with the toys but will enjoy them as they get a bit older. As one mother pointed out to her three sons, "The babies will cry, sleep, and eat, and not much more, and they may be too small to play with you at the beginning." One woman told her daughter, "You can be mommy's special helper."

If twins are not diagnosed prior to delivery, neither you nor your singleton will have any time in advance to talk about this new development. After the arrival, tell your toddler or preschooler that the babies are his or hers, too, and that having two babies is special. Stress that although you enjoy having a special helper, your older child is not responsible for the babies' care. Give your older son or daughter as much extra affection as you can, emphasizing that you love this child as much as you did before the babies were born. One mother of unexpected twins emphasized, "Don't exclude the older child and be sure to give him extra special attention."

School-Age Children

The pre-arrival orientation is usually easier with school-age children. These older children understand the notion of twins, and they are usually enthusiastic about the news. Even at age

sixteen, one boy "just couldn't wait," according to his step-
mother. When the woman was still pregnant with the twins,
her stepson "went out and found jobs babysitting for families
with two or more small children to get himself ready." One
family with two boys ages six and eight hit the jackpot when
boy-girl twins arrived. "One wanted a sister, the other a
brother," remembers their mom, "and they thought I did it
just for them."

Give your school-age child an explanation that is appropriate for his or her age. Talk about what twins are—two babies
born to the same mother after the same pregnancy. For example, you might say, "At the beginning, the woman thinks she
is expecting only one baby, but there are actually two growing
in the mother's womb (uterus) at the same time." Then describe the two types of twins, simplifying when necessary.
"Identical twins have bodies that are designed exactly the
same way. This is why they are always the same sex—two
boys or two girls—and why they look very much alike. Fraternal twins may or may not look alike, and they are no more
similar in body design than any other two children in the
same family. They can be two boys, two girls, or a boy and a
girl. They merely happen to share the same birth date after
being in their mother's womb (uterus) together during the
same pregnancy."

After discussing how twins are formed, talk about how the
babies will affect the household. One mother "explained that
there would be lots of work to do, and that I would be tired."
If the twins come as a surprise on the delivery table, be
honest. Tell your child that you were surprised by the arrival
of two babies, and so was your doctor. When twins were born
to one unsuspecting family, their six year old "was a little
angry that we hadn't told him we were having two babies. We
ourselves didn't even know, and we tried to explain this and
set aside special time for him."

Let your child know that twins require more work but are
also more fun. Tell your singleton how pleased you are to
have him or her at home with you to share this experience.

The Homecoming

Bringing twins home from the hospital can be a joyous event for the whole family, especially if older siblings have been prepared for what to expect. But even if the twins were a surprise, talk to your older child before you bring the babies home. Once at home, let your older child hold the babies as soon as possible. This is an important "icebreaker." Be sure to pick a time when the babies are content, and then point out how the babies are happy to be held by their big brother or sister. Keep your older child involved, especially during these first few hours. For example, if it is feeding time, invite him or her to watch you nurse or to help give bottles. As an active participant, the older brother or sister will be encouraged to see these two new babies as an addition, not a polarizing force within the family.

Toddlers and Preschoolers

Invite your older child to visit with mommy and to meet the twins during the hospital stay. At checkout time, however, you may want to leave your singleton at home. The hospital staff and everyone in the lobby as you depart will fuss over the twins and may ignore your older one. This can be painful to a young and fragile ego. Your toddler or preschooler is curious to see the babies, but what he or she really wants is to have mommy back at home.

One mother made arrangements for her two-and-a-half-year-old son to play at a friend's house when she and the newborn twins came home. Once she was comfortably situated, with babies asleep and suitcase unpacked, her friend brought the older son home. "I gave Paul a great big hug, and we were not distracted or interrupted by crying babies," she remembers. "Then I held him for a while and he asked a lot of questions before we went together to look at the babies."

If your child is at home when you arrive, dad or a friend can bring the babies into the house so that mom can use both arms to hug your waiting child. Many families bring home a special gift from the babies. When one set of twins came home from the hospital, they brought their older brother a baby doll so that "mommy, daddy, and Peter could each have a baby." Some families give two dolls, one from each baby, so that the older child has twins just like mommy and daddy.

School-Age Children

Although small children may have trouble coping with all of the attention focused on the twins at the hospital on check-out day, a school-age child may relish the chance to be with you. Discuss the idea first to see whether your son or daughter would like to be there. Explain that there could be a lot of confusion as you try to get everything and everyone ready to leave, and that people at the hospital may want to stop and get a look at the twins. Then, if your child still wishes to come, make this a family event.

Once at home, school-age children may want to hold the babies, and this is a good way for them to develop an early bond with their new siblings. If your son or daughter offers to help, encourage it. Certain tasks can be anticipated in advance, such as unpacking the car and the suitcases. Helping gives this child a sense of satisfaction, both from feeling needed and from doing something constructive. As with preschoolers, school-age siblings of twins need to feel that they are still special and important. They appreciate getting a little gift from mom and dad when the babies arrive as a reminder that you still care. One eight year old, for example, received a pair of long-awaited roller skates.

The Period of Adjustment

Maintaining Continuity

A dependable daily schedule gives structure and order to your child's life. Regular activities, such as school, sports programs, music lessons, play group, or even just an afternoon nap, become an integral and reliable part of a child's day. Avoid nonessential changes during the month or two before or after the birth because the household routine itself will change dramatically once you have newborn twins at home. One mother counsels, "Resume normal activities as soon as possible."

For toddlers and preschoolers, toilet-training, a room change, or a switch from crib to bed is not usually advisable immediately before or after the new babies are born. Especially with preschoolers, any necessary schedule changes that you can anticipate, such as the beginning of the school year, should be planned and discussed with your child even before the twins are born.

One three and a half year old was having trouble adjusting at first. "She retreated to her room, and we experienced lots of tears," recalls her mother. After the mother was able to resume a normal household routine, such as fixing breakfast for her daughter, the little girl "reverted to her happy, well-adjusted self." A school-age brother or sister is thrust into greater independence with the arrival of a new baby whether willingly or not. When twins arrive, this displacement is more dramatic. The sudden addition of classes or day care after school may be misinterpreted by a child as a sign of your decreasing interest in him or her. Wait a while before making these kinds of changes if you can.

Developing Self-Assurance

Help your singleton maintain a sense of self-worth by showing respect for his or her ideas and by listening to any concerns and answering all questions, no matter how insignificant these issues may seem to you. Also, be sure to give praise as well as criticism. Avoid putting off questions, especially with comments that promote competition, such as "I can't come now; I'm feeding the babies." If you must make your child wait, a better response is, "I'd love to hear about it just as soon as I finish feeding the babies." Even if your son or daughter must then wait five or ten minutes, he or she knows you are interested.

Your older child does not want to lose your love and will need constant reassurance that his or her place of importance is not threatened. From the day twins come home, your older child will be competing for your attention, whether in an obvious or a subtle way. As one mother noted, although "there was much physical work with the babies, there was emotional work with our oldest," and said another, "My four year old was more demanding than the twins." A father of twins with an older child age two felt "learning to share parents and toys is difficult."

Although some children seem to adjust easily, others hold back their feelings until they can no longer carry them inside. This is a characteristic response even after the arrival of a single sibling, but the additional attention given to twins can aggravate the problem.

One three-year-old girl "did well on the surface," according to her mother. "She ignored the babies except when she wished to show them off." Later, despite all the additional attention her parents gave her, she expressed anger and hurt, saying, "I wish the babies would go away. I don't like it when you have those babies." When supertwins arrive, adjustment problems may be magnified. One little boy "felt pushed aside when the triplets were born," recalls his mother, "and for a long time he resented me for bringing the babies home." In their book, *Gemini: The psychology and phenomena of twins*, identical twin psychologists Judy W. Hagedorn and Janet W. Kizziar stress the importance of encouraging singleton siblings to express any negative feelings without being reprimanded. A child should not be permitted to abuse the twins; however abusive behavior may be avoided if the child is given the freedom to express hostilities verbally.

Common sense suggests avoiding comparisons. Do not tell friends how your older child cried more than the twins do, or how the babies are better feeders. Your child overhears this and thinks he or she does not please you as much as the babies do. How can this older child compete at the same level as a baby, and with not one but two tiny rivals? In the child's mind, it is too late to undo whatever he or she did as a baby that made mommy displeased. Nonjudgmental comparisons, however, can sometimes be effective, especially with small children. For example, you can help your toddler or preschooler feel more grown-up with a comment like, "The babies are very tiny and must wear diapers. You're a big girl now, and you can use a real toilet like mommy and daddy." Help promote a warm bond of friendship between your older children and the twins. Do not hesitate to announce publicly, "Amy never smiles as much as when her big sister Becky is playing with her, and Jason will do anything big brother Kevin asks him to do."

Learning to Help

Find things for your older child to do immediately, but only if he or she seems interested. Then be sure to show your appreciation and gratitude. A toddler or preschooler can fetch diapers, baby lotion, or baby clothes. One mother let her three year old "help as much as possible, and let him hold and feed the babies." School-age children can answer the phone, help you put away the laundry, and may even be able to give a bottle or change the babies. Your child will probably be happy to continue helping on a regular basis once he or she feels welcome to participate.

Do not force an unwilling or disinterested child to help, however, and do not ask an older child to clean up after the twins. Stress that although you appreciate having help, you love your child whether or not he or she helps you. With twins, there is a temptation to rely more heavily on your older children's help. This can be an unfair burden on an older sibling. One mother of twins who has three older sons cautions, "Don't place too much responsibility on older children as they will resent it or feel that they are responsible if there are problems." Then she adds, "I never pushed my six and a

half year old into caring for the twins. He may be their brother, but he is not their keeper."

You can, however, expect your child (if old enough) to clean up his or her own toys. A child can assume this responsibility on a regular basis. This may take some coaxing, and you may have to help at first or give an incentive or reward, such as a favorite snack. Try to use a positive rather than a negative approach. Tell your child how proud you are of this helpful behavior. Avoid ultimatums like, "No supper if you don't . . ." or "right to bed unless you . . ." Once your son or daughter is able to do the job alone, he or she will gradually learn to clean up without even being asked.

Finding Privacy

Another source of problems, especially for school-age siblings, is the invasion of their privacy by the babies. Twins, whether they are babies or toddlers, can get into mischief in all directions. Once they can crawl, the babies may become a threat to the quiet and comfort of your older child. When the twins begin to explore, they may be attracted to their older brother's or sister's toys or possessions. Favorite playthings can become broken, or homework disorganized or lost before the curious babies are ever discovered. Incidents of this kind are inevitable but can be minimized by keeping special toys, important papers, and breakable items out of babies' reach. Respect your older child's rights, too. Especially with school-age children, set aside a special place for him or her to keep prized possessions, a place that is out of reach of the babies. Also, give big brothers or sisters the freedom to play apart from the twins some of the time. One mother stresses, "Let older siblings have their own privacy."

Learning to Share

Babies can be especially curious about other people's things. If your older child seems interested in sharing with the twins, encourage him or her to select a small group of discarded toys or stuffed animals that are safe for infants. Then set aside a special time for big brother or sister to offer these gifts. This play session is good for all three children. The twins are delighted at the attention, and the older child is enthusiastic to share.

The more your son or daughter plays with the twins, the more he or she will enjoy their unqualified affection. This was confirmed by the mother of a six and a half year old who paid very little attention to his new sisters at first, but "as they developed and learned to talk and play, he found them very interesting." Small children, however, should not be left alone with babies. A toddler or preschooler may be reluctant to share, grabbing toys from the babies, or may get too rough. Find another activity or project for the older child when conflict seems inevitable.

Learning to Give Up the Limelight

Perhaps hardest of all for older siblings to accept graciously is giving up the limelight. Twins get attention wherever they go. The regular comments about the "adorable baby twins" in the stroller "made me very conscious of my older son," one mother admitted, "and I worried about his reaction." Another woman felt her three year old was happy at first to be a "big brother, but it was hard adjusting to two sisters and all the attention to them afterward." Your job as parents is to see that your older son's or daughter's feelings are considered, too. A simple comment can help if strangers ignore your older child, such as, "Yes, they are twins, and this is my big helper," or "Yes, the twins do look a lot alike, and this is their terrific big sister who looks just like me."

Visitors who bring gifts for the twins and forget the older child further complicate the world of siblings, particularly those under age five. With two baby gifts to buy, cost alone may discourage visitors from bringing an additional little something for big brother or sister. Such a remembrance, however, may be especially important to the sibling of twins whose adjustment may be more difficult than that of a sibling of a single newborn. Adjustment may be even harder if your oldest was an only child until the twins arrived. With toddlers or preschoolers, plan ahead for forgetful visitors with a ready collection of prewrapped trinkets or books. If your school-age child seems distressed about not receiving gifts, a promised future visit to the ice cream parlor or to see a movie will probably do the trick.

Getting Enough Attention

Your older child needs time with you even if he or she seems to be adjusting comfortably. Parents of twins often leave an older child alone as long as he or she is playing happily. This child needs to communicate with others, too, however. Designate at least a half-hour alone with your son

or daughter each day, and make this time an essential part of your daily schedule. Pick a relatively quiet time at home to spend together and read books, talk, or play a game. If this is impossible, find a regular person to watch the twins while you go out for a walk or a ride, or to the park, the library, or even the supermarket.

One mother of twins with an older daughter sets aside "special days with just her and myself." A new mother of two-month-old twins and a four-year-old daughter says, "We do special things with just her—lunch, shopping . . . , but just her, no babies." Most children will find ways to let you know that they need your attention. One four and a half year old "found his own little ways to get mom's help," his mother recalls. "He suddenly couldn't remember how to tie his shoes or to button his shirt."

Your child may feel left out because he or she does not have a twin. The chance to be alone with you will reassure your child that he or she is special, too. This time alone also gives you the opportunity to share your feelings and even to talk about problems if your child is old enough to discuss them with you. A scheduled activity once a week, such as a toddler play group, or time together at a Girl Scout meeting or regular soccer game is meaningful, too.

If you have more than one older child, finding time alone with each one is harder to do. Give each child private time with you whenever possible. Even when you cannot find time for each alone, let them share your attention among themselves, but without the twins.

Small children may latch onto daddy in the early months. In the child's mind, "If mommy belongs to the babies then daddy belongs to me." This exclusive attachment to daddy is usually brief, and mom should not view it as rejection. School-age children may be willing to watch mom attend to the twins all day if they can have her attention in the evening. After waiting patiently all day, this is not an unreasonable expectation, as hard as it may be for mom to comply. One family gave their six year old a special privilege to "stay up after the babies went to bed so she could be alone with mom and dad." Give your child as much attention as possible before bedtime, even if this means just sitting quietly together reading a book or helping with homework.

Toddlers and Preschoolers

Small children may compete with the twins, trying ever harder to be noticed. Regressive behavior, such as a return to thumbsucking, wetting, or baby talk, are some common ways a child may try to get more attention and may be more persistent in siblings of twins than in siblings of singletons. At seventeen months, one little girl had "temper tantrums and wanted to be held a lot more than before the twins came, especially when I held the babies," acknowledges one mother. Another woman with a three year old recalls, "He wanted constant reassurance I still loved him, too, by doing unacceptable things to get my attention."

An older child may even pick on the twins because this is a dependable way to get your attention. Negative feelings toward the babies, such as disappointment because they are too small to be playmates and aggressiveness stemming from jealousy of the twin relationship as well as of mom's attention can be channeled into more positive behavior. Nurture your child's ego and make him or her feel special, too. After the twins arrived, one family gave their sixteen-month-old son "a lot of special outings and attention, and times alone with each parent individually."

Preschoolers can also be very jealous or hurt if excluded from your activities with the babies. "I never took the twins out together without my older son unless he had something special of his own to do," said one mother. On occasion, when you happen to dress the twins alike, your toddler or preschooler may want a matching outfit, too. This can be accomplished simply and inexpensively with a smock or apron modeled after the babies' bibs, or with look-alike bonnets or hats. Even just dressing your older child in the same color as the twins will help him or her feel included. Psychologists

Hagedorn and Kizziar stress, however, that in general you should avoid focusing on similar outfits. This only makes your singleton feel that looking or being like someone else is desirable and important.

School-Age Children

With school-age children, their maturity gives them a greater understanding of the changed family structure brought about by the arrival of twins. This very ability to understand, however, makes your older child more aware of the change in his or her own role within the family. Your school-age child may act withdrawn or despondent, may misbehave at home or at school, or may show off whenever possible. Curious school friends or neighbors, who may never have seen infant twins, may suddenly become very interested in hanging around. Your child may enjoy this sudden popularity, but would prefer to get this attention as a result of his or her own actions, and at first may be jealous or resentful.

The mother of one six and a half year old "felt at times my daughter was left out because of the attention that was given to the twins." These feelings may be magnified as time goes by or by other circumstances beyond your control. One woman gave birth to twin boys on her own birthday. Her older son thought she had purposely planned it that way. "You think the twins are special," he accused. "You even had them on your birthday."

Although school-age children may have adjustment problems when twins arrive, they may have trouble discussing their feelings and fears with you. They may not even be consciously aware of what is bothering them. As one mother suggests, "Get out of the house with your child if he or she seems troubled, even if it means hiring a babysitter for the twins." Have an open discussion, and let your son or daughter know that you do care and do love him or her very much.

Younger Siblings

Attitudes About the Twins

Younger siblings have never experienced life without the twins, so they generally take their circumstances for granted. This was confirmed by one mother of identical sons and a younger daughter, "Merrilee assumes that everybody has two brothers that look alike." In families with twins who do not look or act much alike, younger children often do not even regard the twins as special or different. Said one woman, "Because our twins are boy-girl, our younger daughter never even thinks of them as a twosome." Another woman who has fraternal boys and a younger daughter says her little girl does not think of the twins as different or special. "She just thinks twins are two people who are born on the same day and have the same birthday." Identical or look-alike pairs, however, can be a source of confusion to younger siblings. The younger sister of one set of identical boys "has always been able to tell the twins apart," but another little girl with four-year-old identical brothers calls both by the name of whichever twin is more aggressive that week. Says her mother, "Renee was able to tell the boys apart from the time she could talk, but now I'm not sure if she really does know who's who anymore."

The Relationship Between Twins and Younger Siblings

Some twins are so dissimilar that their younger brothers or sisters rarely respond to them as a team. "Joelle relates to her brothers individually," notes a woman with fraternal sons and a younger daughter. "She relates to them as two brothers who are four years older." Another family's younger son arrived when the boy-girl twins were just over two. "He is now very close to his older brother," maintains his mother. Sometimes, however, the twins do team up either with or against the younger sibling. One such pair tattle on their sister, says their mom, "but by the same token, they make sure she's not going to do anything to hurt herself." Most of the time they look after her, their mother adds. "They're like mother hens!" Once in a while the younger child is invited to participate as part of the team. One set of identical boys and their younger sister are exactly two years apart. An unusual situation developed within this twin-sibling trio in a unique and fascinating

way. "Our boys were late talkers and used their own language," their mother remembers. "Our daughter learned to talk, using the twins' own language and calling the boys by the names they used for each other. They have always thought of their sister as a third one of them."

According to parents of twins in the survey, the bonds of sibling friendship are stronger than jealousy or rivalry. "I don't think Elizabeth is ever going to feel jealous because they are twins," felt one woman, "maybe because they are boys or because they are older, but not because they are twins." Another mother said that although her daughter does compete for the attention given to her twin brothers, "she also likes to have their approval." A third woman feels that in adulthood her twins and their younger sister "are going to be the best of friends." "I definitely would encourage people to have more kids once they have had twins," added another woman. "It gets much easier the next time around."

CHAPTER 11

The Twins

For the nine months before twins emerge from the womb they must share the nutrients from their mother's body and must occupy the same ever-diminishing space. Unlike a single fetus, a developing twin cannot even be soothed by the sound of its mother's heartbeats without the counterpoint of the other baby's beating heart. Twins begin to develop a special bond from the earliest stages of fetal growth. Identicals have a greater predisposition for similarity because they are genetically alike. Both fraternals and identicals, however, have a shared beginning, and it is not until after birth that those around the twins can help strengthen or weaken the ties that bind them.

Although the bond between twins is strong, the parents' attitudes and the personalities of the children also help define the kind of relationship twins have with one another, with their families, and with others around them. Understanding the unique emotional needs of twins, in addition to their physiological development, not only fosters twin children's happy relationship with their parents but also promotes a warm and comfortable bond in their growth as a team and as individuals.

New parents may be able to anticipate the physical demands of caring for two babies, but few are prepared for the psychological impact, including special problems with behavior and socialization. Parents may feel inadequate or unfulfilled because they are unable to give their children much individual attention, but the rewards of twin parenthood are good compensation. Says one mother of five-year-old identicals, "I still feel somewhat cheated because I didn't get to spend a lot of time just holding one baby, but it's really great to watch them grow—raised the same way, yet so different in personality, reaction to the world, etc."

Parental Influences

Focusing on your children's twinness can be fun for you and for the children themselves as they get older. Even at an early age, however, it is also important to let twins discover their separate merits and not to seek attention solely on the basis of their look-alike qualities or their appeal as a twosome. Once they reach adulthood, twins must be able to function effectively within society as two separate and independent people. Some of the early choices you make can contribute greatly one way or the other to the emotional stability and well-being of the children. Selecting rhyming names, identical clothes, and matched toys, for example, stresses similarity rather than individuality and may hinder the children's growth and development as individuals. Thus, you should consider how the decisions you make will affect the twins' social development.

Name Choices

Each family has its own criteria for name selection. Some prefer traditional family names or names that will be easy for the children to recognize and pronounce at an early age. Others want a matching pair (such as Brenda and Glenda, Louis and Louise, or Don and Dan), or two that are distinctly different (such as Brenda and Janice, Louis and Diane, or Don and Allan). For still others, any names will do as long as both parents can agree. Parents of twins find it hard enough to choose appealing combinations for all three possibilities (two boys, two girls, or a boy and a girl). Selecting names that will also consider the children's own feelings and needs as they grow further complicates the process.

Confused identities is one of the most significant problems faced by young twins, particularly identicals. This problem can be magnified by the use of similar names that are often attractive to parents but confusing to the children themselves. Dissimilar names enable each child to develop an awareness of self as separate from his or her ever-present twin. Another consideration is simplicity and importance. Avoid giving one twin an easy or familiar name and the other a name that is awkward or is hard to spell or to pronounce (such as Ann and Brunhilde), and try to give each child an equally important or meaningful name.

Call your children by their names, and do not refer to them as "the twins." Their emotional security and psychological well-being are bolstered by your encouragement and support. Help them recognize that they are two individuals who happen to have a special bond, not two parts of a whole who are not important unless they are together.

Clothing

Most of the families surveyed for this book said they dressed their children alike at least some of the time. Reasons varied from, "It was fun to show them off," and "It was easier to pick out two matched outfits," to "All the baby gifts were identical," and "They wore matching outfits only on special occasions." One mother had another reason. "When we were on outings, it was easier to spot the children when they got away from us." On those occasions, she even dressed her older son in the same outfit. A mother of triplets used the opposite approach. "I went on vacation with the children and didn't dress them at all alike," she noted, "and no one noticed or bothered us."

Some parents would not even consider matched outfits, as one father made clear. "Dressing twins alike is too much like a freak show. They are two individuals and deserve to be treated as such."

Although some parents were adamantly against two-of-a-kind outfits at any time, one woman confessed, "I swore in advance I wouldn't dress the twins alike, but I did because they received look-alike clothes, and when I put them on, I thought it looked cute." You may enjoy dressing your twins alike, especially when they are infants. Matched clothing when worn regularly, however, can become a crutch when the children get older because they may begin to use their look-alike attire as an attention-getting device.

If you do prefer matching wardrobes, color coding (with separate colors regularly assigned to each child) can help others distinguish between twins who look alike. If you have older singletons, you can use hand-me-down clothing for the twins. Although families in the survey had different feelings on the clothing question, at least one mother felt it was much ado about nothing. "I didn't really care what my twins wore," she maintained, "as long as they were clean, dry, and happy."

Toys

Choosing toys for twins can become a complicated process. Some of the common assumptions parents make about twins may not be true. For example, boy-girl sets are not necessarily more willing to accept the idea of different playthings, and identicals do not always share toys more easily than fraternals. The children's own personalities will probably help you decide what to do.

During the possessive toddler stage, despite the expense, some families believe in buying matching toys in order to keep the peace. Others feel that giving different toys to each twin or having a select group of toys for both children promotes sharing and provides diversity in their playthings. Two-of-a-kind toys can prevent unnecessary jealousy in the case of some important gifts. With large items (such as a rocking horse), however, you may not be able to afford two, and one may be adequate.

Safety should always be the top priority in selecting toys. The Consumer Product Safety Commission (see Appendix I for the address and phone number) can provide you with a description of toys that could be unsafe. In addition, when selecting playthings, be sure to consider whether twin children could use these toys to harm one another, either intentionally or accidentally.

Sleeping Arrangements

Families with a large home often wonder whether and at what age to put the twins in separate rooms. Most favor keeping the children together at least during the first year because, as explained by three different parents, "They sleep better together," "Baby care is more convenient," and "They prefer it." Sleep problems may necessitate separating twins at an early age. A temporary crib, playpen, or bassinette in a nearby room can be helpful for especially difficult nights. Separate rooms may be your last resort if one or both are particularly wakeful and regularly keep each other up at night and at nap times. Sharing a room and learning to sleep through the disturbances made by a wakeful twin or sibling also helps children become accustomed to sleeping through normal household noises (the telephone, a dog barking, the vacuum cleaner).

The emotional bond between identicals may be so strong that the children prefer to remain together even as they get older. "Our identical twins sleep in the same room," offered one woman. "At bedtime, after we have tucked them in, they carry on long conversations with each other." Many parents report putting their identicals into separate beds at night only to find them sharing the same bed in the morning. Said one mother of three-year-old boys, "Our twins often get in the same bed and take each other's pajamas and diapers off." How to handle the room situation is less predictable with same-sex fraternals, depending on the ages of the children and how well they get along together. Boy-girl pairs, however, are usually separated before reaching school age, but this, too, is not a rigid rule. If your boy-girl twins are still resistant to make the change by the time they start kindergarten and if you are worried, talk to your pediatrician.

Parents sometimes worry about their children's development as individuals and want to separate them even when they may not be ready. Forcibly separating twins for any reason can be traumatic for them, as one distraught mother of a three-year-old boy-girl pair found out. "We separated the twins at the age of two when they gave up their cribs. This was a real mistake. The doctor felt we should put our boy twin in his older brother's room before our older son began to expect a permanent room of his own. After our daughter was separated from her twin brother she was not able to sleep at night, so we moved them back together again. Finally, at four and a half they [the twins] told me they wanted to have their own rooms." Let the children decide when they are ready and willing to make the change.

School Readiness

The question of school readiness has become a major issue in recent years for parents of twins. Whether or not their chronological age is appropriate for kindergarten, the twins (one or both) may not yet have developed age-appropriate academic, social, and physical skills by age five. In some cases, developmental delays arising out of prematurity or the closeness of the twinship bond may inhibit the children's need to look beyond themselves for playmates or role models. In addition, because they can entertain one another, twins may also be less motivated to explore the physical world around them.

Sometimes a combination of effects leaves parents in doubt about either or both of their twins' school readiness. "My girls are very small for their age," says the mother of four-year-old fraternals who have a September birthday and were born prematurely. "They were tested at our local school for their academic readiness to enter kindergarten next fall. The teacher who gave them the test said they have above average academic skills," she continues, "but I am worried about their adjustment to the big school next year. They have always provided each other with security, but they may not have that luxury in the big school. I feel that if I wait an extra year, they may be more self-confident and they may even be comfortable about separate classrooms."

If one twin is developmentally more mature than the other, he or she may be ready for kindergarten before the other. Letting one enter school ahead of the other may or may not be traumatic to the twins, depending upon such considerations as how independent they are of one another and whether they are identical or fraternal and of the same or of opposite sex. The decision to let one twin begin school before the other, however, should only be made with the help of a psychologist and/or an education specialist.

School Placement

Parents and educators alike disagree on whether to keep twins together in the same classroom or to separate them once they enter school. Those who favor separation feel this stimulates the twins' self-confidence and their growth as individuals, reduces competition between them, promotes achievement and scholarship, and in the case of look-alikes, encourages others to get to know them while discouraging comparisons. Those who support togetherness at school feel twins are often "in tune" with one another and can concentrate better in each other's presence, that some work better as a team than alone, and that any comparisons made by teachers or classmates motivate each of the twins to excel.

In a survey of 320 mothers of twins that was published in 1967 in Amram Scheinfeld's book *Twins and Supertwins*, Scheinfeld asked these women about their school placement preferences for their twins. In their responses, 31 percent of the mothers preferred their twins to remain together in the same classroom, 62 percent wanted the twins to be in separate classrooms from the start, and 7 percent were undecided. These percentages were relatively constant regardless of whether the twins were identicals, same-sex fraternals, or opposite-sex fraternals.

A more recent study done in 1976 examined the attitudes of parents, principals, and twins themselves. The report, by Ramona Emmons, then a Ph.D. candidate at Purdue University, examined twins' class placement at the elementary school level and showed even greater parental preference for separation at school and a strong commitment by principals to place

twins in different classrooms. Twins themselves in this study, however, were less inclined toward separate placement.

Emmons randomly selected 168 principals from state school directories in ten states. She surveyed these principals, the 249 twin pairs enrolled at the schools, and the parents of these twins. Only 55.1 percent of the surveyed twins preferred to be separated, but the percentage of twins who were actually separated was 77.5 percent. The report indicated that 78.5 percent of the parents and 83 percent of the principals favored separate placement. Of the principals, 9.1 percent said that they would send twins to different schools if the number of classrooms did not allow for the twins to be separated, and only 3.7 percent of those principals responding indicated that they were flexible in their placement of twins.

Parents and principals alike identified the principal as the one who decided school placement, but parents indicated the desire to participate in decision-making concerning their twins' class placement.

What works well for some children may not for others. School does not have to be stressful for twins. Psychologist David Hay, director of Australia's ongoing La Trobe University twin study, analyzed 560 sets of school-age twins. He concluded that the best policy for placing twins in school is "no policy, except that each case should be decided on its specific merits." Dr. Hay believes that a wise teacher or school administrator recognizes the need to consider the feelings of the twins themselves and their parents before determining class assignments. The children will be more comfortable with their class assignments if they and their parents have helped make the decision. School placement should be reexamined each year to determine how well the current arrangement is working, more frequently if problems arise. More research is clearly needed to help design appropriate guidelines for twins' school placement.

Twinline, in Berkeley, California, makes five suggestions regarding school placement.

1. Do not separate twins who want to be together. Forced separation can damage self-esteem, inhibit language development, and delay learning.

2. Let nursery school twins be in the same room unless they show a real need to be separated.

3. Do not automatically separate twins in their first school year. Such a separation adds to the stress of starting school and may actually increase twins' need to be together.

4. Allow your twins as much independence as they are ready for. Twins flourish when allowed to separate on their own timetable.

5. Encourage the twins to choose separate classes as they gain confidence in the school situation.

Some parents are not sure how their twins will respond to separation at school and prefer to leave the final decision to the teacher. "I'm willing to take advice from a competent teacher," said one mother. "If the teacher suggested separating them, I would do it." Teachers and school administrators often know less about twins than parents themselves, though. You know your own children, and your own instincts will help you make the best decision for your twins.

Your children will give you warning signals if their school situation is not working out well. As one mother noted, "Last year in preschool, the twins had the same teacher. She compared them all year, and they didn't like it." Look to your children for positive signs, too. The same woman whose twins were unhappy at school last year gives an update, "This year the twins are still in the same classroom, but with two different teachers who think of the boys as two separate people. The twins love it."

If you feel that your twins' class placement or teacher assignment is causing them anxiety or promoting unhealthy competition, talk to the teacher or principal. You as parents are the only ones who can protect your children's interests, and it is your responsibility to help educate teachers on the relationship between twins, particularly your own.

Some parents are concerned about class placement even before their twins reach school age. "My children are at the same day care center. I know they would not want to be split up," insisted one woman. Other parents are more flexible. "They have been separated and they have been together in preschool. Both situations were fine." By the time twins reach school age, however, their parents seem to have an idea of what they want for their children. "My twins were placed in different kindergarten classes at my request," offered one mother, "and they have adjusted very well. They were together in nursery school, but it was hard for them to develop separate friends." For one set of eight-year-old fraternal boys, "separate classes started with kindergarten at our request," noted their mom. "There were tears at first, and then they adjusted. We as parents feel it is the best decision we ever made."

Whether identical or fraternal, some twins have more difficulty separating than others. One set of six-year-old boy-girl twins were reluctant to be apart, according to their mother. "They were in kindergarten together, and they advanced at their own pace. They are in different first-grade classes now. They were apprehensive, but seem to be handling it." Their mother feels "it is good for them to be apart now."

By contrast, in the case of a set of six-year-old look-alike boys, the separation went smoothly. "They were separated for kindergarten, and they both did well in separate classrooms. It was fine with me," acknowledges their mother. "They liked making their own friends, and each worried less about the other's work and accomplishments." Most twins seem to be able to adapt to whichever situation they encounter, and the way other children respond to them in a classroom situation seems to be more closely linked to the twins' personality traits than to their twin type or sex.

The Twin Relationship

The Bond

The bond between twins is manifested in a variety of ways. Some twins are independent and may be highly competitive.

Others do everything as a team, becoming very interdependent. Within still other sets, one twin dominates the other. Examples of these types of intrapair relationships can be found in fraternals and identicals. One mother describes her identical boys as "very close to each other but also competitive. I would like them to be less competitive," she adds, "but to remain very close throughout adulthood." Speaking of her three-year-old look-alike daughters, another mother was "glad they are real individuals and not like the twins I grew up with who were so 'put together' they had no identity." A mother of four-year-old opposite-sex twins asserts, "I think even boy-girl twins have a closer bond than do a brother and sister of different ages—like two old people sitting on the porch not needing to speak because they know what the other is thinking."

Parents may make twins more reliant upon each other, even if unintentionally. For one set of three-year-old fraternal girls, their mother's comments may become a self-fulfilling prophecy. "They have become a group unto themselves," she says. "Often I leave them with a babysitter because it is difficult to handle them together outside the home. But I am afraid they are missing out on a lot of important experiences."

Unlike this team, the three-year-old identical girls of another woman have a very different kind of relationship. According to their mother, one twin is more passive, "easygoing and always seems to give in." The other is more dominant, "strong-willed, always wants her way, and usually gets it."

Twins sometimes split up the territory. For example, one may concentrate on motor skills and the other may perfect social or communication skills. One mother of identical girls describes how "Fiona (first-born) did almost all things first; she was very aggressive and outgoing, and she was hardly afraid of anything. Alissa, the second-born, watched every little thing Fiona did. Then within weeks she'd be doing the same thing. Alissa, however, was first to actually speak, and her vocabulary has been very clear and distinct all along. Fiona now does a lot of mimicking."

Sometimes look-alike twins like to take advantage of their

twinness. Most adult identicals can remember at least one occasion as children when they playfully switched identities. This kind of secret camaraderie may bolster the twins' sense of security as a twosome. It is usually not a source of concern to parents, however, as long as the children do not switch roles constantly or intentionally hurt or embarrass others.

Communication and Language

Twins are together so much of the time that they learn to communicate easily with one another, often with gestures or facial expressions. They may not begin to experiment with speech until later than single children because they do not need it. Twins communicate feelings to one another and may mimic parental behavior, giving affection, praise, and discipline to one another as a parent would give to a child. A woman with thirteen-month-old boy-girl twins notes, "Betsy cautions Kenny, saying, 'no, no, no' whenever he approaches to take a toy away from her. She shakes her finger at him and furrows her brow. I feel like I'm watching myself in 'mini-replay,' " she admits.

Some pairs develop a sophisticated mode of communication, a kind of verbal shorthand, that is not understandable to others. The catch-all term used to describe such "twin talk" is *idioglossia* ("distinct language"). "Twin talk" is not limited to identical twins, contrary to common belief. As one mother of three-and-one-half-year-old fraternals remembers, "They talked to each other in a special language that would elicit laughter, anger, etc."

Research on twins since the 1930s has reported language deficiencies in twins. New evidence from recent studies, however, suggests that this established belief may be unfounded. Dr. Ronald S. Wilson of the University of Louisville School of Medicine who conducted long-range research on twins compared verbal IQ scores of 157 sets of twins and 56 pairs of siblings of twins. Wilson found that 44.5 percent of school-age twins scored as high as or higher than did their older siblings on verbal IQ tests.

An article by Svenka Savic, published in 1979 in the *Journal of Child Language*, observes that toddler twins frequently seem to complete one another's thoughts. Savic identifies three possible reasons why this might happen: (1) because the twins have the same thought in mind; (2) because the adult examiner believes the second twin's response to be a continuation of the first twin's thought; or (3) because of a combination of these two effects. This last possibility provides for the twins' beginning at an early age (perhaps even accidentally) to complete one another's thoughts, a process that may become continuous and acceptable to the children over time. Savic adds that although twins have been reported to make shorter utterances than singletons, this may be due to the unique way in which twin children use their speech rather than to a delay in language development.

Patricia Malmstrom, director of Twinline, conducted a study of toddler twins' language. In her report, which was published in 1980 by the Berkeley Linguistics Society of the University of California at Berkeley, Malmstrom concluded that what may have traditionally been considered deficiencies in twin language development may be a reflection of twin children's worldview and not a developmental lag. She identified three characteristics in the twins' language that reflected their twin-ship: (1) their use of double names for themselves and others; (2) their use of singular verbs with their double names; and (3) their use of "me" to refer to themselves together.

The unique way in which twins use their speech, as Savic and Malmstrom observed, is also identified in a 1982 report by researchers Pamela Waterman and Marilyn Shatz at the University of Michigan. Waterman and Shatz felt that toddler twins' language development is not delayed, but rather that twins undergo an additional step in acquiring names, first acknowledging and naming the twinship and then using individual names.

More research in this field not only may be able to define a "normal" pattern for twin language development but, as Malmstrom suggests, may even be able to help identify the relative strengths of a pair's identity as twins and as separate individuals.

Relationship with Others

Family

Twins get less parental attention than do singletons because they must share their parents. The mother of one pair of seven-month-old girls finds it "hard to pay full attention to one while the other is crying, so I sometimes feel each gets half of me and neither gets all of me." But twins can also reap the benefits of their double arrival and parallel upbringing. They are more independent, play cooperatively, and learn to share at an early age. As a result, the strong bond they have with one another seems to make them less reliant upon the rest of the family than is typically the case with singletons.

"My twins console each other," says the mother of a three-year-old boy-girl pair. "For example, if one gets hurt or is unhapppy, the other offers support. If I am angry at one, the other rushes in to protect the twin who is in trouble. Sometimes I feel left out," she confesses.

As hard as they may try to prevent it, parents may favor one twin over the other, even if only at certain times or under certain circumstances. In the words of a father of two-year-old boy-girl twins, "My son was my favorite at first, even though I always wanted a daughter, but now they share an equal relationship with me."

As parents, you may try to hide preferential feelings, but your singletons may not and may regard each of the twins differently, allowing natural favoritism or antagonism to emerge. This is a healthy response, even if it is distressing to you. Your older child may respond to each of the twins as an individual and not merely as part of a pair. This is helpful not only to the older child but also to the twins themselves as each learns to develop a sense of self-identity. Usually an older sibling's preferences are only temporary.

Older brothers and sisters, like parents, are an important influence on the twins, who may try to emulate an older sibling and may even compete with each other for the older child's attention. One set of identical boys who have a six-year-old sister "will do anything for her," says their mother. "They absolutely idolize her." Younger siblings are often "adopted" by the older twins, who beg to babysit at an early age, sharing the various responsibilities. Because of mom's time commitment to a new baby, the arrival of a younger sibling may push twins into a greater reliance upon one another, but this may be only temporary.

Friends

The close emotional ties between twins may inhibit them from seeking other friendships that are so important to their understanding of the world outside of one another. A close bond between the twins is a source of strength and reassurance to many twin children, but they should also be encouraged to expand their horizons. Introducing twins at an early age to other children can help promote their growth as individuals. In some cases, especially with boy-girl pairs, their interests may be so different that they are eager to have other friends. The mother of one such pair recalls her children's perennial complaint: "Mommy, we have no one to play with."

Strangers

Twins are a source of great interest to the general public and, depending upon how much they look alike, may attract a lot of attention. As babies in a stroller, they will bring you instant acclaim. Later the focus will switch to the children themselves in the case of look-alikes, or fade away in the case of dissimilar twins. Although you may enjoy being "on stage" some of the time, at other times you may become annoyed by the constant attention from curious onlookers.

Of greater concern, however, is the possible long-term effect on the twins themselves and on their brothers and sisters. "I enjoy the attention except for the extra time it takes to get anything accomplished," confided one woman, "but my husband is annoyed and thinks it may be bad both for the girls and for their older sister." The lack of privacy can be an imposition on a regular basis.

Trying to be constantly on good behavior and well attired can be a big burden, especially during the early months. One mother of infant twins expressed her dismay. "We were at the zoo," she began, "when a class of junior high school students who had been watching the monkeys suddenly noticed us. One girl shouted, 'Hey, everybody, look at the twins!' The class made an abrupt about-face and surrounded us. One of the twins began to cry. We had become the monkeys in the cage." As the twins get older, they may enjoy the public attention they attract. Because they get less individual parental attention than singletons do, they may seek additional attention from others as compensation.

CHAPTER 12

The First Year

Twin Care

First Three Months

The first three months with infant twins is more exhausting than with a singleton, and you may have trouble remaining cheerful. Fatigue and disorganization are the norm at first, but you will begin to restructure your home and your family by the end of these three months. You will gradually come to identify your twins' individual preferences and will learn to accommodate the needs and wants of both simultaneously. You will invest a tremendous amount of patience, confidence, and persistence in integrating their life pattern into your regular daily routine, but you will be amazed at how much you accomplish in a single day. The roughest period will soon be over, and the ritual of the next three months will be increasingly easier.

One mother of ten-month-old boy-girl twins described the rewards. "At approximately three months, when the smiles come and the eyes focus on you and a tickle gets a giggling response, it's all worth it. After that it's a piece of cake."

Coming Home

As you leave the hospital you will assume responsibility for the care of not one but two babies. If your twins are identical or look-alike, be sure you know the identity of each infant. Paint a toenail on one of the babies. Then write down which baby you "marked." Do not rely on memory alone. You are likely to forget in the midst of the confusion of your departure and your trip home.

Leaving the hospital with newborn twins, you will be instant celebrities. As one mother acknowledged, "Every passer-by will stop to admire or stare." At first you may feel a bit disconcerted by this new public interest focused on you, especially if you are not used to being in the limelight. In time you will either come to enjoy it or ignore it.

"The moment we got home from the hospital with our twins, the phone and doorbell began to ring," one father remembers. Avoid this by asking your friends to wait a week to ten days before calling or visiting. "Just to be safe," suggests an experienced mom, "put a note on the door with the following message: 'We'd love to have you meet our new babies just as soon as we all get rested and organized. Please call us in a week or two.' "

Phone calls can tire you out as much as visitors, so try to avoid talking on the phone for the first couple of weeks. One mother of quadruplets kept an answering machine on her telephone at all times so that she could call people back at her own convenience. Once you feel you are ready to have calls and visitors, limit the time and the number. Take the phone off the hook when you do not feel like talking, and leave the note on the door to discourage drop-ins.

Feedings and Sleep

Newborns respond primarily to their bodily needs, so they spend most of their time feeding and sleeping. They are aroused from sleep by an empty stomach, and once fed may have only a short period of wakefulness before dozing off again. New babies spend a lot of time sleeping, but the long stretches may never seem to come at the same time or in the middle of the night, when you need your rest. Thus, the primary goal for at least the first month or two is to get both babies to sleep through the middle-of-the-night feeding.

Twins seldom begin to do this at exactly the same time. You may prefer to feed both together during the day, but try not to awaken a sleeping baby during the night, even though his or her twin is up and ready for a feeding. By waking a baby at this hour, you condition him or her to continue demanding a night feeding. For several weeks you may have to feed each baby separately, getting up as many as four times at night. Encouraging both babies to sleep for successively longer periods at night, however, ensures more sleep for you later on.

Infants usually give up a night feeding when they no longer need the additional calories. For babies born at term, whether twins or singletons, this is usually around eleven pounds or twelve weeks (whichever comes first). At this point if your babies are still waking up, check with your pediatrician. He or she may suggest that you let them cry for a little while in the middle of the night before offering to feed them. Babies may go back to sleep without a feeding unless they are really hungry. They may begin to sleep through the feeding after two or three nights of crying for shorter and shorter periods.

You have reached the first important milestone once you have developed a predictable feeding routine for the twins and have "convinced" both to sleep through the night. One-week-old infants sleep 80 percent of the time, but by the end of three months they are usually taking only two regular naps per day (morning and afternoon) and may sleep ten hours at night.

Inevitably there will be fussy times of the day as well as happy, playful periods though the twins may not have these periods at the same time. In general, however, morning is usually relaxed and quiet, but late afternoon is frequently a time for fussiness because everyone is fatigued and tension is greatest. Fitful crying is common at this time of the day, and one twin may even respond to the other as if trying to see who can cry louder or more insistently. Pacifiers, swings, or cradles may help. If not, try a brisk walk or a bath (if the babies are not crying too frantically).

Some babies seem particularly colicky and some do not, and with twins sometimes colic only affects one baby. Do not blame yourselves if your babies have colic. It is unpleasant for parents as well as babies, but is usually outgrown by three months. Try to tune out the noise and to remain calm in spite of your fatigue, rather than dread your babies' usual fussy hours. If you are a nursing mother, your doctor may even suggest a small glass of wine to relax you and to help the milk let down for this otherwise hectic dinner-hour feeding.

As with singletons some twins seem to require additional sucking to calm themselves. This strong sucking urge may be a hereditary tendency. Many infants suck fingers or a thumb as they try to settle down. Thumb sucking, however, is a habit that can be difficult to break and may change the shape of the jaw and palate. This concern is often voiced by doctors and dentists. One old wives' tale maintains that a baby who sucks a thumb was not nursed long enough at the breast. Mothers who nurse generally refute this.

A pacifier may satisfy the sucking needs of some babies. Doctors, dentists and parents alike, however, dispute the pros and cons of pacifiers. If you do offer pacifiers to your babies, observe the safety caution given in Chapter 6 under "Small Articles and Toiletries."* Proponents of pacifiers feel that they can be soothing in the early weeks before most babies have the coordination to find a thumb consistently and that some babies do not develop a dependence on a thumb if a pacifier is offered during the first few days of life.

Many who oppose pacifiers feel they can become a crutch for parents who use them every time a baby whimpers. Some argue that thumbs and fingers are more natural than pacifiers, cannot be dropped or lost, and are always easily accessible. One mother remembers discovering her twins at age three months happily sucking each other's thumbs. "They were both content and were completely unaware of one another."

Hygiene

Bathing two babies can be a major ordeal if you try to conform to a rigid schedule. Try to pick the time of day when your twins are most agreeable. Skip the bath if they are having a particularly fussy day. Many pediatricians feel that a baby does not need a bath every day during the first three months as long as the face and neck, hands, and diaper region are kept clean. A daily bath may be necessary, however, as the babies get older and begin to get dirtier from solid foods or from play.

"I bathed my babies twice a week for the first two months, then daily," said one mother of six-month-olds. Another woman felt, "The baths were easier when they were really

---

*In addition, do not dip a pacifier in a sweetener. Sugar or corn syrup can be harmful to new teeth and can lead to a reliance on sugar. Honey, a known source of infant botulism spores, could be harmful to infants under twelve months (see the end of Chapter 7).

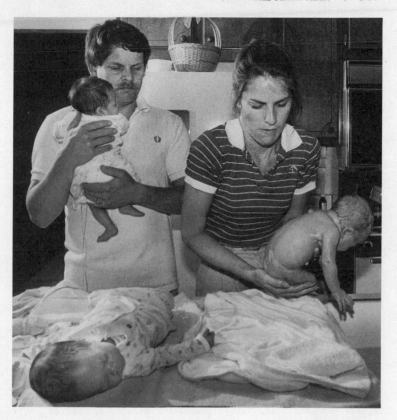

young. It got harder at about three months.'' Although a bath can be soothing, it can also infuriate an already unhappy twin who not only must be undressed and handled but must also wait patiently during the bath of his or her twin. Trying to bathe two fussy infants becomes a battle of wills, and afterward you may be more exhausted and ready for a nap than the babies.

You can bathe your twins in the kitchen sink, or use either a standard or an inflatable infant tub or a bathinette, or even put your infants directly into the big bath tub on a special molded infant sponge. (Baby bath tubs and the special sponge are available at stores that carry baby supplies.) Take the phone off the hook when you give your twins a bath. *Never leave an infant unattended in the bath.* The more quickly and efficiently you bathe the babies, the less you will disrupt their feeding and sleeping routine. They will probably sleep long and restfully after the bath. They may even enjoy their bath by the time they are eight weeks old.

Be sure to clean the diaper region regularly, even if you do not bathe your twins daily. Dirty and wet diapers can be very uncomfortable and can cause skin irritation if left unchanged for too long. Babies may or may not cry when they are wet or messy. Check their diapers often, and always change them before feedings and naps and at any other time it seems necessary. One mother suggests, "Always bathe, feed, and dress both twins at the same time [one right after the other] if possible. It saves time and energy." It also keeps you from wondering which baby has not been changed and provides for fewer interruptions in your own activities.

Attention

New babies need love and attention just as much as food and clean diapers. Their interaction with you is crucial to their social development. Your twins, by necessity, will get less attention than single babies, particularly if you also have older children. As new parents, do not be afraid to handle the babies; try to give each twin a little time alone with each of you. Identicals as well as fraternals have distinct personalities. Spend time alone with each child in order to get to know and enjoy them as separate and unique individuals. The six-year-old brother of one boy-girl pair says, "I play with both of them. I love my brother and my sister."

Giving special time to each baby is easier if their sleep schedules are slightly different so that one baby is awake when the other is sleeping. Spend time with each of them even if they are usually awake at the same time or if one is more demanding than the other. The quiet baby needs your attention just as much as the demanding infant. Offer your attention when you can, but do not worry when you cannot. One mother of fifteen-month-old boys wished she could have been "much more relaxed" during the early months. "I was so afraid the twins wouldn't get enough individual love and attention—and they got plenty."

Three to Six Months

In this three-month period your twins are becoming more attached to you, adapting their needs to your schedule, and you are becoming accustomed to the reorganization of your home and family. The twins are probably less demanding now than during the first three months, and you are now less housebound. The babies are also becoming more responsive, smiling at the sight of your face, at one another, or even at the sound of your voice, and their needs are getting more predictable, too. The exact hour for each function may still be evolving, but you may already be finding it easier to budget your time and plan your day.

It is becoming harder to remember what your life was like before the twins. They have become the dominant force in your home—the major source of your attention—and everything revolves around them. At around six months, just as you think you have become accustomed to their daily routine, however, the babies will begin to explore, venturing out in all directions with you following close behind.

Feedings and Meals

Most babies are efficient feeders by three months, and even burping them gets easier. Turning away from the breast or bottle, twins may begin to smile and "talk" to one another or hold hands while they are feeding. They are also learning to wait patiently (for a short period) while you prepare a bottle or a meal, although one may cry if the other gets fed first.

Your twins may want to sip from the cup you hold for them by the end of these three months.

Pediatricians have different opinions on when to introduce solid foods to a baby's diet. Some doctors advise adding cereal or fruit in the first month or two, but many recommend milk (breast or formula) alone for up to six months. Some parents like to begin with solids (usually after the last milk feeding of the night) even before three months because solids are digested more slowly than either milk or formula and may help a baby sleep longer. Remember that milk is the most important part of your babies' diet until they are a year old, however, so do not rush into cereal or fruit at the expense of the milk feedings. Check with your pediatrician for advice on when to introduce solid foods, how much, and what kind. Be sure your babies are getting enough milk by giving them their milk feeding before offering the solids.

Solid foods add a new dimension to feedings. Put your twins in infant seats or high chairs and position yourself between them, feeding both with the same bowl and spoon. The babies will be exchanging germs anyway since they share

and chew on the same toys. Your twins may help you hold the spoon by the time they are six months and may even want to hold their own teething biscuits or zwieback.

Sleep

Babies need less sleep now and become increasingly alert. They may be up half of the daytime hours by six months. Their daily routine may now consist of two naps, morning and afternoon, though they may not nap at exactly the same hours. They will gradually lengthen their nighttime sleeping hours, until they are getting around twelve hours by the time they are six months old. Your twins may awaken one another at nap time, but they will probably sleep more soundly at night. The babies may even sleep through the disturbances made by one another, as well as any other distracting household noises.

Hygiene

Your twins are now beginning to enjoy their bath. A bath in the tub can be a joyous respite from the daily routine, and the babies will kick and splash with delight. Most babies cannot yet sit up in a bath, however, but by now they are rapidly outgrowing the small baby tub or the sink. Your twins will be able to share a bath in a regular bath tub as soon as they can sit unsupported.

Even diapering twins is not as laborious a chore once they reach three months because they no longer need to be changed as frequently. You are probably still changing both babies before and after naps and before and after feedings, but they are now taking fewer naps and fewer feedings than during the first three months. Their habits are becoming more dependable as their daily routine takes on greater organization. Their messy diapers are also more predictable now, generally coming after feedings. You may not even need to wear the perennial burping diaper over your shoulder anymore, unless you have gassy babies. In many ways, your twins are now developing greater control over their bodily functions.

Six to Nine Months

Your twins will grow increasingly independent during this active three-month period. Just as they begin to venture apart and away from you, however, they will return to their psychological dependence on one another and on you. One father of seven-month-old boy-girl twins compared them to "constantly changing toys. If you don't like the way they act today, just wait until tomorrow."

Feedings and Meals

Feeding gets easier with each new step babies take toward independence. They will probably be able to burp efficiently without help by the time they can sit up. Then, with the introduction of solid foods followed by finger foods, the babies will no longer need as many time-consuming milk feedings. Gradually, the breast or bottle will be replaced by a cup, and your twins will be completely independent and self-feeding.

Breastfed babies may continue to nurse happily for many more months, or they (or their mother) may be ready to quit nursing. Sometimes one twin is ready to be weaned before the other. Some pediatricians recommend switching from formula to cow's milk as early as six months for nonallergic babies who are on bottles or a cup. Check with your doctor.

You may find it difficult to keep enough milk in the house once your twins are on cow's milk. Home delivery is very costly where it is available, and buying a quantity of milk to freeze is also unsatisfactory to many parents because homogenized milk may separate when frozen and may not defrost uniformly. Freezing does not affect the nutritional value of the milk, but some infants are reluctant to drink it once it has separated. Powdered milk may have preservatives or additives.

Your babies will probably be ready for finger foods about halfway through this three-month period. They will poke at small bits of food and catch whatever they can with a clumsy but persistent mittenlike grasp. They will examine each new taste and texture by squeezing it through their hands and smearing it across their trays or faces. "More food will end up 'outside' than 'inside,' " notes one mother. "They are very messy at meals and love to entertain each other with food messes."

The babies' weight-gain pattern may begin to slow down once they are on finger foods. Increasing mobility makes infants more active so they burn up more calories. In addition, as they become more adept at motor skills, they become less interested in eating. As with singletons, the slimming down process often begins by eight or nine months for twins born at term and continues as the children develop from crawlers to walkers and throughout the toddler period of the second year.

By about six months, your twins may also be interested in the way grown-ups eat and may watch you carefully at mealtime. They may want to sample your food or to sip from your glass while you are holding it, even if most of the liquid drizzles down their chins. As they get a bit older, they will want to hold the cup themselves. Give each of them a nontipping baby cup and fill it halfway with water. A bib made of molded plastic with a large catch-all pocket is also useful to catch the spills. Offer juice in the cups once your twins become more skillful. If they are drinking something they like, they may remain interested in the cup.

Some babies are ready to switch to a cup at this stage, and others will not be ready for many more months. "I first gave cups to my twins when they were eight months old," remembers one mother of boy-girl twins. "My son would not give up his bottle. Even at twelve months, he considered the cup a game. My daughter preferred to nurse and had little interest in the cup. I gave up in disappointment after many mistrials with both children. I did not have the patience or the perseverance at this point to coax my children into accepting a cup."

With twins the whole process demands a great deal of your energy. You cannot give a cup to one baby at a time without the other demanding equal treatment. Giving cups to both at once requires that you watch and guide each child individually and give encouragement to both simultaneously. Some babies are willing and ready to give up breast or bottle in favor of a cup by the time they are twelve months old; others are not. Some make the transition more easily if given time to develop greater dexterity. Do not be disappointed if the babies are not interested. Wait a few months and try again.

Sleep

The period around six months marks a distinct growth spurt toward increased motor development and greater mobility. Twins may enter the world of perpetual motion at different times or together. Such a growth period is often preceded by a "lull before the storm," with days of quiet as the babies nap for prolonged periods. Just as you begin to enjoy the additional leisure hours, the children will awaken from their hibernation with weeks of stored energy to let loose. Once this whirlwind has begun, babies may have trouble sleeping. They may be reluctant to quiet down for naps or night sleep with so much pent-up energy and such enthusiasm for every new discovery.

Middle-of-the-night wakefulness may also be a problem. For one set of eight-and-a-half-month-old girls, "the only problem so far is the sleeping through the night," their mom acknowledges. "If we could find the magic key to this, they would have a very happy mom and dad." If your twins are sleeping in the same room, they may keep each other awake as they resist sleep. Once asleep, however, they may not awaken one another if they are sound sleepers. Staggering their nap and bed times by ten minutes may help. Once the first baby dozes off, the second may go to sleep easily. Even a little crying or whimpering from the second-to-bed probably will not awaken the first who is already asleep.

Hygiene

Your babies may be dirtier than ever now that they can crawl and explore new terrain. Food that is well tasted and tested makes great fingerpaint. By now a small infant tub or even the bathroom or kitchen sink is probably too confining for baths. You will probably have to improvise until the twins are old enough to sit up unsupported in a regular bath tub. One mother suggests, "Fill the big bath tub with an inch or two of water and bathe each baby, one at a time. Lie the baby down on a rubber mat or a large sponge." You can bathe both babies together in the big tub as soon as they are comfortable sitting up. This is a great timesaver. Keep the water shallow for safety, and use a rubber mat. An infant can drown in two inches of water, so always take both babies out of the tub before leaving the room. Another quick method for getting two babies clean is to take them into the shower with you one by one. You can even do this on alternate days, as one father did. According to his wife, he "took one baby each day during the last minutes of his morning shower." Each child got a bath every other day and a few minutes of time alone with dad as a bonus.

Wading pools during the summer are a big hit with babies who can sit up on their own, but *never leave your babies unattended*, even to answer the phone or the door. A good rinse in the wading pool can be a big help, even without the soap and shampoo, and you may even be able to postpone a real bath until tomorrow.

You may still find it easier to change both babies at regular times during the day, before and after naps and feedings, changing diapers at least six times a day for each baby. Double-diapering if you are using cloth diapers will save you a lot of extra changes. You may even want to use triple diapers at night by the time the babies are nine months old.

Nine to Twelve Months

The babies' schedule is becoming predictable at this point. They are taking three meals a day (usually at the same time), one or two naps, and may sleep eleven or twelve hours at night. Sometime in these three months your twins may even give up a bottle or nursing at bedtime as they begin to talk themselves and each other to sleep. In addition, the babies are probably dry for long periods now, saving their wet or messy diapers for after meals.

Meals

Mealtime becomes easier as the twins learn to feed themselves. Bottle-fed babies learn to hold their own bottles and even begin to drink from a cup without assistance. Nursed babies become so efficient that they are finished in ten minutes. Finger foods become an integral part of their play and learning experience, as together they explore each food's color and shape as well as its taste and texture. Whatever you give to one twin the other will demand, and the faster eater may lean over to rob what remains of the slower one's meal. A lusty eater may actually tip over his or her own high chair in the process. Be especially careful of this kind of escape artist who, though strapped in securely, will tip over or wriggle out of his or her chair. Babies are self-sufficient feeders by the time they approach their first birthday, and they may even want to wipe their own trays. One set of twelve-month-old boys would even "wipe the floor if they spilled something," says their mother.

Sleep

Many babies now have well-established and predictable sleep patterns. Most are taking two naps (or one long afternoon nap) by twelve months and may sleep a full twelve-hour night. They may begin to have a harder time settling down or sleeping soundly now, however, as they are becoming more physically active. Twins may also awaken one another, especially at nap time.

Hygiene

The twins will no longer be clean-faced now that they are eating finger foods. Nothing is off limits for their total food adventure. They will regularly paint their hair and ears (their own and each other's) with breakfast, lunch, and dinner, not to mention those in-between snacks such as teething biscuits, crackers, and zwieback. As a result, the babies will need more frequent baths now. At this age they will be delighted to share their bath and will sit and play happily in a regular bath tub.

Watching two babies in the tub can be difficult, so keep the water level shallow and use a rubber mat. They may be frightened when you wash their hair, and if one cries, the second one may cry sympathetically. Both wet little bodies may simultaneously scramble to the edge of the tub to cling to you. Splashing contests may also be a favorite activity, so be prepared to get wet. Some parents even wear a rain slicker while giving the twins a bath. Have towels ready after the bath to take the babies out of the tub one by one without delay. *Never leave a baby in the tub if you must leave the room.*

By nine months with twins as with singletons, babies may want to explore their own bodies to find out what has been hiding under the diaper. Bath time provides the perfect opportunity. This curiosity is healthy and normal, and do not be surprised or upset if your twins also examine one another. This, too, is perfectly natural at this age. Leave diapers off for a while if the weather is warm enough.

Diaper changes are needed less frequently now because the babies have developed a pattern for their bodily functions. It may still be easier for you to change both whenever one needs a change, however. You can keep your twins on a diaper-changing schedule (with additional changes as needed) much like a nap or feeding schedule. Plan to change them regularly before and after naps and meals.

Development

The following timetable, which approximates that for single-tons, reflects an average situation for twins born at term without any complications or health problems and is based on the observations reported by parents of twins interviewed and surveyed for this book. Each family's situation is different, however. Your own babies may pass through the various formative stages more slowly, particularly if they were premature or were very small at birth, or they may reach the stages of development more quickly. They may even arrive at each phase at different times. For this reason, the timetable should not be used as a rigid developmental schedule. If your babies were born prematurely, ask your doctor to help you develop an appropriate timetable for your own children.

The First Three Months

Motor

Motor development in human infants, as with babies of most animal species, begins with the upper part of the body and moves downward. The head and neck muscles are the

first to gain strength, as can be seen by a baby's early attempts to raise his or her head. In time, the arms gain greater muscle control, followed by hand and finger coordination. The lower torso and legs are last to mature. Thus, babies have already greatly refined their motor ability by the time they have learned to crawl and later to walk.

The first three months mark a rapid and dramatic period in your twins' growth and development. By the end of these twelve weeks, the two helpless newborns you brought home from the hospital will be transformed into responsive and animated individuals, as alike or different as they may happen to be. They will no longer be ruled by reflexes alone as they develop voluntary muscle control.

By three months, infant twins may be able to lift their heads and watch one another while lying on their tummies with their chests up, and they may hold their heads up quite well when in their infant seats. They are beginning to use their arms to swipe at a cradle gym or dangling toy and may also begin to direct their swiping toward one another.

Twins may already be learning from one another. One mother of two-and-a-half-month-old girls felt that one of her twins was influenced by the other even at this early age. "Right now one flips and looks at the other, and the other one tries to copy her sister, but hasn't mastered the turn over."

Social

During the first three months, twins develop an awareness of an ever-present other baby, who like a second self feels completely familiar. They are beginning to respond to each other with gurgles and smiles. They have an increasing understanding of their own basic needs and are also becoming familiar with the family and the daily routine. They are learning to function within their environment, sleeping during the night hours and becoming more and more wakeful during the daytime. Their hungry times revolve ever more closely around the family's own meal hours as the babies adapt themselves to the patterns of the world around them.

As they develop physically, they are also becoming more aware of their environment and the people who are most important in providing their care and affection. Their crying is becoming less and less frequent, and is now used to express distinct and specific needs, with different kinds of cries to show hunger, discomfort, or frustration. When held, the twins respond according to who is holding them, becoming animated in body movement as well as expressions, especially when held by mommy. They break into instant smiles when they see mom, except if they are hungry, when they protest with insistent wails.

Three to Six Months

Motor

Babies' motor development during this three-month period is far more dramatic than during the previous three months.

Twins from three to six months become more aware of each other and the world around them as they master the skill and command the strength to roll over, sit unsupported, and creep. They have developed enough motor skills by about six months to be able to explore their surroundings alone or together, even if in a limited fashion. Twins almost inevitably influence one another's development. By the end of these three months, the less active baby will be content to watch his or her twin rather than attempt new activities.

Between three and six months, the twins will reach adeptly for each other and for objects that they can guide to their mouths for more careful study. Their legs, which are getting stronger, will push them first backward and later forward, too. Soon they will be able to move anywhere in a room, even if it takes time and determination. This sluggish leg action will be replaced by rapid-action crawling in the next three months.

Social

The twins are becoming more responsive and are also refining the subtleties of their moods. Now they can clearly convey feelings of pleasure, anger, disgust, or fear. They are gradually developing individual personalities, and this can be fascinating to observe. For one father, "watching them interact with one another" was what he enjoyed most about having twins. Now that the babies recognize all members of the family, they delight in the company of their brothers and sisters, as well as mom and dad and one another.

Mommy generally falls into a special class. You are their feeder, provider, diaper changer, playmate, and friend and not only reap the affection of their warmest laughter but must also endure their cries of infuriation and comfort their wails of despair.

Between three and six months a single baby becomes increasingly aware of separateness from mommy and when looking in a mirror learns to distinguish baby from mommy. Infant twins trying to sort out the various images can become confused, however, especially identicals who spend most of the day staring at a look-alike partner.

The babies will probably begin to notice one another around three or four months, though they will not become aware of their separateness for many months to come. By about four months, the twins will provide each other with good company, as they happily babble out loud. Put side by side in crib or playpen, they will "talk" to one another, watch each other's arms wave about, and may even begin "cooing and smiling back and forth," according to one mother of five month olds.

The babies are also delighted to have an older brother or sister talk to them or merely to be in the same room with an older sibling. Siblings are usually flattered by the attention at this stage, when the twins do not yet pose much of a threat because they lack sufficient coordination to challenge big brother or sister for toys. (See also Chapter 10, "Siblings: Older and Younger.")

Six to Nine Months

Motor

This three-month period marks the twins' physical awakening. They are branching out in new and usually opposite directions as they emerge from relative immobility and dependence and burst into activity. Along with this developing sense of freedom comes an insatiable curiosity that is manifested in every aspect of their daily routine. They explore every corner, both individually and as a team, as they learn to crawl. With some sets of twins, the more active baby is the model for the quieter, less mobile one. The first ("the mover") may spend weeks learning and perfecting his or her motor skills in preparation for crawling. The second ("the observer") may watch his or her twin's concerted efforts at crawling and may then catch on in a single day. Other twins develop separately and very independently.

But whether they spend weeks rocking back and forth on all fours and practicing crawling forward or whether they learn quickly by imitation, when your twins begin to move on their own, they will suddenly be in perpetual motion. During this three-month period, safety gates can help protect your babies from hazards such as stairwells, rooms with fireplaces, or utility rooms and to guard your important or fragile possessions such as decorative items, books or important papers, magazines, or even a sewing area. "I find that a gate on their door keeps them in their own room, where they can play with their own safe toys," volunteers an experienced mom.

Some children seem to master many skills at once, such as crawling, sitting up alone, and pulling up to stand. Twins may learn these skills on the same timetable or at different rates. Sometimes twins develop motor skills in different ways, as one mother remembers. "Barbara army-crawled; Amy didn't. Each got from a sitting position to the floor differently, too."

Babies develop a new perspective on all that surrounds them once they are able to sit unsupported, and twins may have distinct responses to this new vantage point. They will even begin to see each other differently and may begin to poke at each other's faces and even to pull one another's hair. Soon they will hug one another and wrestle playfully. Pulling up to stand can be a favorite trick, often before a baby has figured out how to sit back down.

"My son would practice standing up in his crib before falling asleep at night," remembers one mother of boy-girl twins. "Time after time he would cry frantically to be rescued. The night he finally discovered how to get down, our daughter began to cry. She, too, had learned the first half of her brother's trick."

Once they can stand, they will begin cruising along the furniture and opening kitchen drawers. Together twins can easily pull open even the heaviest drawers. All kinds of new hazards are now unleashed. One baby may smash the other's fingers in drawers or doors, and innocent household utensils, such as wooden spoons, may become hammers that can injure. The kitchen cupboard where you store your pots and pans may be safe for a single baby, but twins may sling the pots at one another or one may lock the other inside the cupboard. Keep safety latches on kitchen cabinets, cupboards, and drawers.

The twins are moving around more now and are developing greater dexterity, enabling them to examine small objects that are not always safe. Put all sharp, tiny, or breakable items into storage. If you have older children, put away any of their toys that could be hazardous to a baby, such as anything with small parts (Lego sets, Tinkertoys, toy workbench with tools). Small pieces can easily be swallowed or inserted into nose or ears, and long sharp objects can innocently become weapons. Babies can also be merciless toward fragile games, such as those with paper money or cards. Anything not crumpled or ripped will be chewed or drooled on.

Diaper pins are another potential danger once the twins can pull themselves up. Be careful where you put the pins during changes. Avoid leaving opened pins within reach of one twin while the other is being changed. Fasten diaper pins to your shirt if you are wearing old clothes. A wall-mounted pin cushion is another solution.

Social

By six months infant twins are usually aware that they are separate from mommy, but they still must learn to distinguish themselves as separate from one another. This confusion becomes evident as the children learn to recognize their own names, beginning around six months. Each may respond to either name for many months, however.

Mirrors continue to mystify twins, especially look-alikes. By this age most single babies are learning that a mirror is a reflection, but twins are often confused by reflected images. When a twin touches the inanimate mirror, he or she is bewildered by the cold smooth surface. One mother of identical boys remembers standing in front of a mirror holding one of her babies in her arms. "When he saw himself, he automatically assumed it was his twin, but he couldn't understand why there were two of me."

Sounds are also fascinating to a baby of six to nine months who is enchanted by the sound of his or her own voice. Twins enjoy listening to one another, too. "Our boys would take turns letting out a scream," recalls one mother. For one set of eight-month-old girls, "the big thing is screeching," says their mom, "and it's more a question of 'can you top this?' or 'I can scream louder than you.'"

Twins babble and chatter in turn or simultaneously in harmony, delighting in repeating the string of syllables they have learned. Twins usually learn from one another in these early attempts at speech, and because they have each other, they are less reliant on adults for conversation. The mother of one set of fraternal girls feels, "They learned to talk by being with each other."

By eight or nine months, playpens or other forms of confinement can be frustrating to a single baby who will respond with loud protestations. Twins, however, may be happy to remain in a playpen for many more months. They generally do not resist being confined to the same playpen, corral, or play room because they have each other's companionship. They must be supervised, however, because two can get into mischief even in a playpen.

Growing up together as ready-made playmates, twins do not seem to need the company of other children to the same extent that singletons do. Playing with other children while they are still young is also important, however. This will promote the twins' ability to improve their language and communication skills, to adapt to unfamiliar situations, and to learn to function individually and apart, as well as together as a team. Babies of six to nine months are only observing rather than playing with one another, but they do learn from this experience.

If you know other families with twins the same age as yours, these are useful friendships to encourage even at this early age. You and the other family may even be able to "mix and match" your twins at play time as the children get older, sending one of your twins to their house and bringing one of theirs to yours. This is one way twins can learn to play with other children both together and individually.

Nine to Twelve Months

Motor

Babies become increasingly mobile from nine to twelve months, learning to stand and maybe even to walk, with help and finally alone. Some infants walk before the end of their first year. Twins frequently learn motor skills from one another, and when the first twin begins to walk the second may suddenly stand up and walk, too. Sometimes, however, the second may not have any desire to follow the first twin's lead and may be content to let the leader do all the work, such as retrieving toys and investigating new terrain. Babies at this age also learn to climb up and down from chairs or stairs and may even be able to get out of a high chair, walker, crib, or playpen.

The more active the twins become, the more potential hazards they encounter, separately as well as together, and their play time must be closely supervised. Several available gadgets and devices are designed to help babies improve their motor

skills at this age. Walkers and walker-jumpers open up new territory for the babies to explore. Be prepared, however, for various new kinds of potential dangers and mischief-making. Twins turn into little whirling dervishes in their walkers, spinning all around the house, digging in plants, pulling down cans of food in the pantry, and dumping out the dog food. One twin may be more daring than the other and may lead the other into trouble by suggesting new ideas or by corralling the other and forcing him or her into a corner.

Social

Motor and social development are closely interrelated by the time babies are nine months old. Your twins may acquire new skills on the same timetable, each at his or her own pace, or may learn from one another. Each new accomplishment results in greater awareness and understanding of their environment. Learning to walk, for example, frees a baby's hands for exploration. Ironically, such a major step as walking can also be frightening and may cause a return to greater dependence. Your twins' realization that they can suddenly function apart from you and from each other fosters this separation anxiety, and they may return to greater emotional dependence on you and on each other. According to their parents, twins seem to experience less parental dependence than single babies, in spite of the normal anxieties common to this stage of their development. As each takes a step toward independence, the presence of his or her twin provides a sense of security. This mutual security can be both constructive and destructive, however, for as the babies comfortably relinquish some of their dependence on you, they may also become more reliant on each other.

Twins may spend a lot of time talking to one another at this stage. When one speaks the other listens attentively and then gives a response. They also are now able to express their affection for one another outwardly, as did one set of girls who would "pat heads and kiss." In addition, twins often develop a sense of protectiveness about one another, and one may become upset if his or her partner is threatened.

"My daughter would cry if a dog approached her twin brother, even if she herself was far away and safe," remembers one woman, "or she would become distressed whenever her twin got soap in his eyes during a hairwash. My son, however, has an unshakeable nature and was relatively unconcerned about his sister's fears."

The twins' protective or sympathetic responses toward one another will give way to competition when they are seeking your attention. Jealousy at this stage is constant. You may not be able to give equal time to each baby, but it is important that each sense your willingness to give affection, soothe a hurt, or just participate in play. Sometimes the twins' jealousy may be so constant that you have to feed both babies at exactly the same time and put both to bed simultaneously. Whatever one is eating the other may want, and you will have to give them equal portions of everything. If one has a temporary digestive problem and is on a special diet, you may even have to put their high chairs at opposite ends of the kitchen so that they cannot see that they are getting different foods. Sometimes handling their jealousy may exhaust you, but at other times you may even be amused by the gimmicks your twins will use to get your attention.

Jealousy at this age usually does not extend into play time. Twins are not only able to play happily alongside one another (like most single babies their age), but they may even play together. They probably will not show this same cooperation and favoritism to other babies, however. The twins may play hide-and-seek, may undress one another (particularly socks and shoes), trade their toys, and even hug each other. Their antics may seem innocent and can be great fun, but two babies can quickly get into trouble. Never leave them alone, even in the safest room. Together they are capable of mischief unthinkable for one baby alone. One eleven-month-old pair "pulled a long and heavy drawer down on themselves by sitting at opposite ends and pulling from both sides."

Babies are generally more responsive to children than to adults and are especially eager to please older brothers and

sisters. Infants may try to attract the interest of an older sibling by performing or clowning and will even endure roughhousing just to get big brother or sister's attention. Twins often entertain each other by mimicking an older brother or sister. (See also Chapter 10, "Siblings: Older and Younger.")

Babies between nine and twelve months may be fearful of strangers and may react with contagious crying. The twins are now aware of their identities apart from you and are more reluctant to accept newcomers. Strangers represent an intrusion on the security of their self-centered and twin-centered world. Both babies may even cry vigorously if the newcomer attempts to hold one of them or if the unfamiliar face is a man with a mustache or beard. Giving comfort and reassurance to two infants at once is not easy, and you may have to hold both simultaneously. By now you have undoubtedly become adept at the "double-barreled carry," one baby on each hip. Although the babies are fearful or uneasy around unknown adults, they generally accept new children without difficulty. They may study the child's face, but will usually accept him or her with blind trust.

Health

Colds and Other Viruses

Immunities transmitted by a mother to her developing babies during pregnancy give protection against some illnesses (though not the common cold) during the early months of life. By five or six months, however, these immunities may no longer be effective. Breast milk also has qualities that help protect nursing infants during the early weeks. Even healthy babies can be slowed down by a cold occasionally. Colds and other minor viruses are more common after about three months, especially among infants with older brothers and sisters who transmit the illnesses picked up at school or day care. At this point you will probably be getting out of the house more with the babies than you were during the first three months, and they will be exposed to more people and places outside of your protected home environment.

A rash on the face or body, mucus, watery eyes, general listlessness, and loss of appetite are typical symptoms of viruses, but can also be indications of other more serious conditions, especially if accompanied by a fever. Infants often run a high fever at the beginning of a cold, but to be safe, call your pediatrician if the fever is over 101 degrees (rectal) or if it lasts longer than a day or two. The doctor may prescribe medication such as baby aspirin or an aspirin substitute (*acetaminophen*).

Another common problem is ear infections that can develop as the aftermath of a cold or other virus. Babies with ear infections may not necessarily have a fever. Pulling on the ears or unusual irritability may be indications. All of these conditions warrant a call to the doctor.

Twins usually catch each other's colds or viruses. Isolating the sick twin and maintaining separate feeding routines takes a lot of effort. Even if you are careful to separate them, the second child is often exposed before you realize that the first child is ill.

You also have a responsibility as a parent to take care of yourself (getting more rest, drinking lots of fluids) so that you do not get sick, too. Just worrying about the babies can be emotionally and even physically draining. One father confessed, "I have finally learned not to be so concerned and have learned that they will survive the colds, coughs, and crying."

Congestion that typically accompanies a cold, flu, or other virus can interrupt babies' tranquil sleep, causing them to be more wakeful, restless, and uncomfortable. Infants may have more trouble sleeping soundly, particularly in the winter months during the flu season. They may lapse into a regular pattern of waking at night and may awaken each other. Even babies who have been regularly sleeping through the night may reestablish a pattern of night wakefulness, getting up one or more times during the night. After they have recovered from their colds, you may have to let them cry for a while in the middle of the night until they readjust to a regular sleeping pattern. Congestion not only makes sleeping difficult but also may cause problems at feeding time. A baby with a stuffy nose cannot breathe through his or her mouth while nursing or taking a bottle and may become frustrated and angry. A suction bulb syringe can be used to remove mucus from the nose before a feeding. You may also want to ask your pediatrician for a decongestant that is safe for infants.

Teething

Each baby experiences teething in a different way. Some drool for months, have runny noses, and chew frantically on their fingers (twins may even try to chew on one another's fingers) and on every rattle, toy, or teething ring in sight. They may even run a low-grade fever (under 101 degrees rectal). Others wake up one day with a totally unannounced new tooth. Most infants begin with visible symptoms of teething sometime between three and seven months, even if the first tooth does not erupt until later. The bottom incisors (two front teeth) are usually the first to appear. The gums become swollen as teething progresses. This is often accompanied by discomfort, as evidenced by a baby's crankiness or refusal to suck at the breast or bottle.

Teething rings (especially the fluid-filled kind that can be frozen) or even a cold wet washcloth to suck on can be very soothing. For greater and more immediate relief, however, nonprescription desensitizing gels are available that can be applied directly to the gums. Ask your pediatrician about these gels and about a safe dose of baby aspirin or aspirin substitute (*acetaminophen*) in case of a low-grade fever. Runny noses, colds, irritability, and loose stools may also accompany teething. Teething is usually only a minor annoyance, and discomfort to the babies is usually slight. In addition, it is unlikely that your twins will have teething discomfort on the same days.

Outings and Trips

Getting out of the house with twins requires a lot of energy at the beginning, but it gets easier in time. One mother felt "somewhat tied down at first, but after a few months, we just packed up the diaper bag and took off." Once the twins can ride in a seated position in their stroller, even with blankets or pillows as padding around each, they can watch each other as well as the scenery and may even be content to shop with you. By the time the babies reach six months, their twin stroller can be pared down to "bare bones," and with draft hoods and canopies cast aside, it becomes compact and more portable (see Chapter 6, "Stocking Up: Equipment and Layette").

One mother of eight-month-old twins says, "Weather permitting, we go out for a walk every day." Most parents are happy to expend the additional energy needed to get out of the house with their twins. The babies get their share of fresh air and sunshine, and mom and dad feel more energetic. These times out help the twins become more familiar with "the outside world." One mom even feels that "kids who stay with parents learn faster and learn to act so adults can stand them and want to be with them." After you all return home, you get to relax and unwind while two very tired babies take a long, restful nap.

Some families are eager to travel with their twins. "There was never a question that we would take the children to see their grandparents," insisted one woman. "They were nine months old and were great on the plane." Others are reluctant to go away with the twins. "Most of the time our families came to see us," admitted another woman. "It was hard enough just to get to the doctor's office once a month."

You may have family, friends, or relatives in faraway places who cannot believe you really have twins. Arrange a quiet trip just to see the family, and try to keep your plans simple by avoiding sightseeing. Many parents feel that traveling with twins is easier before six months—before they have begun to develop stubborn attachments to their home surroundings and may no longer be willing to sleep in an unfamiliar setting. In addition, while the twins are still small they may not yet be afraid of strangers and may still smile cheerfully at new faces.

Both parents should travel together if possible, because taking care of two infants during the journey is a two-person job. The time spent en route will be the hardest part of your trip, but this can be made much easier by preparing ahead. Plan to have everyone and everything ready one hour ahead of schedule in order to leave your house on time. You will need this extra hour for unexpected last-minute preparations (such as changing a messy diaper or finding and packing things you have forgotten) or to pack the car if you are driving.

Once you get to your destination the babies may be fussy after the long trip, and you will need an additional pair of hands. "On our first visit back home the twins were nine months old," begins one woman. "We had been on an airplane for five hours and our three year old was with us, too. We were mobbed by family and friends as we arrived, but once they had seen the twins, everyone ran out, leaving us alone to care for two tired, overstimulated babies and a cranky big brother." Make it clear in advance that you will need help right from the beginning.

Consider the length of your trip, the type of weather you might encounter, and the availability of laundry facilities before selecting which clothes to bring and how much. "I always kept a separate suitcase for the twins so that I did not have to rummage through their things to find my own," recalls one mother. Two babies' clothing, crib sheets, blankets, and miscellaneous paraphernalia occupy a lot of space, especially in winter when infants need heavier bedding and garments.

Your twin stroller can also be useful on a trip if you have the space to bring it with you. "We used the stroller a lot when we went sightseeing," noted one woman. Another woman who traveled frequently when her twins were babies felt "the stroller was great at times when we needed to feed babies their solid foods." Other equipment such as cribs, playpens, and even swings can usually be borrowed or rented at your destination. Arrange this ahead of time if possible.

While traveling, you can feed the babies their solids directly from baby food bottles if you buy commercial baby food. The unopened bottles can be easily carried and may not even need to be warmed, depending on your babies' own preferences. Always check the safety seal on top of each bottle before opening. It should be completely flat. If the top is not properly sealed, the food may be contaminated, and it must be discarded. If you need to warm baby food, unscrew the sealed top until it fits loosely. In order to warm the bottle completely, partially immerse it in 2 or 3 changes of hot tap water, changing the water each time it becomes cool. Try to anticipate how much your babies will eat before opening sealed bottles. Open only as many bottles as you need for a single feeding because once the bottles have been opened, they must be stored in a refrigerator. Some baby foods are now also available in dried or powdered form and only need to be mixed with water. This instant baby food is convenient when you travel because you can prepare only as much as you need for one meal and because you only need to add warm water in order to serve a warm meal. When preparing instant foods, however, be sure that the water you are using is safe for drinking. Use sterile bottled water for very young babies and wherever the water source is questionable.

CHAPTER 13

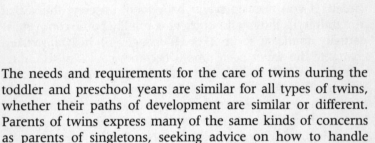

Toddlers and Preschoolers

The needs and requirements for the care of twins during the toddler and preschool years are similar for all types of twins, whether their paths of development are similar or different. Parents of twins express many of the same kinds of concerns as parents of singletons, seeking advice on how to handle toilet training, on fighting and biting, and on how to promote a willingness to share. Nevertheless, even after the first year, raising twins continues to present challenges that parents of singletons do not experience. In particular, the interaction between the twins affects the family dynamics, and can assist, complicate, or delay the learning process.

Single children practice a new skill over and over again until they become confident enough to take the step alone. Twins have an advantage; they can also learn by watching one another and by giving each other approval. "When our son began to walk it was most apparent that his twin sister observed his new stature before following suit two weeks later," noted one woman. In this case, one twin was a positive influence on the other. Sometimes twins are so interdependent, however, that they do not feel as strong a need for parental approval and do not try as hard. In this type of situation they may be slower to learn. Another woman worried that her three-year-old boys entering preschool were "less mature than other children their age because they have always been able to satisfy each other's needs."

Competition and sharing begin even before birth, and the twins' influence on one another often dominates all other influences. "Their desire to do things themselves and their own way creates hassles, mess, and frustration," begins the mother of three-year-old fraternal girls, "but they really keep each other entertained and happy." Educating twins provides many more variables than with singletons, and parents of twins must often chart their own course, finding their own solutions to even the most basic childrearing questions. "Most of the time they are like any two siblings," remarks the mother of four-year-old fraternal girls, "but every so often they unite into some kind of 'magical bond' when they lock out everyone else." Perhaps most of all, says another mother, "You worry that one might not do as well as the other in given areas." She advises parents to "avoid the built-in tendency to compare."

Learning Personal Habits

Eating and Drinking

Twins often respond as a team. This can even be true when they are learning personal skills. Many parents who also have older children feel that twins take care of themselves earlier and need less parental assistance. "The twins have always looked after each other," said the mother of a five-year-old singleton and three-year-old boy-girl twins. One set of identical boys "would feed themselves and each other even before they were two," remembers their mom. Sometimes, however, if the twins do not yet have the skills to master the task they are attempting, more adult help is needed to correct the mistake or clean up the mess. For example, when one set of three year olds decided to set the dinner table, "one poured the milk while the other held the cup. Unfortunately more milk went on the table than in the cups," remembers their mom.

Some toddlers, who in many ways have outgrown their babyhood, may still cling to their bottles for security. "Breaking our twins of the bottle was one of our biggest problems," said one woman. They may insist on bottles before nap and bed, even if they are willing to drink from a cup at mealtime. Ask your pediatrician for advice on the best time to break the bottle habit. Choose a week when the children are feeling well and when they have a normal routine (not when you are about to take a trip, when visitors are staying with you, or when the twins have just begun toilet training).

Most parents advise taking the bottles away all at once. "Our children cried themselves to sleep for two nights and I almost gave in," remembers one mom, "but by the third night they didn't cry at all. Later on, whenever they asked for bottles I just told them that I had given the bottles to a baby who needed them." Be firm; if you give in even once they will expect you to do it again. Do not take one twin's bottle away and let the other continue unless the first child tells you that he or she no longer wants a bottle. Says one mother, "I often wonder who is unwilling to give up the bottle, the mother or the children." Parents are often afraid to take the final step because they worry they have picked the wrong time or because they do not know how to be firm. When you decide the time is right, check with your pediatrician first. Then stay with your instincts. Talk to the doctor again if the children still seem upset after a week or two.

Grooming

Some twins have an unspoken mutual-care agreement, and with preschoolers, for example, one may become upset if the other has shoes on the wrong feet or a shirt on backward. One woman taught her daughters at age two to "dress themselves and put away their dirty clothes." This takes a lot of extra energy at first, but as they assume more responsibility they reinforce each other's sense of pride and accomplishment.

"Let them do for themselves as soon as possible," stresses one mom. Many twins undress and later dress one another, pulling off diapers or pants, socks, and shoes, and as they get older even helping each other to put on these very same items. Says the mother of four-year-olds, "My daughter always ties her twin brother's shoes for him." Some twins like to brush each other's hair, and some even enjoy scrubbing one another in the bath. "My twins love to wash each other's hair," offers one mother of three year olds, "but when one gets shampoo in the other's eyes they think it's my fault."

Toileting

Toilet training is a major issue with toddlers and preschoolers. Twins frequently learn as a team, either mimicking one another's performance on the toilet or jointly rebelling against the whole idea. This can be very frustrating for some parents who

would love to be finished with what one woman called "that whole messy business." Another anxious mother complains, "Potty training is not going well. At two and a half they aren't even willing to try." But an experienced mom counsels "patience, time, and lots of love."

Some parents devise a reward system—such as a cookie each time a child successfully uses the toilet. This can create undesirable competition between the twins, and the unsuccessful one who does not get a cookie may become resentful rather than motivated. Rewarding both children each time either one is successful may encourage both to try harder.

Many parents, however, feel that rewards are not the answer. One experienced mother of twins asserts, "Bribery for good performance is bad policy. After training five children I know they will train themselves when *they* are *ready*. Parents should relax!"

Give your twins encouragement at the times when they seem interested. Offer gentle praise when they are successful, but never compare one twin's success to the other's failure, and do not scold them for their accidents or their disinterest. In time they will want to emulate mommy and daddy, older

brothers and sisters, other children their age, or even one another. The motivation must come from within, and fortunately with many twins the enthusiasm is contagious.

Sleep

Night wakefulness is very common in young children who can conjure up scary monsters or creatures, especially at bedtime and especially in the dark. With twins, one's fear is often contagious to the other. Fear of the dark and of being alone (without a grown-up's protection) may be magnified as they lie in their beds and talk to each other. These fears can develop suddenly and without warning, soon becoming an established pattern. Talk to the children about what frightens them, and try to reassure them as they go to bed. Leave a lamp with a low-watt bulb (not just a night light) burning in the children's room in case they wake up in the middle of the night. Take a tour of the whole room together before bed. Look under beds, in closets and drawers, and behind curtains to show the children that no creatures are hiding there. Leave closets and drawers closed at night so no imagined monsters can jump out.

Some children are comforted by having a friendly stuffed animal monster of their own to take to bed each night for protection and security. Let them go to the toy store with you to pick out a creature-companion. "Give the children a kiss and added reassurance when you put them to bed," advises one mom, "but try to maintain your usual bedtime routine because children can also make a big deal out of nightmares just to get more attention."

"Parents need to be extra firm when putting their twins to bed," insists a woman with a three-and-a-half-year-old boy-girl pair. "Otherwise they can and will take advantage of you with constant and alternating demands to go to the toilet, to get a drink of water, to get one more good night kiss, and to have mommy or daddy lie down with them, first one and then the other." The bedtime ritual with twins can also be a headache for their parents because as one mother complains, "One always keeps the other awake." This can also happen periodically throughout the night.

If space permits, some parents temporarily separate their twins at night until they have outgrown this pattern of interrupted sleep. This does not work in every case, however, and some twins who are very close resist any kind of night separation. Although getting up with two restless children night after night can be very taxing on parents, psychologists generally advise against bringing little children into the parents' bed at night for comfort. This can become a regular expectation on the part of the child even long after the actual problem—the nightmare, illness, or hurt—has gone away.

One mother learned this the hard way. "We used to bring Betsy to bed with us on a regular basis whenever she would wake up at night because we didn't want her to wake her twin brother. Soon she began to expect this and would run into our room two and three times a night. As hard as it is, my husband or I now go to the twins' room to comfort Betsy at night. Sometimes we must actually lie down with her for a short while, but she is getting up less often now, not even every night anymore, so we think the problem is improving."

Resolving these kinds of sleep problems can take several months. Just giving up an afternoon nap may be the answer for some children, but as another mother of twins observed stoically, "Constant lack of sleep comes with the job. You just have to learn to adjust."

Good Behavior

Your children will like to please you and will feel proud when you give them praise. Toddlers and preschoolers, however, cannot be expected "to be seen and not heard," and even the best-behaved child is naughty some of the time. Twins often give each other incentive to be cooperative, but may also lead one another into mischief, whether intentionally or not. Here is one mother's example:

" 'Let's go pick flowers in Mrs. Edwards' yard,' I heard my three-year-old son say to his twin sister. They didn't realize this was not a nice thing to do, and I was glad I caught them in time."

Be patient with your children and explain the reasons why certain behavior is unacceptable. Show them you are pleased when they are thoughtful or well behaved. This was not so easy in one mother's case. In another flower-picking incident, the twins "cut all of their dad's prized roses and came in with huge bouquets. Their faces were glowing as they announced, 'We picked these just for you, mom.' I couldn't decide whether to hug them or cry."

When your twins are deliberately naughty, do not threaten them or take away privileges. Tell them you are disappointed and that you know they can behave better. Let them know when you are proud of their actions, too. Trying to discipline one naughty twin can be difficult, especially when you do not know which one was the culprit. Sit down quietly with both children together and explain why you are angry or disappointed. Tell them that you still love them, that you do not care who was to blame, but that you do not want it to happen again. Ask each child to repeat what you have just said or to promise not to repeat the undesirable behavior.

Keeping Their Belongings in Order

Twins can create at least twice the mess a single child can make and can also be very hard on their toys. Together they are more active and curious than even the most energetic singleton. When their interest turns to something belonging to mom or dad, "they take constant watching," says one mom. "What one doesn't think of the other one does." For this reason another woman warns, "It is imperative to child-proof the house." Until the twins have learned respect for their own personal possessions and those of others, usually by the time they reach school age, most need constant encouragement to put away their toys and books and to pick up their dirty clothes and deposit them in a designated place.

Sometimes, however, twins learn responsibility for their belongings earlier than singletons. They may help one another with cleanup, and the more willing child may be able to coax the more disinterested one even if the parents have been unsuccessful. One mother of two-year-old identical girls lets them "play with some of my things" because "they are always good about putting things back."

Learning to Function Together

Competition

Although or perhaps because they understand each other so well, twins can be very competitive. They share their parents, their possessions, and even their privacy, but not always willingly. One set of four-year-old identical boys have an up-and-down relationship according to their mother. "They are and have been either best friends or worst enemies," she says. "They either fight or hug and kiss each other."

During the second and third years when the children focus on their own ego needs and desires, they begin to become more self-centered, which may cause friction between them. "It was so much fun watching them develop," noted one mom, "but the biting and fighting was a surprise!" One set of identical girls "started fighting, hair pulling, scratching, or pinching" as early as eighteen months, but a pair of boy-girl twins, "play well together except when he takes her toy."

Fighting over toys presents you with a dilemma. Who should get the toy and for how long? When toddlers struggle over the same toy you need to supervise, giving each child a brief period of time. Using an egg timer or just counting to ten will sometimes satisfy the children. Encourage sharing so that later, as the children get old enough to control their own toys, they will be willing to share.

She bites him . . .

. . . he hits her back

Teething toddlers sometimes bite each other the way puppies chew on slippers. At first the biting baby has no intention of hurting. He or she will be startled by the outcries of the victim. At this stage, it is important to comfort the biter as well as the bitten child. In time, however, a child may begin to use biting to express anger or frustration, or to get attention. If this happens, separate the twins at the times when one or both are biting, and try to channel the biter's anger into a more constructive direction by offering something that is acceptable and satisfying to bite, such as a teething ring or hard crackers.

Some parents believe in biting back when their children behave this way. This gives mixed messages, since you are also telling them that biting is wrong. One mother gives her son his own hand to try whenever he bites his twin sister. "If you want to bite something, try this and see how it feels," is his mom's standard line, but she confesses that this method "doesn't exactly bring the results I had hoped for. He does stop biting his sister for the moment, but instead he directs his anger at me."

Jealousy seems to increase dramatically around the age of

two. "I thought they would play together more than they did," remembers a mother whose boys are now over three. "I wasn't ready for two 'terrible two's.' " Grandma's visits cause trouble for one set of identical girls. "One twin gets very upset if grandma holds the other," says the girls' mother. "She thinks grandma is hers." Fighting over mom and dad is even more common. "They compete for my attention," volunteers one frustrated mother of four year olds, "and I feel I can't ever give anything (food, love, etc.) without being questioned about why the other one can't have it (or go with me)."

Twins are not competitive all of the time, some more or less than others. One four-year-old pair, a boy and a girl, "are terrific playmates and very caring of each other," says their mother. Speaking of her fraternal girls now almost two, another mom notes, "One brings a toy for comfort when the other one has hurt herself." Even a woman who says her identical daughters have minds of their own, also describes them as "close—always together. They hold hands a lot." "Having a twin is like having a partner in life," maintains the mother of two-year-old girls, "sometimes in the way, but mostly someone to share everything with."

Although parents of twins sometimes feel like referees, at other times they are witnesses to the very special moments their twins share. "The obvious problems have been the double dose of temper tantrums, whining, mischievousness, and carrying two thirty-pounders at once," began one mother of three-year-olds. "But to see them share their food, toys, and love with each other, to observe their sophisticated pretend games, and to watch their special relationship to each other grow has been an incredible joy."

Now that her sons have graduated to school age, another mother can savor the memories of their preschool years together. "They were a built-in home entertainment center," she remembers. "We older members of the family have spent many hours playing with them and watching them jump, laugh, and play together and with us. We never tired of their antics, and the fact that there were two of them made it twice as fascinating."

Parents also describe the personal benefits they derived from watching their twins grow. "It's been a great learning process for us," says one woman whose three-year-old son and daughter are her only children. "We know ourselves better from seeing us in them."

Attracting Attention

While the twins are still in the stroller stage, attention is focused on you, their parents. Once the children no longer need a stroller, you may get little attention, and the twins themselves may even go unnoticed if they do not look alike or if they are not dressed alike. "Our twins look completely different," notes the mom of one set of three-year-old fraternals, "so they don't attract attention at all." A woman with four-year-old boy-girl twins claims, "People don't even notice my children are twins anymore. The boy is noticeably taller than his sister now, and people just assume that one is mine and I am babysitting for the other."

Look-alike twins, who continue to be noticed, may enjoy the attention, may dislike it, or may even be disinterested or unaware of it. One pair of identical girls "didn't realize they were twins until they were three," their mother maintains. "Now they act like a 'set' to satisfy public curiosity." These children may feel as though others only like them when they are together. A mother of identical boys maintains, "I think it bothers my children that people mix them up. People talk about it in front of them, and that's very insensitive. When Danny fell and got a black-and-blue bump on his forehead, he turned to his grandma and said, 'Now, I'm not a twin because I don't look like Sean anymore.'" Another woman confides, "I don't think they realized that they were twins until they went to school and saw that others couldn't tell them apart." Yet another woman whose identical boys are now three says, "Our twins seem to be oblivious to the attention they attract in public."

Some twins, however, are self-conscious about attention

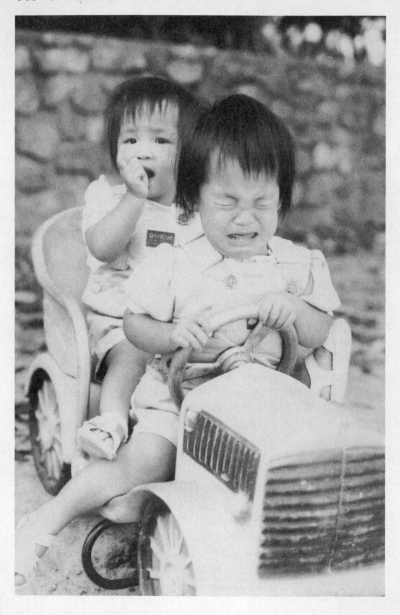

focused on them. "Our boys are very shy at times," notes one mother. Another who has a fifteen-month-old boy and girl feels her children like to be in the spotlight. "They enjoy it very much—the girl more than the boy." But, says a third woman whose twins are now six, "They either ignore it [public attention] or show off."

With twins, even those who do not look alike, people often call them by the wrong name or refer to them as "the twins." To avoid this, "I personalized their clothing so people would call them by their names," says a woman whose four-year-old girls are fraternals. "Like royalty, twins grow up expecting to be noticed," asserts one mother, "but unlike royalty, the twins are not recognized alone, only as part of a twosome."

Parents have a responsibility to protect their twins from insensitive comments or comparisons. As young children, twins begin to get messages through the remarks made by others. For example, if one child is labeled as the smarter twin, the other may become less motivated or may develop resentment toward his or her twin. As parents of twins, you must help educate the public, stressing that each twin is a real person with feelings and is entitled to consideration, thoughtfulness, and respect. You have an important responsibility as their parents to help each of your twins feel like a unique and special individual, particularly during these early years.

Leader/Follower

Twins necessarily spend a lot of time together. Parents describe three basic types of play relationships—joint activities with both children playing together and participating equally, separate activities with each child playing alone, and leader-follower activities. Some twins seem to prefer only one arrangement; others have more flexible play relationships. For example, one woman says her boys have no prearranged format. They "play independently, but also play well together."

Some twins seem to have an unspoken agreement with carefully defined roles, as with one set of fraternal boys whose mother says, "Brett is always the aggressor and Daniel the whiner." Others have a changeable arrangement. "My boys switch roles all the time," says one woman about her identicals. And a mother of a set of fraternal girls notes, "They alternate being the leader. There isn't an obviously more aggressive twin."

Occasionally, however, the plan seems to backfire. One mother tells how this happened with her identical boys. "When Jason, who had always been the follower, decided to assume the leadership role, Alexander began to have temper tantrums and began to cling to me. I couldn't figure out why Alexander was suddenly so upset until the boys' preschool teacher brought this to my attention. Alexander was unwilling to give up the leadership role at that point."

Even if your twins seem to prefer specific roles in their relationship with one another, encourage them to be as adaptable as possible. They will be encountering many different kinds of real-life situations as they grow, and they need to be able to function as both leader and follower, and apart as well as together.

Learning to Function Apart

Learning to be unique and separate individuals is often difficult for twins who spend so much of their time together. The children themselves may wonder whether they are two parts of a single being, particularly if they look alike and others constantly mistake one for the other. One mother of eight-year-old boys advises, "Prepare your twins for independence from each other by providing periods of separation as early as possible." She says her own children "seemed to have little need for friends until they started school and were separated."

Practice separations are necessary for many twins long before the children reach school age. Without these rehearsals, the twins may be devastated when they are suddenly forced to separate for school or anytime later in life. The mother of a

five-year-old boy and girl counsels, "Try to help each child develop his or her potential as an individual. Think of them as two separate beings." This is true for identicals as well as for fraternals. Some twins are more interdependent than others. One set of four-year-old fraternals "depends on each other and each really misses the other when she's not around," observes their mother. Another three-year-old pair is more independent. "When separated, they just ask where the other one is. They are not unhappy about it," notes their mom, "but they've never been separated for more than a day." A long separation, however, can be difficult for even the most adaptable twins. "At fifteen months, my wife took one boy on a long trip," begins one father. "The boy at home moped around the house because he had no one to interact with. It took him a week to come out of it."

Sometimes twins become more reliant on one another because of circumstances around them. For example, one set of two-and-a-half-year-old identical boys were more reluctant to leave one another for even short periods when their parents became separated. Says their father, "The boys sense anxiety, fear, tension, and resentment between the two households, and they are still affected by unresolved issues of the separation."

Twins are separate individuals and must necessarily be apart from one another at least some of the time. As they get older, they must begin to find interests that each can pursue individually as well as together. With one six-year-old set, "more definite tastes are developing that are pulling them apart," observes their mother. "Now one may go one way and the other another, where it has always been everything together. They seem somewhat reluctant to accept this fact. One is less mature than the other, and it is extremely hard not to compare them—as it has been all along." Keep in mind that they are two separate people and cannot be expected to act as one. Let them know that you understand this and give them time alone with each of you. As one mother stresses, "Use whatever resources you have to give them separate and individualized attention."

Learning to Socialize with Others

Making Friends

Some twins are easily able to expand their horizons to include other children when it comes to making friends. "They make friends easily and play well with others," says one mother about her own four-year-old boys. Branching out is not as easy for other pairs. The twins have "just recently begun to make friends," confides the mother of a five-year-old boy-girl pair. "They didn't at all before the age of four." A set of three-year-old identical boys "often said in the past that they don't like other children—only each other," remarks their mother. "Now they have just begun preschool and seem to be making their own friends for the first time."

Twins approach the subject of new friends in various ways. Some divide up the territory, with each child choosing his or her own playmates. Two-year-old twin girls who are currently in the same toddler program "interact as individuals with the other children and rarely with each other," according to their mom. "They are very comfortable with it," she continues, "yet, they also seem to be comfortable knowing the other one is there." This same kind of arrangement works well for a set of three-year-old boy-girl twins. Their mom says, "One plays with one group, and the other plays with other kids."

Sometimes, however, only one of the twins makes friends easily. The other may cling to his or her twin, to mom, or to the teacher, may retreat to a corner, or may have temper tantrums. In the case of one set of twenty-month-old fraternal girls, "One is more outgoing, a flirt and a 'ham'; the other is a 'momma's girl,' " observes their mother.

For a three-year-old boy-girl pair, making friends is relatively easy, but each child has a different approach. "Andrea goes to other people to make friends," her mother notes, "but Rick waits for others to come to him."

Some pairs generally share their friends, as with a pair of four-year-old girls who "seem to choose the same friends at preschool as if they have to agree on a choice." One mother says her three-year-old identical boys even "talk about the same people." Other twins are content with more than one type of arrangement. "They make friends easily and each has her own friends," said a mother of four-year-old girls, "but they also have friends in common."

Some twins remain very close to one another, each considering the welfare of the twosome before making friends with others. Sometimes the twins may not agree on how much time to give to other children, or one may try to structure the other's friendships. "My son always wants to hang around with his twin sister and her little friends," begins the mother of a three-and-a-half-year-old pair. "He wants to organize their activities and to be included in their play. My daughter gets angry when he intrudes, and she sometimes pushes him away or asks him to leave, which hurts his feelings. I have learned that each must have time alone with friends. Now whenever one of the twins gets an invitation, I let the other invite a friend to our house."

Making outside friendships and developing separate interests are important from an early age because doing so becomes increasingly difficult as the twins get older. Twins have a warm and loving bond and need their time together, but they also need to prepare themselves individually for the responsibilities of later life.

Protecting Each Other

With twins, concern for the other may be as great as concern for oneself. This may become more apparent as the children get older. If other children pick on one of the twins, both may retaliate. One mother of fraternal boys says, "They are best friends and very protective of each other." A set of three-year-old boy-girl twins are "protective of one another when around other children," their mom notes. The twins may be competitive or aggressive toward one another at home, but when together away from home, they suddenly become each other's best defender. "Right now Allan is very protective of Jacob," says one mom of her identical three-year-olds, "but sometimes they switch roles."

Some parents of boy-girl twins say that one of their twins plays the role of defender for both, but contrary to popular stereotypes, the boy is not necessarily the protector. With one three-year-old boy-girl set, "the girl is more aggressive and outspoken than the boy," when it comes to taking care of the needs of either or both, according to their mother.

Sharing

Sharing is a necessity of life during twins' prenatal existence. Then, as babies, they share their parents' love and attention and, in the case of breastfed twins, even their mother's milk. Although twins grow up learning to share with one another, some of their items should be individualized and personal. At a minimum, each child should have his or her own bed (or crib), favorite toys, clothing, and hygienic items (such as toothbrush, comb and brush, and even underwear).

Perhaps because twins must share so much with one another from the beginning, they may or may not be willing to extend this courtesy to others. Twins may not easily share each other with other children, as has already been discussed under "Making Friends," but they do seem to be more generous with their personal possessions.

Since they have always had to share, young twins generally assume that all children share. "When Andy and Jonah were two and a half, Andy said that nobody liked him," began one woman. "I discovered that one of his regular playmates would not share his toys with Andy, so Andy assumed that the boy didn't like him. How could he know," she added with insight, "that two-year-old singletons haven't yet learned to share?"

Birthday Celebrations

Parents often wonder how to make their twins' birthday a special day for both children. By their third or fourth birthday, each child can separately select party invitations and choose a few special friends to invite. "For our twins' fourth birthday they had a single, shared party," one woman recalls, "but I took them to the store and let them pick out separate invitations. I put one card from each twin in all of the envelopes to save money on postage." The children can select separate party accessories, such as favors, plates, or hats.

Whether to have one or two birthday cakes is also an issue with twins. One mother of adult twins remembers, "When they were little, my twins couldn't agree on the kind of cake they wanted, and since we were inviting lots of kids, I baked two—one chocolate and one vanilla." Although sharing a birthday cake may not be fair to the children, baking or buying separate cakes for them is either very time-consuming or expensive. Cupcakes sometimes provide an easy solution to this dilemma—each twin can decorate half of the cupcakes.

Or, each twin can be responsible to plan for half of the children; one can choose the ice cream flavor and the other a favorite kind of cake.

As far as gifts are concerned, "it's terrible to have to share a present with your twin," says an eight-year-old identical twin. "If you feel that buying two separate presents will be too expensive for your guests," offers one mother of five-year-olds, "plan ahead by asking each guest to bring something for only one of the twins. When our boys were four, I asked half of the children to bring gifts for Tom and half for Stephen. I had extra gifts in the closet in case some of the children could not come so that each of our boys would have the same number of presents."

Other children's parties can also cause friction between the twins if only one is invited. Arrange a special activity for the child who is not included, such as a few hours with mom and dad at the zoo or a movie. This lets both children feel important. Buying gifts for others can be expensive when both children are regularly invited to the same birthday parties. Save money by getting two-part gifts, such as crayons and a drawing pad, or bubble liquid and a giant bubble-blower. Wrap the two gifts separately so that each of the twins has something to present to the birthday child.

Travel

The key to a successful trip with toddler or preschool age twins is organization. "Traveling with twins isn't much different than traveling with one or more singletons," claims one experienced mother of three-year-old twins and a five year old. "A lot depends on the energy and mood of the adult or adults traveling with the children," she adds. "Take a traveling companion," advises another, "especially if you are going by plane." Get lots of rest before a trip. A good night's sleep will increase your own energy level and patience, and children who are well rested will be more cooperative.

Try to anticipate the children's needs while you will be traveling. "I come equipped with lunches, juice, a wide variety of snacks and treats, games, new and favorite toys, and changes of clothes," says one well-prepared mom. A mother of two-year-olds suggests bringing "two little bags of everything, such as stickers, crayons, and paper." "If each child can have a seat or space where he can sit without bumping into another child," observes a woman with three-year-olds, "another cause of friction is eliminated." Traveling with twins becomes increasingly easier once they are finished with bottles, once they no longer need some of the heavy baby equipment (such as high chairs, cribs, and strollers), and once they are toilet trained.

A P P E N D I X   I

Resource Guide

Listings given in the resource guide are current as of the time of this writing. Many of these organizations and books are the author's personal choices. The others have been recommended by reputable specialists.

Pregnancy and Childbirth

Organizations in the United States and Canada

American Academy of Husband-Coached Childbirth (the "Bradley Method")
P.O. Box 5224
Sherman Oaks, CA 91413
(800) 423-2397; (818) 788-6662 (California)

Write or call this organization for information on the Bradley childbirth method and for a list of affiliated teachers in your area.

American Society for Psychoprophylaxis in Obstetrics, Inc. (ASPO/ Lamaze)
1840 Wilson Boulevard, Suite 204
Arlington, VA 22201
(703) 524-7802

ASPO /Lamaze provides information to expectant parents on the Lamaze (psychoprophylactic) method of childbirth and on family-centered maternity care. The organization, which publishes *Lamaze Parents' Magazine,* also operates a free referal service to provide names of local, ASPO-certified childbirth educators to expectant parents.

C/SEC, Inc. (Cesareans/Support, Education, and Concern)
22 Forest Road
Framingham, MA 01701
(617) 877-8266

C/SEC gives emotional support to Cesarean parents and provides information and education on Cesarean childbirth, Cesarean prevention, and vaginal birth after a Cesarean. The organization publishes *Frankly Speaking: A Book for Cesarean Couples.* Ask for referral to a support group in your area. Send a stamped, self-addressed business envelope for a free copy of the organization's brochure.

InterNational Association of Parents and Professionals for Safe Alternatives in Childbirth (NAPSAC)
P.O. Box 646
Marble Hill, MO 63764
(314) 238-2010

This organization is dedicated to exploring, examining, implementing, and establishing childbirth programs that meet the needs of families while also promoting safe medical care of the mother and babies. Be sure to indicate that you are expecting twins when you write or call.

International Childbirth Education Association (ICEA)
P.O. Box 20048
Minneapolis, MN 55420
(612) 854-8660

ICEA provides referrals to local childbirth educators and family-centered facilities. It also publishes and distributes pamphlets, books, and periodicals relating to childbearing. The association has a mail-order book center. Send for catalog, *ICEA Bookmarks.*

National Genetics Foundation, Inc.
555 West 57th Street
New York, NY 10019
(212) 586-5800

This voluntary health agency serves individuals and families with known or suspected genetic problems. The foundation provides information about genetic evaluation, counseling, and treatment, as available. The foundation can also arrange referrals to genetic centers for the above genetic services. Write for copies of their pamphlets *Can Genetic Counseling Help You?* and *How Genetic Disease Can Affect You and Your Family,* and *For the Concerned Couple Planning a Family* (single copies free). Also write for details about their new computerized "Family Health History Analysis," in which both members of a couple complete family history questionnaires. The analysis can pinpoint genetic risks to yourselves as well as to your (future) children. The analysis should take place before the tenth week of a pregnancy, or preferably before a pregnancy is attempted, and the results are sent to your physician. (There is a charge for this analysis.)

Read Natural Childbirth Foundation, Inc.
P.O. Box 956
San Rafael, CA 94915
(415) 456-8462

The Read Foundation provides information on the method of child-birth preparation developed by English physician Grantly Dick-Read. Write for a free information packet describing their philosophy and for information on the annotated bibliography and class manual available for purchase.

Organizations Abroad

International Childbirth Education Association (ICEA)
c/o Jan Cornfoot, International Coordinator
42 Lenori Road, Gooseberry Hill
Perth, Western Australia 6076
Australia

See entry under Organizations in the United States and Canada.

National Childbirth Trust of Great Britain
9 Queensborough Terrace
London W2 3TB
England
(01) 221-3833

This organization services England, Wales, and Scotland, by offering prenatal classes, postpartum support, and breastfeeding counseling through its branches nationwide. In Britain send a stamped, self-addressed envelope for a catalog, price lists, and an events list.

Books

Childbirth Without Fear, by Grantly Dick-Read. Revised and edited by Helen Wessel and Harlan F. Ellis, M.D. New York: Harper & Row, 1984. Outlines the philosophy behind the Read method of childbirth preparation.

Dear Elisabeth Bing, We've Had Our Baby: The Adventure of Birth, by Elisabeth Bing. New York: Pocket Books, 1983.

The First Nine Months of Life, by Geraldine Lux Flanagan. New York: Simon and Schuster, 1982. Illustrates fetal development.

Having a Baby After Thirty, by Elisabeth Bing and Libby Colman. New York: Bantam, 1980.

Husband-Coached Childbirth, by Robert A. Bradley, M.D. New York: Harper & Row, 1981. Outlines the philosophy behind the Bradley method of childbirth preparation.

Making Love During Pregnancy, by Elisabeth Bing and Libby Colman. New York: Bantam, 1982.

Moving Through Pregnancy, by Elisabeth Bing. New York: Bantam, 1980.

New Hope for Problem Pregnancies: Helping Babies Before They're Born, by Dianne Hales and Robert K. Creasy. New York: Harper & Row, 1982. Includes one chapter on twins.

Nine Months Reading: A Medical Guide for Pregnant Women, by Robert E. Hall, M.D. New York: Bantam, 1973.

Pregnancy, Birth, and Family Planning, by Alan F. Guttmacher, M.D. New York: Signet/New American Library, 1973. Includes one chapter on twins.

Six Practical Lessons for an Easier Childbirth, by Elisabeth Bing. New York: Bantam, 1982. Based on the Lamaze method.

Thank You, Dr. Lamaze, by Marjorie Karmel. Revised edition. New York: Harper & Row, 1981.

Maternal and Child Health

Organizations in the United States and Canada

American Academy of Pediatrics
Publications Department
P.O. Box 927
Elk Grove Village, IL 60007

Write for a price list of publications on first aid and poisoning prevention, nutrition, breastfeeding, and other subjects concerning child health.

American Dental Association
Department of Public Information and Education
211 East Chicago Avenue
Chicago, IL 60611
(312) 440-2590

Ask for a copy of *Your Child's Teeth,* free to parents.

Association for the Care of Children's Health (ACCH)
3615 Wisconsin Avenue, N.W.
Washington, DC 20016
(202) 244-8922

ACCH is an international organization that provides resources to parents and professionals to humanize the health care environment through education, research, advocacy and networking. ACCH publishes and disseminates information on such topics as infant care, chronic illness, and developmental disabilities. Write for a list of their publications.

Children in Hospitals (CIH)
c/o The Federation for Children with Special Needs
31 Wilshire Park
Needham, MA 02192
(617) 482-2915

CIH offers support and education to parents who wish to keep in close touch with their children during a hospital stay. The organization offers counseling, a newsletter, information sheets, and meetings.

Organizations Abroad

National Association for the Welfare of Children (NAWCH)
Argyle House
29–31 Euston Road
London NW1 2SD
England

NAWCH supports sick children and their families and works to ensure that health services are planned for them.

Books

The Allergy Encyclopedia, edited by the Asthma and Allergy Foundation of America and Craig T. Norback. New York: Plume/New American Library, 1981.

Child Health Encyclopedia, by the Boston Children's Medical Center and Richard I. Feinbloom, M.D. New York: Delacorte, 1975.

Healthy Mothers Coalition Directory of Educational Materials, by the U.S. Department of Health and Human Services. Washington, D.C.: Public Health Service, November 1985. Free.

Brings together voluntary, professional, and government health agencies in an effort to promote maternal and infant health—a listing of hundreds of useful materials published by the various member organizations.

Write: Healthy Mothers and Healthy Babies Coalition
ACOG
600 Maryland Avenue, S.W.
Suite 300 E
Washington, D.C. 20024

A Sigh of Relief: The Revised Edition of the First Aid Handbook for Childhood Emergencies, by Martin I. Green. New York: Bantam, 1984.

Breastfeeding

Organizations

La Leche League International, Inc. (LLL)
P.O. Box 1209
Franklin Park, IL 60131-8209
(312) 455-7730 (twenty-four hour referrals, office hours Monday through Friday, 8 to 3)

This organization promotes the mother-infant relationship through breastfeeding. LLL groups are located throughout the United States and Canada and in countries throughout the world. Check your library or local phone book, or write or call the international headquarters to find the LLL leader nearest you. Send a self-addressed, stamped envelope for information or to request a copy of the *La Leche League International Catalogue*. Publications of particular interest include *Mothering Multiples* (no. 267), a book by Karen Kerkhoff Gromada, and the La Leche League handbook, *The Womanly Art of Breastfeeding* (no. 250), both listed separately under "Books," the information sheet "Breastfeeding Your Premature Baby" (no. 13) by Sandy Countryman, and *Nighttime Parenting*, by William Sears, M.D. (no. 276).

Books

Breastfeeding Twins, Triplets, and Quadruplets: 195 Practical Hints for Success, edited by Donald M. Keith, Sheryl McInnes, and Louis G. Keith, M.D. Chicago: The Center for Study of Multiple Birth, 1982.

Mothering Multiples, by Karen Kerkhoff Gromada, R.N. Franklin Park, Ill.: La Leche League International, 1985. Publication no. 267.

Nursing Your Baby, by Karen Pryor. New York: Pocket Books/Harper & Row, 1977.

You Can Breastfeed Your Baby . . . Even in Special Situations, by Dorothy Patricia Brewster. Emmaus, Pa.: Rodale Press, 1979.

The Womanly Art of Breastfeeding, by La Leche League International. Revised edition. Franklin Park, IL: La Leche League International, 1981. Publication no. 250.

Nutrition

Organizations in the United States and Canada

Society for Nutrition Education
1700 Broadway, Suite 300
Oakland, CA 94612
(415) 444-7133

The society primarily services professionals in nutrition education but also publishes the *Family Health Cookbook* and a complete series of films and videos on nutrition during pregnancy, lactation, infancy and the preschool years. Write for their catalog of titles and prices.

Books

The Family Health Cookbook, edited by Alice White and the Society for Nutrition Education. Oakland, Calif.: Society for Nutrition Education, 1980.

Feed Me, I'm Yours, by Vicki Lansky. New York: Bantam, 1981.

Pickles and Ice Cream: A Complete Guide to Nutrition During Pregnancy, by M. A. Hess and A. Hunt. New York: McGraw-Hill, 1982.

To Baby With Love: Your Prenatal Nutrition Diary, by Marilyn Hanson and Robert Segura. Palo Alto, Calif.: Bull, 1982.

Write: Bull Publishing Co.
        P.O. Box 208
        Palo Alto, CA 94302

The Total Nutrition Guide for You and Your Baby: From Pregnancy Through the First Three Years, by Alice White. New York: Ballantine, 1983.

Safety

Organizations in the United States

American Academy of Pediatrics
Publications Department
P.O. Box 927
Elk Grove Village, IL 60007

Send for price list of their publications on automobile safety, car seats, and car seat loan programs.

Consumer Product Safety Commission
Washington, DC 20207
(800) 638-CPSC (2772) (toll free)

Ask for free fact sheets and information on toy and baby equipment safety and on poison prevention. Two helpful free publications are "The Safe Nursery" and "The Super Sitter."

National Passenger Safety Association (NPSA)
1050 17th Street, N.W.
Suite 770
Washington, DC 20036

The NPSA provides information about child safety seats and child passenger safety issues through brochures, research, information packages, and newsletters. Send a stamped, self-addressed envelope to receive a price sheet of resources.

National Highway Traffic Safety Administration
Office of Occupant Protection (NTS-10)
U.S. Department of Transportation
Room 5118
400 7th Street, S.W.
Washington, DC 20590

Write for free information on automobile safety seats and for the address of your state's highway safety office.

Physicians for Automotive Safety
P.O. Box 798
Maple Street Extension
Kent, CT 06757
(203) 927-4668

For a nominal fee (50¢ at the time this book went to press) you can order this organization's useful pamphlet, *Don't Risk Your Child's Life,* which gives current information on car seats and automobile safety. Send check or coins along with a stamped, self-addressed legal-size envelope.

Twin Care and Research

Organizations in the United States and Canada

The Center for Study of Multiple Birth
Suite 476
333 Superior Street
Chicago, IL 60611
(312) 266-9093

This nonprofit organization conducts medical research on the subject of multiple birth and assists expectant parents and those who are already parents of multiples. The center answers inquiries from countries throughout the world and has a mail-order bookstore (the "one-stop twin bookshop"). Write for a book list. Pamphlets and research reports are also available upon request. In addition, the center can refer you to the appropriate medical facility or research institution if your twins have medical or health problems requiring specialized attention.

International Twins Association (ITA)
P.O. Box 28611
Providence, RI 02908
(401) 274-8946

ITA is a nonprofit organization promoting the spiritual, intellectual, and social welfare of multiples throughout the world. A twin convention is held each year in a different city over the Labor Day weekend.

National Organization of Mothers of Twins Clubs, Inc. (NOMOTC)
12404 Princess Jeanne, N.E.
Albuquerque, NM 87112-4640
(505) 275-0955

NOMOTC is a network of clubs devoted to research and education with chapters throughout the United States. Call or write for referral to a local club. Fathers, grandparents, adoptive or foster parents, and parents of supertwins are also welcome to join. The *MOTC's Notebook* is the organization's official quarterly newspaper, available to members (free) and to non-members. New and expectant parents can send for a copy of *Your Twins and You*, which gives helpful hints for twin care and facts about twins. Purchase the booklet *How to Organize a Mothers of Twins Club* if there is no club in your area and you would like to start one.

Parents of Multiple Births Association (of Canada) (POMBA)
283 7th Avenue South
Lethbridge, Alberta T1J 1H6
Canada
(403) 328-9165

POMBA provides referrals to local clubs or helps parents start one. The organization also conducts scientific, social, and consumer-oriented research on multiple births. Reports are available. A mail-order book service offers books, booklets, and pamphlets on multiple births, pregnancy through school age, and includes materials on twins, triplets, and quads. Write for a price list and for information about the quarterly news magazine, *Double Feature*, and the organization's other publications.

Supertwin Statistician
"Miss Helen" Kirk
P.O. Box 254
Galveston, TX 77553
(409) 762-4792

"Miss Helen," as she is fondly known, has historical and current records and a wealth of information on twins and supertwins throughout the world.

TWINLINE, Services for Multiple Birth Families
P.O. Box 10066
Berkeley, CA 94709
Hotline: (415) 644-0863 (Monday, Wednesday, Friday, from 10 to 2, Pacific Time, and twenty-four-hour message machine)
Business number: 644-0861 (Monday through Friday, from 10 to 4, Pacific Time)

TWINLINE's hotline and educational materials provide support to multiple-birth families and the professionals who serve them throughout the United States. The organization also offers classes and respite care in the San Francisco Bay Area. TWINLINE does research on twin development and care and is a resource for social service agencies that help multiple-birth families. Call for information or send a self-addressed, stamped envelope for a description of services and publications.

The Twins Foundation
P.O. Box 9487
Providence, RI 02940-9487
(401) 274-TWIN (8946)

This nonprofit organization established by twins has three major programs: the research library, the museum and traveling exhibits, and the hall of fame. The research library houses educational, historical, sociological, and scientific information about multiples and helps pilot new research through seminars and conferences. The organization is developing a museum and traveling exhibits that will offer displays on the educational, historical, and humanistic aspects of multiples. Through its hall of fame, the foundation recognizes major achievements of accomplished twins and is in the process of establishing scholarships for twins and developing a bureau of speakers, films and other audio-visual materials. The organization also publishes a newsletter, *The Twins Letter*. Write for membership information.

The Triplet Connection
c/o Janet Bleyl
2618 Lucile Avenue
Stockton, CA 95209
(209) 474-3073

The Triplet Connection provides help and encouragement to expectant mothers and fathers of supertwins, offers ideas and support to parents after the birth of the children and as they grow, and helps connect families and supertwins themselves who are looking for others in a similar situation. Members receive the organization's monthly newsletter.

Organizations Abroad

ABC Club
Helga Grutzner
Strohweg 55
D-6100 Darmstadt
West Germany

This club provides support and information for families of triplets and larger multiples, and it serves various countries. The director speaks English.

Australian Multiple Birth Association (AMBA)
P.O. Box 105
Coogee 2034
New South Wales
Australia

This voluntary, self-help organization is concerned with the care and management of multiple-birth children and with the well-being of their parents and families. Write for information on membership and for a list of leaflets, publications, and sound or slide programs.

New Zealand Multiple Birth Association
P.O. Box 1258
Wellington
New Zealand

This organization offers help, support, and advice to parents of multiples, acts as a liaison between New Zealand clubs and overseas organizations with similar objectives, and publishes a quarterly. Write for information on how to order . . . *and One Makes Two: A Practical Guide for New Parents of Twins*, by Jo Broad (Wellington, New Zealand: Wellington Gemini Club, 1980).

South Africa Multiple Birth Association (SAMBA)
National Executive Head Office
P.O. Box 20115
Crystal Park
Benoni 1515
Transvaal
Republic of South Africa
(011) 849-5119

SAMBA offers emotional support to parents and guardians of multiple-birth children. The organization helps parents understand developmental patterns and childrearing questions that are unique to twins.

Twins and Multiple Births Association (TAMBA)
Katy Gow, Secretary
20 Redcar Close
Lillington
Leamington Spa, Warwickshire CV32 7SU
England

This self-help organization, founded in 1978, has local chapters throughout Great Britain. TAMBA provides encouragement and support to parents of multiples and attempts to create greater public awareness of the needs of multiple-birth children and their families. Please send a self-addressed envelope with inquiries.

Newsletters and Magazines Available in the United States, Canada, and Abroad

Double Talk
P.O. Box 412
Amelia, OH 45102
(513) 753-7117

A quarterly newsletter that focuses exclusively on multiples and the special parenting problems they present.

Twins Magazine
P.O. Box 12045
Overland Park, KS 66212
(913) 722-1090

Published bimonthly, the national publication *Twins* Magazine is directed at parents, multiples, teachers, health professionals, twins themselves, and anyone who has an interest in "the unique world of multiples." The magazine regularly contains over a dozen columns including prematurity, supertwins, family health, and an individual story about each stage of the growing years—pregnancy through adulthood. Features focus on key issues facing parents of twins and adult twins, examine new research in the field, and give an inside look at famous twins and parents of twins.

Books and Booklets

All About Twins: A Handbook for Parents, by Gillian Leigh. Boston: Routledge and Kegan Paul, 1984.

The Care of Twin Children: A Common-Sense Guide for Parents, by Rosemary Theroux, R.N., and Josephine Tingley, R.N. Edited by Louis G. Keith. 2nd edition. Chicago: The Center for Study of Multiple Birth, 1984.

A Full House, by Feenie Ziner. Chicago: The Center for Study of Multiple Birth, 1983 (reprinted). The autobiographical story of a mother of triplets.

Gemini: The Psychology and Phenomena of Twins, by Judy W. Hagedorn and Janet W. Kizziar. Chicago: The Center for Study of Multiple Birth, 1983 (reprinted).

Having Twins: A Parent's Guide to Pregnancy, Birth and Early Childhood, by Elizabeth Noble. Boston: Houghton Mifflin, 1980.

Mothering Multiples, by Karen Kerkhoff Gromada. Franklin Park, IL: La Leche League International, 1985. Publication no. 267.

Multiple Births: Preparation, Birth, Management Afterwards, by J. Linney. New York: Wiley, 1983. For health professionals.

The Parents' Guide to Raising Twins, by Elizabeth Friedrich and Cherry Rowland. New York: St. Martin's Press, 1984.

The Psychology of Twins: A Practical Handbook for Parents, Doctors, Nurses, Counselors and Teachers, by Herbert Collier. 3rd revised edition. Phoenix, AZ: O'Sullivan, Woodside, 1980. Available by mail order only.

Write: Books
4227 North 32nd Street
Phoenix, AZ 85018

Twins: From Conception to Five, by Averil Clegg and Anne Woollett. New York: Van Nostrand Reinhold, 1983.

Twins on Twins, by Frances McLaughlin Gill and Kathryn McLaughlin Abbe. New York: Clarkson Potter/Crown, 1980. A book with beautiful photos taken by well-known identical twin photographers.

Twins: Nature's Amazing Mystery, by Kay Cassill. New York: Atheneum, 1984.

What Is a Twin? by Judy W. Hagedorn and Janet W. Kizziar. Chicago: The Center for Study of Multiple Birth, 1983 (reprinted). A book for twin children explaining what twinship means.

Parenting

General Organizations in the United States and Canada

Family Resource Coalition
230 North Michigan Avenue
Chicago, IL 60601
(312) 726-4750

This organization represents family resource programs in the United States and Canada and maintains a clearinghouse for information about these programs. The coalition provides a national referral service to parents. It also publishes the *FRC Report* and produces publications on family resource programs.

National Self-Help Clearinghouse
33 West 42nd Street
New York, NY 10036
(212) 840-1259

Contact the clearinghouse for a list of self-help (nonprofessional) parent support groups in your area.

Specialized Organizations in the United States and Canada

Parents Without Partners (PWP)
8807 Colesville Road
Silver Spring, MD 20910
(301) 588-9354, or (800) 638-8078

This national organization has local chapters that provide various activities for single parents and their children. In the United States and Canada, write for chapter referral and for a list of their available materials aimed at the problems faced by single parents.

Stepfamily Association of America (SAA)
602 E. Joppa Road
Baltimore, MD 21204
(301) 823-7570

This national association offers workshops and support groups, provides professional referrals, and acts as a national advocate for stepparents, remarried parents, and their children. SAA publishes a quarterly newsletter for stepfamilies and has a national conference each year. Write or call for information on the chapter nearest you and for a list of publications and their prices.

Books for Parents

Baby and Child Care, by Dr. Benjamin Spock. New York: Pocket Books, 1984.

Between Parent and Child, by Dr. Haim G. Ginott. New York: Avon, 1969.

Discipline Without Shouting or Spanking: Practical Options for Parents of Preschoolers, by Jerry Wyckoff, Ph.D., and Barbara C. Unell. Deephaven, MN: Meadowbrook, 1984.

Handbook for New Parents, by Alvin N. Eden, M.D. New York: Berkley, 1984.

How to Discipline with Love (From Crib to College), by Fitzhugh Dodson, Ph.D. New York: Signet/New American Library, 1978.

How to Parent, by Fitzhugh Dodson, Ph.D. New York: Signet/New American Library, 1973.

The Magic Years: Understanding and Handling the Problems of Early Childhood, by Selma H. Fraiberg. New York: Scribners, 1984.

Ourselves and Our Children: A Book by and for Parents, by the Boston Women's Health Book Collective, Inc. New York: Random House, 1978.

The Parenting Advisor, by the Princeton Center for Infancy. Garden City, NY: Anchor/Doubleday, 1977.

Toilet Learning: The Picture Book Technique for Children and Parents, by Alison Mack. Boston: Little, Brown, 1978.

What Now? A Handbook for New Parents, by Mary Lou Rozdilsky and Barbara Banet. New York: Scribners, 1975.

Books for Mothers

The Mother's Almanac, by Marguerite Kelly and Elia Parsons. New York: Doubleday, 1975.

Working Mother's Complete Handbook, by Gloria Norris and Jo Ann Miller. Revised edition, New York: Plume/New American Library, 1984.

Books for Fathers

The Father Book: Pregnancy and Beyond, by Rae Grad, et al. Washington, DC: Acropolis Books, 1981.

The Father's Almanac, by S. Adams Sullivan. New York: Dolphin/ Doubleday, 1980.

How to Father, by Fitzhugh Dodson. New York: Signet/New American Library, 1975.

Books for Special Interests

Black Parents' Handbook: A Guide to the Facts of Pregnancy, Birth and Child Care, by Clara J. McLaughlin. New York: Harcourt Brace Jovanovich, 1975.

The Joint Custody and Co-Parenting Handbook, by Miriam Galper. Revised edition. Philadelphia: Running Press, 1980.

The Single Parent Experience, by Carole Klein. New York: Avon, 1973.

Stepparenting, by Jean and Veryl Rosenbaum. Novato, CA: Chandler & Sharp, 1977.

Write: Chandler & Sharp
      11A Commercial Boulevard
      Novato, CA 94947

Child Care and Babysitting

Books

Choosing Child Care: A Guide for Parents, by Stevanne Auerbach. New York: Dutton, 1981.

My Day Care Book, by Jeffrey Brand and Nancy Gladstone. Mt. Rainier, Md.: Gryphon, 1985.

Write: Gryphon House, Inc.
        3706 Otis Street
        P.O. Box 275
        Mt. Rainier, MD 20712

Child Development

Books

The First Month of Life: A Parent's Guide to Care of the Newborn, by Glenn R. Stoutt, Jr. New York: Signet/New American Library, 1981.

The First Three Years of Life: A Guide to Physical, Emotional, and Intellectual Growth of Your Baby, by Burton L. White. New York: Avon, 1984.

The First Twelve Months of Life: Your Baby's Growth Month by Month, edited by Frank Caplan. New York: Bantam, 1978.

The Gesell Institute's Child from One to Six: Evaluating the Behavior of the Preschool Child, by Louise Bates Ames, Ph.D., et al. New York: Harper & Row, 1979.

Infant and Child in the Culture of Today: The Guidance of Development in Home and Nursery School, by Arnold Gesell, M.D., et al. New York: Harper & Row, 1974.

Infants and Mothers: Individual Differences in Development, by T. Berry Brazelton, M.D. New York: Dell, 1983.

Oneness and Separateness: From Infant to Individual, by Louise J. Kaplan, Ph.D. Franklin Park, IL: La Leche League International, 1983. Publication no. 372.

The Second Twelve Months of Life: A Kaleidoscope of Growth, by Frank Caplan. New York: Bantam, 1980.

Toddlers and Parents: A Declaration of Independence, by T. Berry Brazelton, M.D. New York, Dell, 1976.

Prematurity

Organizations in the United States and Canada

Parent Care, Inc.
University of Utah Health Sciences Center
50 North Medical Drive
Salt Lake City, UT 84132
(801) 581-5323

Parent Care, Inc. offers information, referrals, and other services to families, parent support groups, and health care professionals concerned with infants who require intensive or special care after birth. The organization has a directory listing parent support groups in the United States, Canada, and abroad, and other resources and products, such as breast pumps, preemie diapers, and preemie clothing. The directory is a benefit of membership in this nonprofit organization, along with the quarterly newsletter *Parent Care . . . News Brief.*

Books and Booklets

Born Early: The Story of a Premature Baby, by Mary Ellen Avery, M.D., and Georgia Litwack. Boston: Little, Brown, 1983. A picture book.

Born Too Soon: Preterm Birth and Early Development, by Susan Goldberg and Barbara A. DiVitto. New York: W. H. Freeman, 1983.

Premature Babies: A Handbook for Parents, by Sherri Nance. New York: Arbor House, 1982.

The Premature Baby Book: A Parent's Guide to Coping and Caring in the First Year, by Helen Harrison, with Ann Kositsky, R.N. New York: St. Martin's Press, 1983.

Your Premature Baby: The Complete Guide to Preemie Care During That Crucial First Year, by Robin Marantz Henig, with Anne B. Fletcher, M.D. New York: Rawson, 1983.

Breastfeeding Your Premature Baby, by Sandy Countryman. Franklin Park, IL: La Leche League International, 1980. Publication no. 13 (booklet).

Coloring Book

The Frogs Have a Baby, a Very Small Baby, by Jerri Oehler, R.N. Free copies available at many hospitals, or send $1.50 to cover postage to:
   Jerri Oehler
   Route 7, Box 197B
   Durham, NC 27707

Disabled Children

Organizations in the United States and Canada

Alexander Graham Bell Association for the Deaf, Inc.
3417 Volta Place, N.W.
Washington, DC 20007
(202) 337-5220 (voice and TTY)

This association helps hearing-impaired children and adults become active, participating members of their community through the use of speech and by maximizing their residual hearing. Members can take advantage of conferences, publications, and audio-visual aids. Write for a list of their publications for parents. The association serves families and professionals in any country requesting information.

American Foundation for the Blind (AFB)
15 West 16th Street
New York, NY 10011
(212) 620-2000

The foundation provides information and assistance to the blind and visually impaired and to their families. The AFB has a lending library and also has publications for purchase as well as materials available free of charge. Write for their descriptive catalog of publications and for a free sample copy of their bimonthly newspaper.

Association for Children and Adults with Learning Disabilities
4156 Library Road
Pittsburgh, PA 15234
(412) 341-1515

The association has a resource library of over 600 publications for sale, has a film rental service, and publishes a newsletter, *Newsbriefs*, six times annually. Write for information, a list of available publications, and referral to a local chapter.

Clearinghouse on the Handicapped
U.S. Department of Education
Switzer Building, Room 3132
Washington, DC 20202
(202) 732-1245

The Clearinghouse has a *Pocket Guide to Federal Help for the Disabled Person* and a newsletter called *O.S.E.R.'s* News in Print*. Both publications are free. (*Office of Special Education and Rehabilitation)

Federation for Children with Special Needs
312 Stuart Street, 2nd floor
Boston, MA 02116
(617) 482-2915

This is a center for parents and parent organizations to work together to serve children with special needs better. The federation publishes a newsletter, *Newsline*. All services are provided free of charge.

March of Dimes Birth Defects Foundation
1275 Mamaroneck Avenue
White Plains, NY 10605
(914) 428-7100

The March of Dimes Birth Defects Foundation fights birth defects by funding research, medical services, and education programs. Write the organization's community services department or call the chapter listed in your local telephone directory. Ask for a list of free materials on the subject of maternal and child health, genetic counseling, birth defects, and parenting. Two useful pamphlets are *Be Good to Your*

Baby Before It is Born, and *Data: Drugs, Alcohol, Tobacco Abuse During Pregnancy.*

National Association for Hearing and Speech Action (NAHSA)
10801 Rockville Pike
Rockville, MD 20852
(800) 638-TALK (8255) (Monday through Friday, 8 to 4)

This association provides information on all communicative disorders through its "Helpline" (the number listed above). Write for a price list of their brochures.

National Information Center for Handicapped Children and Youth (NICHCY)
P.O. Box 1492
Washington, DC 20013

NICHCY is a free information service that helps parents, educators, care-givers, advocates and others to improve the lives of children and youth with handicaps. The organization answers questions, develops and shares new information through fact sheets and newsletters, provides advice to people working in groups, and connects people across the country who are solving similar problems.

Books

About Handicaps, by Sara Bonnett Stein. New York: Walker, 1974. For children with their parents.

A Difference in the Family: Life with a Disabled Child, by Helen Featherstone. New York: Basic Books, 1980.

Helping Your Exceptional Baby: A Practical and Honest Approach to Raising a Mentally Handicapped Baby, by Cliff Cunningham and Patricia Sloper. New York: Pantheon Books, 1981. Primarily deals with handicapped children, but also assists with any children with developmental problems or delays.

Selecting a Preschool: A Guide for Parents of Handicapped Children, by Pam Winton, Ann Turnbull, and Jan Blacher. Austin, TX: Pro-Ed., 1984.

Write: Pro-Ed., Inc.
    5341 Industrial Oaks Boulevard
    Austin, TX 78735

Special Children, Special Parents: Personal Issues with Handicapped Children, by Albert Murphy. Englewood Cliffs, NJ: Prentice-Hall, 1980.

We Have Been There: Families Share the Joys and Struggles of Living with Mental Retardation, edited by Terrell Dougan, Lynn Isbell, and Pat Vyas. Nashville, TN: Abingdon Press, 1983.

Miscarriage/Death of Child

Organizations in the United States, Canada, and Abroad

Support After Neonatal Death (SAND)
Alta Bates Hospital
3001 Colby Street at Ashby
Berkeley, CA 94705
(415) 540-0337 (Janet Kirksey, R.N.), or (415) 540-1571 (for recorded message or to leave a message)

SAND offers support, consultation, and educational services to parents who have lost a baby through miscarriage, abortion or stillbirth or whose infant has died during or after birth. These services are provided by trained parents and professionals who have also lost an infant.

The Compassionate Friends, Inc. (TCF)
National Headquarters
P.O. Box 3696
Oak Brook, IL 60522-3696
(312) 990-0010

This organization provides understanding and support to bereaved families after miscarriage or death of a child. TCF offers assistance through local support groups, telephone friends, and a quarterly newsletter. Write for brochures, a book list, and referral to a local chapter. Two booklets available for purchase from TCF are *The Grief of Parents . . . When a Child Dies,* by Margaret S. Miles, and *When a Baby Dies,* by Martha Jo Church, Helen Chazin, and Faith Ewald.

In Canada, write or call: The Compassionate Friends
National Center–Winnipeg
685 Williams Avenue
Winnipeg, Manitoba R3E 0W1
(204) 787-2460

In England, write or call: The Compassionate Friends
c/o Brenda Trimmer
2 Nordon Road, Blandford
Dorset DT11 7LT
(02) 58 52760

In Australia, write or call: The Compassionate Friends
Lindsay and Margaret Harmer
Rear 205 Blackburn Road
Syndal 3149–Victoria
(03) 232-8151

In New Zealand, write*: Bereaved Parents Group
2/5 Badderley Avenue
Kohimarama
Auckland 5
(*not affiliated with TCF)

National Sudden Infant Death Syndrome (SIDS) Foundation
8200 Professional Place
Suite 104
Landover, MD 20785
(301) 459-3388, and (800) 221-SIDS (toll free)

The foundation has a network of volunteer chapters throughout the United States that can be helpful to parents of victims of SIDS and to families with high-risk infants. Write for a list of their publications and for referral to a local chapter.

Books

After a Loss in Pregnancy: Help for Families Affected by a Miscarriage, a Stillbirth, or a Newborn's Death, by Nancy Berezin. New York: Fireside/ Simon and Schuster, 1982.

The Bereaved Parent, by Harriet Sarnoff Schiff. New York: Penguin/ Crown, 1978.

The Long Dying of Baby Andrew, by Peggy and Robert Stinson. Boston:

Atlantic/Little, Brown, 1983. Deals with ethics of neonatal intensive care, the rights of parents, and the death of a baby.

Surviving Pregnancy Loss, by Rochelle Friedman and Bonnie Gradstein. Boston: Little, Brown, 1982.

When Pregnancy Fails: Families Coping with Miscarriage, Stillbirth and Infant Death, by Susan O. Borg and Judith Lasker. Boston: Beacon Press, 1981.

Coloring Book

The Frog Family's Baby Dies, by Jerri Oehler, R.N. Free copies available at many hospitals, or send $1.50 to cover postage to:
  Jerri Oehler
  Route 7, Box 197B
  Durham, NC 27707

APPENDIX II

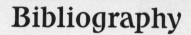

Bibliography

Albright, George A. *Anesthesia in Obstetrics: Maternal, Fetal, and Neonatal Aspects.* Menlo Park, CA: Addison-Wesley, 1978.

Altschuler, Geoffrey. "Medical implications of basic concepts in gemellology," chap. 68. In *Principles and Practice of Obstetrics and Perinatology,* ed. Leslie Iffy and Harold A. Kaminetzky, Vol. 2. New York: Wiley, 1981.

Apgar, Virginia. "A proposal for a new method of evaluation of the newborn infant." *Anesthesia and Analgesia* 32(1953):260.

Arnon, Stephen S., et al. "Honey and other environmental risk factors for infant botulism." *Journal of Pediatrics* 94(2)1979:331–336.

Atkins, A. J., et al. "The influence of posture upon cardiovascular dynamics throughout pregnancy." *European Journal of Obstetrics, Gynecology and Reproductive Biology* 12(6)1981:357–372.

Atkinson, S. A., et al. "Human milk: difference in nitrogen concentration in milk from mothers of term and premature infants." *Journal of Pediatrics* 93(1)1978:67–69.

Barrett, Jeffrey M., et al. "The effect of type of delivery upon neonatal outcome in premature twins." *American Journal of Obstetrics and Gynecology* 143(3)1982:360–367.

Bean, William J., and Rodan, Bruce A. "Pelvimetry revisited." *Seminars in Roentgenology* 17(3)1982:164–171.

Benirschke, Kurt, and Kim, Chung K. "Multiple pregnancy 1." *New England Journal of Medicine* 288(24) 1973: 1276–1284.

———. "Multiple pregnancy 2." *New England Journal of Medicine* 288(25)1973:1329–1336.

Berger, Gary S., et al. "The Northwestern University Multihospital Twin Study: III. Obstetric characteristics and outcome." *Progress in Clinical and Biological Research* 69(pt. A)1981:207–215.

Bernstein, Beth A. "Siblings of twins." *Psychoanalytic Study of the Child* 35(1980):135–154.

Bouchard, Thomas J., Jr., et al. "The Minnesota Study of Twins Reared Apart: project description and sample results in the developmental domain." *Progress in Clinical and Biological Research* 69(pt. B)1981:227–233.

Bracken, Michael B. "Oral contraception and twinning: an epidemiologic study." *American Journal of Obstetrics and Gynecology* 133(4)1979:432–434.

Brazelton, T. Berry. *Neonatal Behavioral Assessment Scale.* Philadelphia: Lippincott, 1973.

Brown, Lawrence W. "Commentary: infant botulism and the honey connection." *Journal of Pediatrics* 94(2)1979:337–338.

Bulmer, M. G. *The Biology of Twinning in Man.* Oxford: Clarendon Press, 1970.

Bureau of Radiological Health, Food and Drug Administration, Public Health Service. *The Selection of Patients for X-ray Examinations: The Pelvimetry Examination.* HHS publication (FDA) 80-8128. Rockville, MD: U.S. Department of Health and Human Services, 1980.

Campbell, D. M., and MacGillivray, Ian. "Maternal physiological responses and birthweight in singleton and twin pregnancies by parity." *European Journal of Obstetrics, Gynecology and Reproductive Biology* 7(1)1977:17–24.

Christian, J. C. "The use of twin registers in the study of birth defects." *Birth Defects* 14(6A)1978:167–178.

Clegg, Averil, and Woollett, Anne. *Twins from Conception to Five Years.* New York: Van Nostrand Reinhold, 1983.

Committee on the Fetus and Newborn. *Standards and Recommendations for Hospital Care of Newborn Infants.* 6th ed. Evanston, IL: American Academy of Pediatrics, 1977.

Dubowitz, L. M., Dubowitz, V., and Goldberg, C. "Clinical assessment of gestational age in the newborn infant." *Journal of Pediatrics* 77(1970):1–10.

Eastman, Nicholson, J., and Hellman, Louis M., eds. *Williams' Obstetrics.* 13th ed. New York: Appleton-Century-Crofts/Meredith, 1966.

Elias, Sherman, Gerbie, Albert B., and Simpson, Joe Leigh. "Amniocentesis for prenatal diagnosis in twin gestation." (letter). *Clinical Genetics* 17(4)1980:300–301.

Elias, Sherman and Simpson, Joe Leigh. "Ultrasound and amniocentesis," pp. 165–177. In *Diagnostic Ultrasound Applied to Obstetrics and*

Gynecology, ed. Rudy E. Sabbagha. Hagerstown, MD.: Harper & Row, 1980.

Ellis, R. F., et al. "The Northwestern University Multihospital Twin Study: II. Mortality of first versus second twins." *Acta Geneticae Medicae et Gemellologiae* (Rome) 28(4)1979:347–352.

Elwood, J. Mark. "The end of the drop in twinning rates." (letter) *The Lancet* 1(8322)1983:470.

Emmons, Ramona F. W. "The placement of twins in elementary school." Ph.D. dissertation. Purdue University, 1976. (unpublished) (See *Dissertation Abstracts International* 37(8)1977:4720-A.)

Evrard, John R., and Gold, Edwin M. "Caesarean section for delivery of the second twin." *Obstetrics and Gynecology* 57(5)1981:581–583.

Field, Barbara, and Picker, Richard. "Genetic amniocentesis in twin pregnancy." *Australia and New Zealand Journal of Obstetrics and Gynaecology* 22(2)1982:71–73.

Gaddis, Margaret and Vincent. *The Curious World of Twins.* New York: Hawthorn, 1972.

Ganesh, Vijaya, Apuzzio, Joseph, and Iffy, Leslie. "Clinical aspects of multiple gestation," pp. 1183–1192. In *Principles and Practice of Obstetrics and Perinatology,* ed. Leslie Iffy and Harold Kaminetzky. Vol. 2. New York: Wiley, 1981.

Gaston, Anne H. "Small for gestational age (SGA) infants," pp. 172–175. In *Pediatrics.* ed. Abraham M. Rudolph. 16th ed. New York: Appleton-Century-Crofts, 1977.

Gedda, Luigi. "The human twin." *Acta Geneticae Medicae et Gemellologiae* (Rome) 29(2)1980:85–90.

Greenhill, J. P., ed. "Problems of twin pregnancy," pp. 242–244. In *Year Book of Obstetrics and Gynecology.* Chicago: Year Book Medical, 1972.

———. "The second twin," pp. 244–245. In *Year Book of Obstetrics and Gynecology.* Chicago: Year Book Medical, 1972.

Gromada, Karen Kerkhoff. *Mothering Multiples* (publication no. 267). Franklin Park, IL: La Leche League, 1985.

Gross, Steven J., et al. "Nutritional composition of milk produced by mothers delivering preterm." *Journal of Pediatrics* 96(4)1980:641–644.

Gushurst, Colette A., et al. "Breast milk iodide: reassessment in the 1980's." *Pediatrics* 70(3)1984:354–357.

Guttmacher, Alan F. *Pregnancy, Birth and Family Planning.* New York: Signet/New American Library, 1973.

Hagedorn, Judy W., and Kizziar, Janet W. *Gemini: the psychology and phenomena of twins.* Chicago: Center for Study of Multiple Birth, 1983.

Harrison, Helen. *The Premature Baby Book.* New York: St. Martin's Press, 1983.

Hartmann, Heinz. "A review of *Twins: A Study of Three Pairs of Identical Twins,* by Dorothy Burlingham." *Psychoanalytic Study of the Child* 36 (1981):45–70.

Hrubec, Zdenek, and Robinette, C. Dennis. "The study of human twins in medical research." *The New England Journal of Medicine* 310(7)1984:435–441.

Hunter, Alasdair G. W., and Cox, David M. "Counseling problems when twins are discovered at genetic amniocentesis." *Clinical Genetics* 16(1)1979:34–42.

James, William H. "Twinning rates." (letter) *The Lancet* 1(8330)1983:934–935.

Jennings, Betty, and Edmundson, Margaret. "The postpartum period: after confinement—the fourth trimester." *Clinical Obstetrics and Gynecology* 23(4)1980:1093–1103.

Keith, Donald M., McInnes, Sheryl, and Keith, Louis G., eds. *Breastfeeding Twins, Triplets and Quadruplets.* Chicago: Center for Study of Multiple Birth, 1982.

Keith, Louis, et al. "The Northwestern University Multihospital Twin Study: I. A description of 588 twin pregnancies and associated pregnancy loss, 1971 to 1975." *American Journal of Obstetrics and Gynecology* 138(7)1980:781–789.

Keith, Louis, and Hughey, Michael J. "Twin gestation," chap. 74. In *Gynecology and Obstetrics,* ed. J. J. Sciarra, vol. 2. Hagerstown, MD: Harper & Row, 1979.

Keith, Louis, and Keith, Gail. "Zygosity determination among twins." *Journal of Continuing Education in Obstetrics and Gynecology* 20(1978):15–25.

King, Janet, Associate Professor of Nutrition, University of California, Berkeley. Personal Communication to Terry Pink Alexander. May 5, 1982.

Klaus, Marshall H., and Fanaroff, Avroy A., eds. *Care of the High-Risk Neonate.* Philadelphia: Saunders, 1973.

Koch, Helen. *Twins and Twin Relations.* Chicago: University of Chicago Press, 1966.

Landy, Helain J., et al. "The vanishing twin." *Acta Geneticae Medicae et Gemellologiae* (Rome) 31(3-4)1982:179–194.

Leonard, Linda G. "Breastfeeding twins: maternal–infant nutrition." *JOGN Nursing* 11(3)1982:148–153.

———. "Twin pregnancy: maternal–fetal nutrition." *JOGN Nursing* 11(3)1982:139–145.

Levinson, Gershon, and Shnider, Sol M. "Anesthesia for abnormal positions, presentations and multiple births." chap. 12. In *Anesthesia for Obstetrics*, ed. Sol M. Shnider and Gershon Levinson. Baltimore: Williams and Wilkins, 1979.

Linney, Judi. *Multiple Births: Preparation, Birth, Managing Afterwards.* New York: Wiley, 1983.

MacGillivray, I., and Campbell, D. M. "The physical characteristics and adaptations of women with twin pregnancies." *Progress in Clinical and Biological Research* 24(pt. C)1978:81–86.

Malmstrom, Patricia M. "Manifestations of twinship in toddler language." In *Proceedings of the Sixth Annual Meeting of the Berkeley Linguistics Society*, ed. Bruce R. Caron et al. Berkeley: Berkeley Linguistics Society, University of California, 1980.

Malmstrom, P. M., et al. "Respite care—A lifeline for low-income multiple-birth families." *Acta Geneticae Medicae et Gemellologiae* (Rome) 36( ) 1987. (In press)

Malmstrom, P. M., Faherty, T. F., and Wagner, P. "Essential nonmedical perinatal services for multiple-birth families." *Acta Geneticae Medicae et Gemellologiae* (Rome) 36( )1987. (In press)

Malmstrom, P. M., and Malmstrom, E. J. "Maternal recognition of twin pregnancy." *Acta Geneticae Medicae et Gemellologiae* (Rome) 36( )1987. (In press)

Malmstrom, P. M., and Silva, M. N. "Twin talk: manifestations of twin status in the speech of toddlers." *Journal of Child Language* 13 (1986): 293–304.

Mantle, M. J., Greenwood, R. M., and Currey, H. L. "Backache in pregnancy." *Rheumatology and Rehabilitation* 16(2)1977:95–101.

Mantle, M. J., Holmes, J., and Currey, H. L. "Backache in pregnancy II: prophylactic influence of back care classes." *Rheumatology and Rehabilitation* 20(4)1981:227–232.

Matheny, Adam P., Jr., et al. "Behavioral contrasts in twinships: stability and patterns of differences in childhood." *Child Development* 52(2)1981:579–588.

Metcalf, James, McAnulty, John H., and Ueland, Kent. "Cardiovascular physiology." *Clinical Obstetrics and Gynecology* 24(3)1981:693–710.

Metneki, Julia, and Czeizel, A. "Twinning rates." (letter) *The Lancet* 1(8330)1983:935.

Myrianthopoulos, Ntinos C. "An epidemiologic survey of twins in a large, prospectively studied population." *American Journal of Human Genetics* 22(6)1970:611–629.

Naeye, Richard L., and Ross, Samuel. "Coitus and chorioamnionitis: a prospective study." *Early Human Development* 6(1)1982:91–97.

National Center for Health Statistics, Public Health Service. "Advance report of final natality statistics, 1981." In *Monthly Vital Statistics Report*. PHS publication no. 84–1120, vol. 32, no. 9, supplement. Hyattsville, MD: U.S. Department of Health and Human Services, December, 1983.

———. "Advance report of final natality statistics, 1982." In *Monthly Vital Statistics Report*. PHS publication no. 84–1120, vol. 33, no. 6, supplement. Hyattsville, MD: U.S. Department of Health and Human Services, September, 1984.

———. "Multiple Births, 1964," pp. 1–13. In *Vital and Health Statistics Data from the National Vital Statistics System*. PHS publication no. 1000, series 21, no. 14, Washington D.C.: U.S. Department of Health, Education, and Welfare, 1967.

———. *Vital Statistics of the United States, 1978, Vol. 1: Natality*. Table 1-75. Hyattsville, MD: U.S. Department of Health and Human Services, 1982.

Newton, Warren, et al. "The Northwestern University Multihospital Twin Study: IV. Duration of gestation according to fetal sex." *American Journal of Obstetrics and Gynecology* 149(6)1984:655–658.

Noble, Elizabeth. *Having Twins: A Parents' Guide to Pregnancy, Birth, and Early Childhood*. Boston: Houghton Mifflin, 1980.

Phibbs, Roderic H. "Multiple births," pp. 170–172. In *Pediatrics*, ed. Abraham M. Rudolph. 16th ed., New York: Appleton-Century-Crofts, 1977.

Pitkin, Roy M., ed., and Scott, James R., asst. ed. "Collision and interlocking of twins," pp. 154–155. In *Year Book of Obstetrics and Gynecology*. Chicago: Year Book Medical, 1978.

Pitkin, Roy M., and Zlatnick, Frank J., eds. "Delivery of the second twin," pp. 134–135. In *Year Book of Obstetrics and Gynecology*. Chicago: Year Book Medical, 1983.

———. "Effect of type of delivery on neonatal outcome in premature twins," pp. 133–134. In *Year Book of Obstetrics and Gynecology*. Chicago: Year Book Medical, 1983.

Pitkin, Roy M., ed., and Zlatnick, Frank J., asst. ed. "Assessment of gestational age in twins," pp. 201–202. In *Year Book of Obstetrics and Gynecology*. Chicago: Year Book Medical, 1979.

Pitkin, Roy M., ed., and Zlatnick, Frank J., assoc. ed. "Bed rest in twin pregnancy: identification of a critical period and its cost implications," pp. 98–99. In *Year Book of Obstetrics and Gynecology*. Chicago: Year Book Medical, 1980.

———. "Diagnosis of multiple pregnancy," p. 91. In *Year Book of Obstetrics and Gynecology*. Chicago: Year Book Medical, 1981.

———. "Genetic amniocentesis in twin gestations," pp. 187–189. In

Year Book of Obstetrics and Gynecology. Chicago: Year Book Medical, 1982.

————. "Selective birth in twin pregnancy with discordancy for Down's Syndrome," pp. 189–190. In *Year Book of Obstetrics and Gynecology.* Chicago: Year Book Medical, 1982.

Pitkin, Roy M., ed., and Zlatnick, Frank J., assoc. ed. "Value of bed rest in twin pregnancies," pp. 196–197. In *Year Book of Obstetrics and Gynecology.* Chicago: Year Book Medical, 1979.

Pitkin, Roy M., ed., and Zlatnick, Frank J., asst. ed. "Zygosity and intrauterine growth of twins," pp. 93–94. In *Year Book of Obstetrics and Gynecology.* Chicago: Year Book Medical, 1981.

Popp, Lothar, and Thomsen, Russel J. *Ultrasound in Obstetrics and Gynecology.* Washington, DC: Hemisphere/McGraw-Hill, 1978.

Powers, W. F. "Twin pregnancy: complications and treatment." *Obstetrics and Gynecology* 42(6)1973:795–808.

Pritchard, Jack A., MacDonald, Paul C., and Grant, Norman F., eds. *Williams Obstetrics.* 17th ed., chap. 26. Norwalk, CT.: Appleton-Century-Crofts, 1985.

Purohit, Dilip M., Levkoff, Abner H., and Pai, Sharada. "Management of multi-fetal gestation." *Pediatric Clinics of North America* 24(3)1977:481–490.

Recommended Dietary Allowances, 9th rev. ed. The National Research Council of the National Academy of Sciences, 1980.

Riese, Marilyn L. "Assessment of gestational age in twins: lack of agreement among procedures." *Journal of Pediatric Psychology* 5(1)1980:9–16.

Rovinsky, Joseph J., and Jaffin, Herbert. "Cardiovascular hemodynamics: III. Cardiac rate, stroke volume, total peripheral resistance, and central blood volume in multiple pregnancy. Synthesis of results." *American Journal of Obstetrics and Gynecology* 95(6)1966:787–794.

Sando, W. C., et al. "Risk factors for microwave scald injuries in infants." *Journal of Pediatrics* 104(6)1984:864–867.

Sarasohn, Charles. "Care of the very small premature infant." *Pediatric Clinics of North America* 24(3)1977:619–632.

Savic, Svenka. "Mother–child verbal interaction: the functioning of completions in the twin situation." *Journal of Child Language* 6(1976):153–158.

Schanler, Richard J., et al. "Composition of breast milk obtained from mothers of premature infants as compared to breast milk obtained from donors." *Journal of Pediatrics* 96(4)1980:679–681.

Scheinfeld, Amram. *Twins and Supertwins.* Baltimore: Penguin, 1967.

Shearer, Madeleine H. "A survey of the literature on ventilation and hyperventilation in childbirth." *Childbirth Education* 2(4)1969:7–10.

———. "Teaching prenatal exercise: part I, posture." *Birth and the Family Journal* 8(3)1981:105–108.

Shrock, Pamela, Simkin, Penny, and Shearer, Madeleine. "Teaching prenatal exercise: part II, exercises to think twice about." *Birth and the Family Journal* 8(3)1981:167–175.

Siegel, Sheila, and Siegel, Michael. "Practical aspects of pediatric management of families with twins." *Pediatrics in Review* 4(1)1982:8–12.

Theroux, Rosemary T., and Tingley, Josephine F. *The Care of Twin Children.* Chicago: Center for Study of Multiple Gestation, 1978.

United States Bureau of the Census, *Statistical Abstract of the United States: 1982–1983.* (103rd edition). Washington, DC, 1982.

United States Bureau of the Census, *Statistical Abstract of the United States: 1983–1984.* (104th edition). Washington, DC, 1983.

Vital Statistics of the United States, 1978, Vol. 1: Natality. Hyattsville, MD: U.S. Department of Health and Human Services, 1982.

Waterman, Pamela, and Shatz, Marilyn. "The acquisition of personal pronouns and proper names by an identical twin pair." *Journal of Speech and Hearing Research* 25(1982):149–154.

Watts, Denise, and Lytton, Hugh. *Twinships as handicap: fact or fiction? Progress in Clinical and Biological Research* 69(pt. B) 1981:283–285.

Wilson, Ronald S. "Concordance in physical growth for monozygotic and dizygotic twins." *Annals of Human Biology* 3(1)1976:1–10.

———. "Growth standards for twins from birth to four years." *Annals of Human Biology* 1(2)1974:175–188.

———. "Twin growth: initial deficit, recovery, and trends in concordance from birth to nine years." *Annals of Human Biology* 6(3)1979:205–220.

———. "Twins: measures of birth size at different gestational ages." *Annals of Human Biology* 1(1)1974:57–64.

———. "Twins and siblings: concordance for school-age mental development." *Child Development* 48(1977):211–216.

White, Alice. *The Total Nutrition Guide for Mother and Baby.* New York: Ballantine, 1983.

Wolf, Deborah A., et al. "Genetic amniocentesis in multiple pregnancy." *Journal of Clinical Ultrasound* 7(3)1979:208–210.

Woodward, Susan L. "How does strenuous maternal exercise affect the fetus? A review." *Birth and the Family Journal* 8(1)1981:17–24.

Index